GĪTĀ SUBODHINĪ

Enriching the Experience of Bhagavad-gīta Study

yatra yogeśvaraḥ kṛṣṇo
yatra pārtho dhanur-dharaḥ
tatra śrīr vijayo bhūtir
dhruvā nītir matir mama

"Wherever there is Kṛṣṇa, the master of all mystics, and wherever there is Arjuna, the supreme archer, there will also certainly be opulence, victory, extraordinary power, and morality. That is my opinion."

(*Bhagavad-gīta 18.78*)

GĪTĀ SUBODHINĪ

Enriching the Experience of Bhagavad-gīta Study

GAURANGA DARSHAN DAS

Bhaktivedanta Vidyapitha
ISKCON Govardhan Eco Village, Galtare, Hamrapur (P.O),
Wada (Taluka), Palghar (District), 421303 - Maharashtra, India

Published and Printed by:
Tulsi Books (A division of Sri Tulsi Trust)
7. K. M. Munshi marg, Girgaum Chowpatty, Mumbai – 400007
www.tulsibooks.com | tulsibookssales@gmail.com
Author's website: www.gaurangadarshan.com

GĪTĀ SUBODHINĪ
ISBN: 978-93-81283-60-8
First Six Printings – 20,000 Copies

Dedicated to

HIS DIVINE GRACE
A. C. BHAKTIVEDĀNTA SWĀMĪ PRABHUPĀDA

Founder Ācārya: International Society for Krishna Consciousness

yair īdṛśī bhagavato gatir ātma-vāda
ekāntato nigamibhiḥ pratipāditā naḥ
tuṣyantv adabhra-karuṇāḥ sva-kṛtena nityaṁ
ko nāma tat pratikaroti vinoda-pātram

"How can such persons, who have rendered unlimited service by explaining the path of self-realization in relation to the Supreme Personality of Godhead, and whose explanations are given for our enlightenment with complete conviction and Vedic evidence, be repaid except by folded palms containing water for their satisfaction? Such great personalities can be satisfied only by their own activities, which are distributed amongst human society out of their unlimited mercy."

[*Śrīmad-Bhāgavatam* 4.22.47]

CONTENTS

PART III: JÑĀNA-YOGA

THEMATIC COMPILATIONS

APPENDIX

ACKNOWLEDGEMENTS

Words fall short in expressing my gratitude to Śrīla Prabhupāda who presented the *Bhagavad-gīta As It Is* with his lucid explanations, without which it would have been difficult for me to study the *Gīta*. I am indebted to Śrīla Viśvanātha Cakravarti Ṭhākura and Śrīla Baladeva Vidyābhūṣaṇa for their commentaries that further helped me understand the contents and flow of the *Gīta*. My sincere thanks to His Holiness Bhānu Swami Mahāraja for presenting them in English. *Gīta Subodhinī* is nothing but a concise representation of the *Bhagavad-gīta* based on the explanations of these great *ācāryas*.

I express my earnest gratitude to my beloved *guru* His Holiness Radhanath Swami Maharaja for enlightening me on the ideal mood of scriptural study and encouraging me with his kind blessings. I am forever indebted to Gauranga Prabhu, my guide and source of inspiration in all my humble endeavors. It is his ardent desire to see the scriptures being studied systematically by the devotees, and it is my great fortune to get an opportunity to be of some assistance to him in this effort.

I thank His Grace Bhūrijana Prabhu for his wonderful overview of the *Gīta* – 'Surrender unto Me,' published by the VIHE. I am deeply grateful to our dear teacher Gauranga Priya Prabhu, who provided a comprehensive study guide for the *Gīta,* with an amazing analysis of Śrīla Prabhupāda's purports. I thank Chaitanya Charan Prabhu for his insightful talks on the *Gīta* that inspired me. All the above sources greatly contributed to my understanding of the flow of the *Gīta* and thus in the making of *Gītā Subodhinī*.

My heartfelt thanks to Revativallabh Prabhu for his encouragement in my writing efforts and going through the manuscript, editing and giving his valuable suggestions. I am grateful to Sakha Gadadhar Prabhu for drawing the Kṛṣṇa-Arjuna images in this book. I am very thankful to Sakha Subal Prabhu, Vikas Prabhu and Hemarupa Chaitanya Prabhu for their kind assistance in the appendix and thematic compilations.

My sincere gratitude to the Tulsi books team for publishing the book. Special thanks to dear friend Raas Gopal Prabhu for his coordination and assistance.

It is not possible to name all my friends at Govardhan Ecovillage whose warmth and support inspire me in my services.

– Gauranga Darshan Das

Introduction

In the rainy season, mud paths in villages are often not used, and thus they get covered with grass. Similarly, when authentic scriptures are not studied for long, pure knowledge becomes covered by speculative and unwanted theories that misdirect the human society.

Scriptures present pristine wisdom descending directly from the Supreme Lord, showing us the path of transcending miseries and going back to Godhead. When thick grass covers a pathway, it is difficult to walk on that path or sometimes the path is not even recognized. Similarly, if one generation chooses not to study, understand, apply and spread the knowledge of the scriptures, the later generations would have no precedence and inspiration to study or follow them, or even become aware of them.

Therefore, it becomes the responsibility of sincere spiritual seekers to read and assimilate the scriptural principles and guide the future generations. This *Gītā Subodhinī* is a humble attempt to facilitate and simplify the study of our most vital scripture, the *Bhagavad-gīta,* by giving its structure, flow and gist in a concise form.

Bhagavad-gīta is the greatly enlightening philosophical song sung by Lord Śrī Kṛṣṇa, the Supreme Lord, to instruct bewildered Arjuna on the battlefield of Kurukṣetra. The *Gīta* is known for its philosophical depth and practical relevance in day-to-day life. The five truths that embody the teachings of the *Bhagavad-gītā* are *īśvara* (God), *jīva* (living entity), *prakṛti* (material nature), *kāla* (time), and *karma* (activities).

Bhagavad-gīta systematically presents the knowledge of the eternal soul, temporary body, the art of working without reactions, the three modes that influence all beings, regulated habits, how to speak, how to eat, how to recreate, how to donate, mind control, sense control, meditation, the art of rendering service to the Supreme, various powers of God, attachment, detachment and so on. Thus *Bhagavad-gīta* is a standard reference manual for all human beings who seek to know the truth, refine their intellect and uplift their consciousness.

The expanse and depth of the *Bhagavad-gīta* is better appreciated from the commentaries of great *ācāryas*, or spiritual teachers. In *Gītā Subodhinī*, I have made a humble attempt to present the flow of the *Bhagavad-gīta* concisely based on the explanations of Śrīla Prabhupāda, Śrīla Viśvanātha Cakravarti Ṭhākura and Śrīla Baladeva Vidyābhūṣaṇa. For a detailed explanation of each verse, one may refer to the commentaries of these great *ācāryas*.

Initially I restrained writing this book, as there are already various study guides for the *Bhagavad-gīta* presented by many experienced teachers and authors. They are very helpful and I too personally took help from them for my own understanding of the *Gīta*. Yet several devotees including many seniors who appreciated my earlier works – *Bhāgavata Subodhinī* and *Caitanya Subodhinī* – requested me to present the *Bhagavad-gīta* in a similar concise format. Therefore, although I hesitated and delayed significantly, I finally submitted to the desires of devotees and now offering this *Gītā Subodhinī* to the readers of the *Gīta*.

Features of Gītā Subodhinī

Both new and seasoned readers of the *Bhagavad-gītā* can relish the profound knowledge of the *Gīta* as presented in the *Gītā Subodhinī* owing to its simplified presentation. The following are the features of the book.

- *Overview chart:* Provides a bird's eye view of the major sections and subsections of a chapter in a block diagram.
- *Section:* A group of verses that fall under the same heading.
- *Subsection:* A sub-group of verses within a section.
- *Verse synopsis:* A brief summary of a verse highlighting its import as explained by the *ācāryas*. All the verses are duly numbered and some keywords of the Sanskrit verse are given in brackets.
- *Verse:* A most vital Sanskrit verse of the chapter, which is worth memorizing, presented in the flow, sometimes with its line-by-line meaning in a tabular form. Sometimes a series of verses that present a list of characteristics is presented in a tabular form, with the corresponding Sanskrit and English key words duly color-coded. This is to help the reader get familiar with the important Sanskrit words.
- *Table:* A list of items under a section.
- *Flow chart:* Gives a bird's eye view of a sequence of stages in a process.
- *Note:* A vital comment or a brief explanation on a verse or section, mainly related to the flow of the chapter, for enhancing the understanding.

- Link: The connection between two verses, sections, subsections or chapters
- *Footnote:* Deeper insights, additional information and application perspectives.

The links, notes and footnotes are based on the commentaries of Śrīla Prabhupāda, Śrīla Viśvanātha Cakravarti Ṭhākūra and Śrīla Baladeva Vidyābhūṣaṇa.

Thematic compilations present lists of verses on various prominent themes of the *Bhagavad-gīta*, duly categorized. The objective of this section is to make the reader appreciate the cross-sectional prominence of a specific theme revealed in various chapters.

Appendix presents extensive lists of reference material from the *Gīta*. Unlike thematic compilations, they are more direct in nature with little or no analysis, such as, names of Lord Kṛṣṇa and Arjuna and analogies of the *Gīta*.

To keep the reading of *Gītā Subodhinī* relatively simple, the referencing for verses is done in a standard format. The following abbreviations represent their equivalent expanded forms given against them:

- 1.2 → *Bhagavad-gīta*, Chapter 1, Verse number 2
- 1.2 P → Śrīla Prabhupāda's purport for 1.2
- Q1 → Question number 1
- A1 → Answer to Q1

With all the above features, the *Gītā Subodhinī* aims to enrich the experience of your *Bhagavad-gīta* study.

Preparing mood for Gīta Study

As mentioned earlier, scriptural study is of vital importance to a spiritual seeker, and the study of the *Bhagavad-gīta* is considered foundational for one's spiritual understanding. At the onset I wish to briefly present a beautiful episode from the divine pastimes of Lord Śrī Caitanya Mahāprabhu on the study of the *Bhagavad-gīta*. I believe that this pastime and Śrīla Prabhupāda's explanation on it reminds us of key requirement for understanding of the *Gīta,* apart from our intellectual efforts.

At Śrī Raṅga-kṣetra, a *brāhmaṇa* Vaiṣṇava used to recite the *Bhagavad-gīta*. But he could not pronounce the words correctly. So, people would criticize and laugh at him. As he read the *Gīta*, his hairs stood on end, tears welled up in his eyes, and his body trembled and perspired. Lord Śrī Caitanya Mahāprabhu, who is none other than Lord Śrī Kṛṣṇa, the speaker of the *Bhagavad-gīta*, saw the *brāhmaṇa* and became very happy. He asked the *brāhmaṇa* which portion of the *Gīta* was giving him so much joy. The *brāhmaṇa* replied, "I am an illiterate. I am reading the *Gīta* as per the orders of my *guru*. When I read the *Gīta*, I only see Kṛṣṇa sitting as Arjuna's charioteer. Taking reins in His hands, He appears very beautiful and blackish. Seeing Kṛṣṇa instructing Arjuna, I am filled with ecstatic happiness."

Lord Caitanya told him, "You are an authority in the reading of the *Bhagavad-gīta*. Whatever you know constitutes the real purport of the *Gīta*." The Lord embraced him, and revealed to him that He was Lord Kṛṣṇa Himself.

The Lord is pleased by devotion and faithful submissiveness to the instructions of *guru*, but not by erudite scholarship or sharp intelligence. The real import of the Gīta or any other Vaiṣṇava scripture is revealed to one who has faith in the Supreme Lord and *guru*. It doesn't depend on external things like pronunciation or scholarship.

Scholarship could be a by-product of one's scriptural study, but the intended end product is the development of good character, and ultimately love for the Supreme Lord Kṛṣṇa. Reaching such a pristine goal begins with the baby steps of practicing various elements of *sādhana* prescribed by our *ācāryas*, of which scriptural study in the association of devotees is one of the important elements.

I sincerely hope and pray that this book is of some assistance in the study and revision of the sincere readers of the *Gīta*, translated and commented by Śrīla Prabhupāda and the other *ācāryas*. I seek forgiveness for any unintended discrepancies in this work and would like to be informed of any improvements required. I invite you to dwell on the glorious teachings of the *Bhagavad-gīta* and experience its enlivening effect.

For systematic verse-by-verse lectures on entire Bhagavad-gita, and short videos on vital verses and lessons from the Gita, by the author, please visit https://gaurangadarshandas.com/gita-subodhini/

THE STRUCTURE OF BHAGAVAD-GĪTA

Gīta, the jewel box

Bhagavad-gīta, the crown jewel of all knowledge, is like a beautiful golden box containing the most valuable secret treasure. The eighteen chapters of the *Gīta* are divided into three sections with six chapters each. The first section concerning *karma-yoga* is the lower covering of the box. The last section about *jñāna-yoga* is the jewel-studded lid of the box. The middle section on *bhakti-yoga* is the most excellent shining jewel inside the box, more valuable than anything in the three worlds—which brings Lord Śrī Kṛṣṇa under control. Śrīla Viśvanātha Cakravarti Ṭhākūra gives this beautiful comparison.

Yoga means to link one's consciousness with the Supreme Absolute Truth. Śrīla Prabhupāda writes, "When the linking process is predominantly in fruitive activities it is called *karma-yoga*, when it is predominantly empirical it is called *jñāna-yoga*, and when it is predominantly in a devotional relationship with the Supreme Lord it is called *bhakti-yoga. Bhakti-yoga*, or Kṛṣṇa consciousness, is the ultimate perfection of all *yogas*." (6.46 Purport)

The essential message of the *Bhagavad-gīta* is *bhakti* or devotional service unto the Supreme Lord Kṛṣṇa. The first six chapters present how to attain *bhakti* by one's work or *karma-yoga*. The last six chapters describe how to attain *bhakti* by knowledge or *jñāna-yoga*. The middle six chapters directly present *bhakti*. This fascinating structure of the *Gīta* ultimately concludes that seeking shelter of Lord Kṛṣṇa by *bhakti-yoga* is the essence of human life.

Karma-yoga (Chapters 1-6)

Karma-yoga means to perform one's prescribed duties and offering them to the Supreme Lord. Such work done with detachment from results is specifically called *niṣkāma-karma-yoga,* which consists of *jñāna* or knowledge developed by such work.

Seeing the armies on the battlefield of Kurukṣetra, Arjuna becomes overwhelmed with compassion for his relatives and gives various reasons why he cannot fight. (1)

Responding to Arjuna's concerns, Kṛṣṇa first gives him the knowledge of the soul (*ātmā-jñāna* or *sāṅkhya*) and says that doing one's prescribed work gives happiness either in victory or defeat (*sakāma-karma*). Kṛṣṇa then recommends doing such work with detachment by which one attains steady knowledge (*sthita prajñatā*). This process is called *niṣkāma-karma-yoga*. (2)

Arjuna gets confused about which of the two – renunciation and action – is better! Kṛṣṇa explains that action based on *niṣkāma-karma-yoga* is preferable to premature renunciation based on *jñāna-yoga*. Even if Arjuna is qualified for renunciation, he should still do *niṣkāma-karma-yoga* to set the right example. Kṛṣṇa also warns about lust, the formidable enemy on the path of *yoga*. (3)

Then Kṛṣṇa teaches transcendental knowledge about Himself – His divine descents, reciprocation with devotees, creation and so on – understanding which many liberated souls did their work with detachment. A *karma-yogī* or a detached worker, although working, doesn't incur reactions. All kinds of sacrificial work culminate in knowledge (*jñāna*), by which one can renounce action (*sannyāsa*). (4)

Arjuna again gets confused about Kṛṣṇa's simultaneous emphasis on *karma-yoga* and renunciation (*sannyāsa*). Kṛṣṇa again clarifies that they both are not contradictory and are the same, but *karma-yoga* is easier. A *niṣkāma-karma-yogī* can be a true *sannyāsī* and be free from all bondage and attain liberation. Then Kṛṣṇa briefly mentions about *aṣṭāṅga-yoga* and the supremacy of *bhakti-yoga*. (5)

Then Kṛṣna speaks of *dhyāna-yoga* or *aṣṭāṅga-yoga* that has two stages – *yogārurukṣa* (beginning) to *yogārūḍha* (advanced). The various practices of *aṣṭāṅga-yoga* are aimed at attaining the perfection of realizing the Supersoul. In *yoga* it is necessary to control the mind by practice and detachment. *Karma-yoga* is a more practical and easier method for Arjuna. However, *bhakti-yogī* is the topmost *yogī*. (6)

Thus, although Kṛṣṇa describes *karma-yoga, jñāna-yoga* and *aṣṭāṅga-yoga* in the first six chapters of the *Gīta,* the main emphasis of this section is *karma-yoga*. *Niṣkāma-karma-yoga* contains within it *jñāna*, and culminates in *aṣṭāṅga yoga*.

Bhakti-yoga (Chapters 7-12)

The middle six chapters that categorically describe *bhakti-yoga* or direct surrender unto Śrī Kṛṣṇa are the essence of the *Gīta*. *Bhakti* essentially means to be in Kṛṣṇa consciousness (*mat-citta*), as Lord Kṛṣṇa says several times in the *Gīta*.

Submissive hearing is the primary aspect of *bhakti* that reveals knowledge about Kṛṣṇa's energies and all-pervasiveness. Kṛṣṇa's inferior material energy constitutes the elements such as earth, water, air and so on. Kṛṣṇa's superior spiritual energy consists of the living entities (*jīvas*). The *jīvas* are prone to be conditioned by the three material modes and thus suffer. Surrendering to Kṛṣṇa in *bhakti-yoga* delivers them. However, impious people do not perform *kṛṣṇa-bhakti;* some worship the devatās; some even consider Kṛṣṇa to be impersonal. And some perform *bhakti* with various intentions – to come out of distress, being inquisitive, desiring wealth and knowledge. But a pure devotee who does unalloyed *bhakti* (*kevala bhakti* or *ananya bhakti*) just to please Lord Kṛṣṇa is the topmost *bhakti-yogī*. A sinless person can do determined *bhakti*. (7)

Whatever one remembers at the time of death will surely attain that object. One who always remembers Kṛṣṇa while doing his duties and performs *ananya-bhakti* can remember Kṛṣṇa at the time of death. He reaches the eternal spiritual abode of Kṛṣṇa and never takes birth again in this miserable material world. *Jñānīs* and *yogīs* attain liberation by the path of light and *karmīs* who take the path of darkness come back to this world. But a *bhakta* attains Kṛṣṇa's abode. (8)

The knowledge of pure *bhakti* is most confidential, and is the king of all education. It gives direct experience of the Absolute Truth and causes ultimate joy. Under Kṛṣṇa's supreme direction, His material energy creates, maintains and destroys this material world, but that work doesn't bind Kṛṣṇa. Different people approach Kṛṣṇa in different ways: fools consider Him as an ordinary human, devotees worship Him constantly with devotion and the three kinds of *jñānīs* worship Him by – considering themselves God, worshiping the universal form and worshiping *devatās* for quick material results. But the process of direct *bhakti* to Kṛṣṇa is most simple and easy. Kṛṣṇa accepts even a leaf, flower, fruit or water offered with devotion. Kṛṣṇa is equal to all, but specially inclined to a devotee and excuses him for accidental mistakes. People of even sinful birth can attain Kṛṣṇa by *bhakti*. So perform direct *bhakti* to Kṛṣṇa. (9)

Lord Kṛṣṇa, the object of *bhakti*, is the source of everything in the material and spiritual worlds. No one including the great sages and *devatās* can know Him. Kṛṣṇa is especially merciful to His devotees who are absorbed in enlivening discussions about Him. Arjuna acknowledges Kṛṣṇa's supreme position, which is also confirmed by great authorities. At Arjuna's request, Kṛṣṇa describes the most prominent of His infinite opulences (*vibhūtīs*), which are just a spark of His splendor. By a single fragment of Himself, Kṛṣṇa pervades and supports this entire universe. (10)

Arjuna desired to see that all-pervading form of Kṛṣṇa. Kṛṣṇa reveals His unlimitedly expansive Universal form (*viśva-rūpa*) by giving Arjuna the divine vision to behold it.

Witnessing that frightening display, Arjuna describes Kṛṣṇa's supremacy and His form of time (*kāla-rūpa*) that devours everything. Kṛṣṇa then shows Arjuna the future outcomes of the war and asks him to be just as an instrument in His mission. Arjuna offers prayers and apologizes Kṛṣṇa for his offenses. At his request, Kṛṣṇa again shows His original two-handed personal form. Pure *bhakti* is the prerequisite to see any form of Kṛṣṇa and attain Him. (11)

A personalist devotee always worships Kṛṣṇa and his path is easy and simple. An impersonalist meditates on the unmanifest Brahman and his path is troublesome. *Bhakti* accommodates people at various levels. Ideally, one should fix one's mind and intelligence on Kṛṣṇa always. But if that is not possible, one can practice to do so by *sādhana-bhakti*. If that is also difficult, one can work for Kṛṣṇa or at least give up the results of one's work for some good cause. A devotee possesses several glorious qualities - like non-envy, equanimity, mercy, tolerance and so on – that make him dear to Lord Kṛṣṇa. (12)

Thus the middle six chapters glorify the path of *kṛṣṇa-bhakti*. In the first six chapters Kṛṣṇa explains the identity (*svarūpa*) of the living entity and in the middle six chapters He speaks of His own identity and the means to realize Him.

Jñāna-yoga (Chapters 13-18)

Jñāna-yoga involves knowing the precise characteristics of the living entity (*jīva*), the material nature (*prakṛti*) and the Supreme Lord (*īśvara*). They are briefly described in the first six chapters and are elaborated in the last six chapters. *Jñāna* assists us in developing detachment from matter and subsequent attachment to Kṛṣṇa. Thus *jñāna* serves as the door to *bhakti*, which is described in the middle section. Without the touch of *bhakti* both *karma* and *jñāna* are useless.

The material body is the field of activities (*kṣetra*) and its knowers are the soul and Kṛṣṇa (*kṣetra-jñas*). Knowledge (*jñānaṁ*) consists of twenty elements including humility, tolerance and so on. The objects of knowledge (*jñeyaṁ*) are the soul and Supersoul. The living entity (*puruṣa*) situated in the material nature (*prakṛti*) associates with the three modes and thinks himself the enjoyer and thus changes bodies. The real *puruṣa* or the enjoyer is the Supreme Lord. The *jīva* is not the only doer of activities. By the vision of knowledge (*jñāna-cakṣu*) one can see the *jīva*, *prakṛti* and the Lord properly. (13)

The Supreme Lord impregnates *prakṛti* with the *jīvas*. Therefore, Kṛṣṇa is the father and *prakṛti* is the mother of all *jīvas*. The *jīvas* get conditioned by the material modes (*guṇas*) namely – goodness, passion and ignorance (*sattva, rajas* and *tamas*). The modes compete with each other for prominence and influence the *jīva's* actions and destinations. By unalloyed *bhakti* unto Lord Kṛṣṇa, one can transcend the modes and become *guṇātīta*. (14)

The material world is like an upside-down banyan tree. One should cut it with the axe of detachment and surrender to Kṛṣṇa and thus attain the spiritual world. The *jīva* is a fragmental part of Kṛṣṇa, but due to the material mind and senses, the *jīva* transmigrates. Kṛṣṇa is the maintainer of all. As Paramātma He is the initiator of all activities. He is above the fallible (*kṣara*) and infallible (*akṣara*) living entities and is the Supersoul of all. Knowing Kṛṣṇa means knowing everything. (15)

Godly men are endowed with divine qualities (*daivī sampada*). Demoniac people have degraded qualities (*asura sampada*) and activities that make them enter hell and lower species. Following scriptures causes elevation and disregarding them causes degradation. (16)

Arjuna inquires about the unauthorized worship of those who have some other faith not based on scriptures. Kṛṣṇa explains that the three modes determine people's faith, which can be known by the nature of their foods, sacrifices, austerities and charity. *Oṁ tat sat* indicates the Supreme Absolute Truth Viṣṇu. (17)

Summarizing all His teachings in the *Gīta*, Kṛṣṇa explains *tyāga* or renunciation in three modes and the five factors of action. He describes knowledge, work, worker, intelligence, determination and happiness in the three modes and purification through prescribed duties of *varṇāśrama*. He then describes Brahman platform (confidential knowledge), surrender to Supersoul (more confidential knowledge) and surrender to Kṛṣṇa (most confidential knowledge). Arjuna and Sañjaya present their realizations. (18)

Yoga ladder

The *Bhagavad-gīta* presents the path of *yoga* as a ladder with multiple rungs to reach the Supreme Lord Kṛṣṇa. This *yoga* ladder that begins from the lowest material condition of the *jīva* and rises up to perfect self-realization in pure spiritual life.

Śrīla Prabhupāda writes, "*Yoga* actually means *bhakti-yoga*; all other *yogas* are progressions toward the destination of *bhakti-yoga*. From the beginning of *karma-yoga* to the end of *bhakti-yoga* is a long way to self-realization. *Karma-yoga*, without fruitive results, is the beginning of this path. When *karma-yoga* increases in knowledge and renunciation, the stage is called *jñāna-yoga*. When *jñāna-yoga* increases in meditation on the Supersoul by different physical processes, and the mind is on Him, it is called *aṣṭāṅga-yoga*. And when one surpasses the *aṣṭāṅga-yoga* and comes to the point of the Supreme Personality of Godhead Kṛṣṇa, it is called *bhakti yoga*, the culmination. Factually, *bhakti-yoga* is the ultimate goal, but to analyze *bhakti-yoga* minutely one has to understand these other *yogas*." (6.47 P)

Śrīla Viśvanātha Cakravarti Ṭhākūra considers the following two verses spoken by Lord Kṛṣṇa, as the servants of *bhakti*. Śrīla Prabhupāda calls them the essence of the *Bhagavad-gīta*.

man-manā bhava mad-bhakto
mad-yājī māṁ namaskuru
mām evaiṣyasi satyaṁ te
pratijāne priyo 'si me

"Always think of Me, become My devotee, worship Me and offer your homage unto Me. Thus you will come to Me without fail. I promise you this because you are My very dear friend." (18.65)

sarva-dharmān parityajya
mām ekaṁ śaraṇaṁ vraja
ahaṁ tvāṁ sarva-pāpebhyo
mokṣayiṣyāmi mā śucaḥ

"Abandon all varieties of religion and just surrender unto Me. I shall deliver you from all sinful reactions. Do not fear." (18.66)

These two pure verses consisting of sixty-four syllables are like the jewels embedded on the lid (last six chapters) of the golden box of the *Gīta*.

BHAGAVAD-GĪTA AT A GLANCE

Part I: KARMA-YOGA (Chapters 1-6)

1. Arjuna observes the armies and becomes overwhelmed by compassion for relatives. Foreseeing no enjoyment in victory, fearful of sinful reactions and concerned about the harmful effects of destroying families, Arjuna decides not to fight.

Dhṛtarāṣṭra becomes hopeful of not losing the kingdom for his sons, but Sañjaya describes how Kṛṣṇa inspires Arjuna to fight.

2. Summary of the Gīta: Arjuna accepts Kṛṣṇa as guru and Kṛṣṇa describes – Jñāna (knowledge of body and soul), sakāma-karma (doing duty and attaining enjoyment), Buddhi-yoga – Niṣkāma-karma-yoga (working with detachment and knowledge) and the qualities of a sthita-prajña.

In 2.49, Kṛṣṇa told Arjuna to keep all abominable actions far away by buddhi-yoga. So, Arjuna asks which of the two - renunciation and action - is better (3.1).

3. Karma-yoga: Kṛṣṇa prescribes action based on niṣkāma-karma-yoga rather than premature renunciation based on jñāna-yoga. Even if Arjuna is qualified for renunciation, he should still do niṣkāma-karma-yoga to set the right example. Lust is a formidable enemy on the path of yoga and one has to conquer it by deliberate spiritual intelligence.

Kṛṣṇa presents transcendental knowledge by which one can be protected from the bondage of lust.

4. Transcendental knowledge descends from Kṛṣṇa in disciplic succession. Knowing the divine nature of Lord Kṛṣṇa's appearance gives liberation. Karma can be understood on the platform of jñāna and one can attain jñāna through yajña (sacrifice), and from a bona fide guru.

Kṛṣṇa spoke of attaining peace by jñāna (4.39) and renouncing karma by jñāna (in 4.41), but again asked Arjuna to take up karma-yoga (in 4.42). So, Arjuna again asks about renunciation (sannyāsa) and action (karma-yoga) (5.1).

5. Karma-yoga – Action In Kṛṣṇa Consciousness: Kṛṣṇa says they both are equal but karma-yoga is easier. Niṣkāma-karma-yoga frees one from bondage. One can attain liberation by focusing on the Supreme. Aṣṭāṅga-yoga and bhakti-yoga give liberation.

Having mentioned about aṣṭāṅga-yoga in brief, Kṛṣṇa now describes it in greater detail.

6. Dhyāna Yoga or Aṣṭāṅga-yoga has two stages – yogārurukṣa (beginning) to yogārūḍha (advanced). Aṣṭāṅga-yoga has various practices and its perfection is to realizing the Supersoul. In yoga it is necessity to control the mind by practice and detachment. Even an unsuccessful yogī is given another opportunity to attain perfection. Bhakti-yogī is the topmost yogī.

In 6.47, Kṛṣṇa says that bhakti is the highest form of yoga. From Chapter 7, He describes bhakti-yoga elaborately.

Part II: BHAKTI-YOGA (Chapters 7-12)

7. Knowledge of the Absolute: Hearing reveals knowledge about Kṛṣṇa's material and spiritual energies. Four types of pious people worship Kṛṣṇa and four types of impious people don't. Some worship devatās and some become impersonalists. One who is free from sins can do determined bhakti.

In 7.29-30, Kṛṣṇa mentions several items starting from Brahman. He elaborates them in Chapter 8.

8. Attaining the Supreme: Whoever remembers Kṛṣṇa at the time of death attains Him. Jñānīs and yogīs attain liberation by path of light and karmī comes back to this world. But a bhakta quits this material world full of miseries and attain Kṛṣṇa's spiritual abode by pure bhakti.

Having described the glory of an ananya-bhakta, Kṛṣṇa describes how to become such an ananya-bhakta.

9. Most confidential knowledge is the knowledge of pure bhakti. Kṛṣṇa creates, maintains and destroys this world by His majestic powers. Fools and jñānīs approach Kṛṣṇa in different ways. But direct bhakti to Kṛṣṇa is the best. Kṛṣṇa is specially inclined to a devotee and forgives him for accidental mistakes.

In 9.34, Kṛṣṇa instructed to fix one's mind in Him. In Chapter 10, Kṛṣṇa describes His opulences on which one can fix his mind and remember Him.

10. The opulences of Kṛṣṇa are unlimited. He is the origin of everything and is especially merciful to His devotees. Arjuna accepts Kṛṣṇa's supreme position and at his request Kṛṣṇa describes all His opulences (vibhūtīs) which are just a spark of His splendor. He is the all-pervading Supersoul of everything in the cosmos.

In 10.42, Kṛṣṇa said that He pervades and supports the entire universe. In 11.1-4, Arjuna desires to see that all-pervasive universal form.

11. The Universal form (viśva-rūpa) of Kṛṣṇa consists of everything within the universe. Frightened upon seeing the form of time (kāla-rūpa) that devoured everything, Arjuna offered prayers and requested Kṛṣṇa to manifest His pleasing two-handed form.

In 11.55, Kṛṣṇa established the supremacy of bhakti-yoga unto His personal form. So, in 12.1 Arjuna inquires about personalists and impersonalists.

12. Devotional service is the highest of all spiritual paths. Kṛṣṇa differentiates between the personalists and impersonalists and gives the progressive levels of bhakti that enable people at various stages to connect with the Supreme. A devotee possesses several glorious qualities that ender him to Kṛṣṇa.

Having describes bhakti-yoga in six chapters, Kṛṣṇa describes jñāna-yoga in the last six chapters.

Part III: JÑĀNA-YOGA (Chapters 13-18)

13. Nature, the enjoyer and consciousness: Upon Arjuna's inquiry Kṛṣṇa explains six topics: (i) kṣetra – field of activities or body; (ii) kṣetra-jñam – knowers of body, the soul and Kṛṣṇa; (iii) jñānaṁ – 20 elements of knowledge; (iv) jñeyaṁ – objects of knowledge, soul and Supersoul; (v) prakṛti – material nature; (vi) puruṣa – jīva and Lord. A true seer has the right vision of jīva, prakṛti and Paramātma.

In 13.22, Kṛṣṇa said that the jīva takes up repeated birth and death due to association with the material modes. In Chapter 14, Kṛṣṇa explains how those modes bind the jīva and the way out.

14. Modes of material nature: The Supreme Lord impregnates the jīvas into the womb of prakṛti that consists of the three material modes. There is competition amongst the modes and one of them becomes prominent and influences the jīva's actions and destinations. By pure bhakti one can transcend the modes (guṇātīta).

In 14.26, Kṛṣṇa said that one can transcend modes by bhakti. But attachment to Kṛṣṇa, needs developing detachment to this world. In Chapter 15, Kṛṣṇa describes the process of detachment.

15. The yoga of the Supreme Person: The material world is like an upside down banyan tree. One should cut it with the axe of detachment and surrender to Kṛṣṇa. Due to material mind and senses, the jīva, although a fragmental part of Kṛṣṇa, transmigrates. Kṛṣṇa is the maintainer of all and is above the fallible (kṣara) and infallible (akṣara) living entities and is the Supersoul.

In Chapter 15, Kṛṣṇa described the Banyan tree of material world, but its fruits are not described. In Chapter 16, Kṛṣṇa describes the good fruits (divine qualities) and bad fruits (demoniac qualities).

16. The divine and demoniac natures: Godly men are endowed with 26 divine qualities (daivī sampada). Demoniac people have degraded qualities (asura sampada) and their activities make them enter hell and lower species. Following the scriptures causes elevation and disregarding them causes degradation.

In 16.23, Kṛṣṇa said that those who disregard scriptures and behave whimsically do not attain happiness in this life or the next. In 17.1, Arjuna asks Kṛṣṇa about the unauthorized worship of those who have some faith not based on scriptures.

17. The divisions of faith: Kṛṣṇa explains that the three modes determine people's faith which can be know by the nature of their foods, sacrifices, austerities and charity. Oṁ tat sat indicates Supreme Absolute Truth Viṣṇu.

In the previous chapters, various systems of yoga and the supremacy of bhakti-yoga have been explained. In the last chapter, Kṛṣṇa gives an overview of Bhagavad-gīta, and stresses that surrender unto Kṛṣṇa in bhakti is the ultimate goal of life.

18. Conclusion, the perfection of renunciation: Kṛṣṇa explains – tyāga in three modes; five factors of action; knowledge, work, worker, intelligence, determination and happiness in three modes; and purification through prescribed duties of varṇāśrama. Then Kṛṣṇa describes Brahman platform, surrender to Supersoul and to Kṛṣṇa.

Part I
Karma-yoga
Chapters 1-6

1. Observing the Armies on the Battlefield of Kurukṣetra

1: Dhṛtarāṣṭra's Inquiry to Sañjaya
- Blind Dhṛtarāṣṭra, partial to his own sons, inquires what his sons and the Pāṇḍavas did on the battlefield.

2-11: Duryodhana's Fear and Diplomacy in Describing the Armies
- Duryodhana goes to Droṇācārya and describes the warriors of the Pāṇḍavas' army and his own army and compares them.

12-19: Blowing of Conchshells (Signs of Victory of the Pāṇḍavas)
- Lord Kṛṣṇa and the Pāṇḍavas blow their conchshells shattering the hearts of the opposite party.

20-27: Arjuna Observes the Armies
- 20-25: Desiring to see the supporters of Duryodhana, Arjuna asks Kṛṣṇa to take the chariot between the two armies.
- 26-27: Seeing different kinds of relatives, Arjuna becomes overwhelmed with compassion.

28-46: Arjuna's Reasons Not to Fight
- 28-30: First reason – Compassion for relatives and the resultant bodily symptoms
- 31-35: Second reason – Foreseeing no enjoyment in victory
- 36-38: Third reason – Fear of sinful reactions
- 39-43: Fourth reason – Harmful effects of destroying the family
- 44-46: Arjuna, being griefsriken, decides not to fight.

1: DHṚTARĀṢṬRA'S INQUIRY TO SAÑJAYA

Background: Dhṛtarāṣṭra was blind from birth. Unfortunately, he was also bereft of spiritual vision. His hundred sons, headed by Duryodhana, were equally blind in the matter of religion. Pāṇḍavas were the sons of Pāṇḍu, Dhṛtarāṣṭra's brother. They were virtuous and Dhṛtarāṣṭra's sons usurped their rightful kingdom by inappropriate means. Now a fight ensued between both the parties at a holy place called Kurukṣetra. Dhṛtarāṣṭra was doubtful about the influence of the holy place on the fate of the battle. Therefore he asked Sañjaya, his assistant, about the situation on the battlefield. By the mercy of Śrīla Vyāsadeva, Sañjaya was able to envision the Battlefield of Kurukṣetra.

1. Dhṛtarāṣṭra asked Sañjaya: "After my sons (*māmakāḥ*) and the sons of Pāṇḍu (*pāṇḍavaḥ*) assembled in the holy place of pilgrimage (*dharma-kṣetra*) at Kurukṣetra, desiring to fight, what did they do?"

dhṛtarāṣṭra uvāca
dharma-kṣetre kuru-kṣetre samavetā yuyutsavaḥ
māmakāḥ pāṇḍavāś caiva kim akurvata sañjaya

Dhṛtarāṣṭra was partial to his own sons and separated his nephews, the Pāṇḍavas, although both parties belonged to the same family. Although he himself had said that they had assembled *to fight*, still he asked Sañjaya what they did, because, he was –

- *desirous* that his sons get the kingdom.
- *doubtful* of the possibility of his sons' victory.
- *fearful* because the holy place Kurukṣetra might influence his sons to compromise.
- *hopeful* that under the holy influence, the Pāṇḍavas may renounce their claim, to avoid bloodshed.

Kṛṣṇa's plan: Just as in a paddy field (*kṣetra*), unnecessary weeds are taken out, similarly in the religious 'field' of Kuru-kṣetra, in the presence of the father of religion, Kṛṣṇa, unwanted harmful weeds like Dhṛtarāṣṭra's sons would be wiped out.

The rest of the chapter is Sañjaya's description of the scene on the battlefield in response to Dhṛtarāṣṭra's inquiry. He first described the acts of Duryodhana, who didn't have any intentions to compromise in the battle, as feared by Dhṛtarāṣṭra.

2-11: DURYODHANA'S FEAR AND DIPLOMACY IN DESCRIBING THE ARMIES

2. Duryodhana approached Droṇācārya, after seeing the army of the Pāṇḍavas and spoke the following words (*verses* 3-11):

3-6. Pāṇḍavas' army: "O teacher, behold this great army, expertly arranged by your intelligent disciple, the son of Drupada. It has many great fighters equal to Bhīma and Arjuna: Yuyudhāna (Sātyaki), Virāṭa, Drupada, Dhṛṣṭaketu, Cekitāna, Kāśirāja, Purujit, Kuntibhoja, Śaibya, Yudhāmanyu, Uttamaujā, Abhimanyu (son of Subhadrā) and the five sons of Draupadī (Prativindhya, Śrutasena, Śrutakīrti, Śatānīka and Śrutakarma). All these people are *mahā-rathas.*"

Duryodhana feared internally seeing the Pāṇḍavas' army. But, being political, he hid his fear by showing that he had come personally out of his respect to *guru*, Droṇa.

Duryodhana points out Droṇācārya for liberally imparting the military secrets to Dhṛṣṭadyumna, despite knowing that he was born to kill Droṇa. Duryodhana wanted Droṇa not be similarly lenient in battle with the Pāṇḍavas, his affectionate students.

Duryodhana wanted to anger Droṇa, by revealing the disrespect of the Pāṇḍavas, who arrogantly came with their army, not considering Droṇa's exalted position as a teacher and a warrior. Also, by addressing Dhṛṣṭadyumna as the son of Drupada, he wanted to remind Droṇa of his previous enmity with Drupada.

Thinking that Droṇācārya might perceive that he was fearful of the Pāṇḍavas' army, Duryodhana then spoke boldly about his own army to cover his inner fears.

7-9. Duryodhana's army: "The captains in my army are personalities like you, Bhīṣma, Karṇa, Kṛpa, Aśvatthāmā, Vikarṇa and Bhūriśravā who are always victorious in battle. There are many other experienced heroes, well equipped with weapons, prepared to lay down their lives for my sake[1] (*madarthe tyakta jīvitāḥ*)."

10-11. Comparison: "Our army, protected by the most experienced general Bhīṣma, is immeasurable (*aparyāptam*[2]), whereas the army of the Pāṇḍavas, protected by less experienced Bhīma, is limited (*paryāptam*). All of you must protect Bhīṣma from all sides, standing at your respective strategic positions."

Duryodhana considered that others might feel less important as he praised Bhīṣma. So he diplomatically said that Bhīṣma, although the greatest hero, was old and needs protection from everyone.

Duryodhana was confident of the full support of Bhīṣmadeva and Droṇācārya in the battle because they did not speak when Draupadī had appealed to them for justice while she was being forced to appear naked.

---

[1] Indirectly it means that they will surely die for taking the side of sinful Duryodhana.

[2] The word "*aparyāptam*" could also mean "insufficient," and "*paryāptam*" could mean "sufficient." Thus Duryodhana's army is inadequate to fight with the Pāṇḍavas.

12-19: Blowing of Conchshells (Signs of Victory of the Pāṇḍavas)

12-13. Then Bhīṣmadeva blew his conchshell loudly, making a sound like the roar of a lion, giving Duryodhana joy. Thereafter, the conchshells, drums, bugles, trumpets and horns were all sounded, and the combined sound was tumultuous.

Bhīṣmadeva's nuanced prediction: Bhīṣma, without saying a word, blew the conchshell, informing his depressed grandson Duryodhana that he had no chance of victory, because the Supreme Lord Kṛṣṇa was on the other side. But still, it was his duty to conduct the fight, and no pains would be spared in that connection.

14. Lord Kṛṣṇa and Arjuna, stationed on a great chariot drawn by white horses, sounded their transcendental conchshells (*divyau śaṅkhau*).

tataḥ śvetair hayair yukte mahati syandane sthitau
mādhavaḥ pāṇḍavaś caiva divyau śaṅkhau pradadhmatuḥ

15-16. Names of the conchshells blown by various personalities:

	Personality	Conchshell
1	Hṛṣīkeśa (Lord Kṛṣṇa)	Pāñcajanya
2	Dhanañjaya (Arjuna)	Devadatta
3	Vṛkodara (Bhīma)	Pauṇḍra
4	Yudhiṣṭhira	Ananta-vijaya
5	Nakula	Sughoṣa
6	Sahadeva	Maṇipuṣpaka

Kṛṣṇa is called **Hṛṣīkeśa,** because He is the owner of all senses. He directs the senses of all living entities in terms of their surrender. Here in the battle, He directly controls the transcendental senses of Arjuna.

Arjuna is called **Dhanañjaya,** because he helped his elder brother in fetching wealth when it was required by the king to conduct different sacrifices.

Bhīma is called **Vṛkodara,** because he could eat as voraciously as he could perform herculean tasks, such as killing the demon Hiḍimba.

17-18. Others like Kāśīrāja, Śikhaṇḍī, Dhṛṣṭadyumna, Virāṭa, Sātyaki, Drupada, the sons of Draupadī and Abhimanyu, all blew their respective conchshells.

Sañjaya informed Dhṛtarāṣṭra very tactfully (by the words "*divyau śaṅkhau*" in 1.14 and further by speaking the next verse) that the signs already clearly indicated that the whole Kuru dynasty would be killed in that great battle, and his unlawful policy to deceive the Pāṇḍavas wasn't very laudible. The whole catastrophe was due to King Dhṛtarāṣṭra, because he encouraged the policy followed by his sons.

19. Kurus' hearts shattered: The blowing of various conchshells became uproarious. Vibrating both in the sky and on the earth, it shattered the hearts of the sons of Dhṛtarāṣṭra.

Pāṇḍavas' confidence in Kṛṣṇa: The sound of the conches of Bhīṣma and others on Duryodhana's side did not cause any heart-breaking for the Pāṇḍāvas. One who takes shelter of Lord Kṛṣṇa has nothing to fear, even in the midst of the greatest calamity.

20-27: Arjuna Observes the Armies

20. Arjuna took up his bow and prepared to shoot arrows, after looking at the sons of Dhṛtarāṣṭra drawn in military array. The battle was about to begin. Arjuna, with Hanumān's insignia on his flag (*kapi-dhvajaḥ*), then spoke to Lord Kṛṣṇa:

The emblem of Hanumān is another sign of victory for Arjuna, because Hanumān helped Lord Rāma to be victorious over Rāvaṇa. Lord Kṛṣṇa is Rāma Himself, and thus His eternal servitor Hanumān and His eternal consort Sītā (goddess of fortune), were also present with Arjuna now.

21-23. Arjuna said to Kṛṣṇa, "O infallible one (*acyuta*), please draw my chariot between the two armies so that I may see those present here, who desire to fight, wishing to please the evil-minded son of Dhṛtarāṣṭra, and with whom I must fight."

Kṛṣṇa is called **Acyuta,** because He *never fails* in His affection for His devotees and takes pleasure in serving them. Here, as a charioteer, He carried out Arjuna's orders without hesitation. Yet, in all circumstances, His supreme position remains intact.

Arjuna had no desire to fight with his cousins, because he is a pure devotee. But he was forced by the obstinacy of Duryodhana, who was never agreeable to any peaceful negotiation. Arjuna wanted to make an estimate of the strength which he had to face.

24-25. Lord Hṛṣīkeśa then drew the chariot between the two armies, at the request of Guḍākeśa (Arjuna). In the presence of Bhīṣma, Droṇa and all the other chieftains, the Lord said, "Just behold, Pārtha, all the Kurus assembled here."

Arjuna is called **Guḍākeśa,** because he conquered sleep (*guḍākā* means sleep). Sleep also means ignorance. So Arjuna conquered both sleep and ignorance because of his absorption in the remembrance of the beauty and qualities of his close friend, Kṛṣṇa.

Kṛṣṇa is called **Hṛṣīkeśa,** because He could understand the mind of Arjuna. Although He is the controller of everyone's senses, He is now controlled by Arjuna's words.

Kṛṣṇa called Arjuna as **Pārtha,** because he is the son of Pṛthā, or Kuntī, the sister of His father Vasudeva. As a friend, He had agreed to be Arjuna's charioteer, but now by saying "Behold the Kurus", He predicted Arjuna's mind of giving up fighting in joking.

26-27. Arjuna sees all kinds of relatives			
i	*pitṝn*	Fathers	Bhūriśravā
ii	*pitāmahān*	Grandfathers	Bhīṣma, Somadatta
iii	*ācāryān*	Teachers	Droṇācārya, Kṛpācārya
iv	*mātulān*	Maternal uncles	Śalya, Śakuni
v	*bhrātṝn*	Brothers	Duryodhana, Vikarna and others
vi	*putrān*	Sons	Lakṣmaṇa kumāra and others
vii	*pautrān*	Grandsons	Sons of Lakṣmaṇa
viii	*sakhīṁs*	Friends	Aśvatthāmā
ix	*śvaśurān*	Fathers-in-law	Drupada
x	*suhṛdaś*	Well-wishers	Kṛtavarmā (this word best applies to Kṛṣṇa)
Seeing all the above categories of people, Arjuna was overwhelmed by compassion and spoke. (This compassion is the first reason due to which Arjuna didn't want to fight).			

Kṛṣṇa has put Arjuna under illusion. Being the merciful Lord of all beings, Kṛṣṇa desired to deliver the universe through instructions to His dear associate Arjuna. He thus made Arjuna feel that his duty to fight was against religious principles, through a distortion of the philosophy of non-violence mentioned in the *śruti* scriptures.

28-46: Arjuna's Reasons Not to Fight

In this section, Arjuna presents four reasons not to fight in the battle. In the next chapter, he becomes indecisive whether to fight or not (See 2.6). Kṛṣṇa addresses these concerns and confusions of Arjuna in the later chapters as shown below.

Why Arjuna didn't want to fight? –		Kṛṣṇa addresses them in –
i	Compassion for friends and relatives (1.28-30)	2.11-30
ii	No enjoyment even if victorious (1.31-35)	2.31-37
iii	Fear of sinful reactions (1.36-38)	2.33, 38-53
iv	Destruction of family traditions (1.39-43)	2.45-46, 3.24
v	Indecision (2.6)	2.41

28-30: First reason – Compassion for relatives and the resultant bodily symptoms	
dṛṣṭvemaṁ sva-janaṁ kṛṣṇa	My dear Kṛṣṇa, seeing my friends and relatives
yuyutsuṁ samupasthitam	present before me in such a fighting spirit, –
sīdanti mama gātrāṇi	(*i*) the **limbs** of my body are quivering,
mukhaṁ ca pariśuṣyati	(*ii*) my **mouth** is drying up,
vepathuś ca śarīre me	(*iii*) my whole **body** is trembling,
roma-harṣaś ca jāyate	(*iv*) my **hairs** are standing on end,
gāṇḍīvaṁ sraṁsate hastāt	(*v*) my Gāṇḍīva **bow** is slipping from my hand,
tvak caiva paridahyate	(*vi*) my **skin** is burning.
na ca śaknomy avasthātuṁ	(*vii*) I am unable to **stand** here any longer.
bhramatīva ca me manaḥ	(*viii*) I am forgetting myself, and my **mind** is reeling.
nimittāni ca paśyāmi viparītāni keśava	(*ix*) I see only causes of **misfortune** and opposite results, O Kṛṣṇa, killer of the Keśī demon.

Arjuna felt compassionate to his own soldiers and even for the soldiers of the opposite party, foreseeing their imminent death. This is due to his softheartedness, a characteristic of a pure devotee.

By Kṛṣṇa's will, Arjuna is showing ignorance of his real self-interest, which is to satisfy the Supreme Lord. Thus he displayed impatience and weakness of mind. Excessive attachment for material things puts a man in such bewilderment, fear and loss of mental equilibrium. When one sees only frustration in his expectations, he thinks, "Why am I here?" Arjuna considered his victory to be a cause of lamentation.

31-35: Second reason – Foreseeing no enjoyment in victory

31. No desire for kingdom	
na ca śreyo 'nupaśyāmi	I do not see how any good can come
hitvā sva-janam āhave	from killing my own kinsmen in this battle –
na kāṅkṣe vijayam kṛṣṇa	nor can I, my dear Kṛṣṇa, desire any victory,
na ca rājyam sukhāni ca	kingdom, or happiness.

No interest in kingdom: Attracted to bodily relationships, sometimes people forget even the causes of material happiness. A *kṣatriya* requires a kingdom for his subsistence, and as a *kṣatriya,* Arjuna's sole opportunity for reclaiming the kingdom lies in fighting with his cousins. However, Arjuna lost interest in fighting, just as a person who has lost interest in food has no interest in cooking. Instead, Arjuna considers living in the forest as more commendable for him.

Arjuna now relates the reason for his disinterest in the kingdom and victory.

32-35. No pleasure without relatives: O Govinda, what is the use of a kingdom, happiness or life[1], when those for whom we desire them – teachers, fathers, sons, grandfathers, uncles and other relatives – are ready to give up their lives and wealth in the battle? Why should I wish to kill them, even if they kill me? O Madhusūdana, I can't fight with them even in exchange for the three worlds[2], let alone this earth. O Janārdana, what pleasure will we derive from killing the sons of Dhṛtarāṣṭra?

Kṛṣṇa is called **Govinda** because He knows (*vindati*) the functions of everyone's senses (*go*). Arjuna called Kṛṣṇa as Govinda, expecting Kṛṣṇa to understand his mind.

Everyone wants to show his opulence to friends and relatives, but Arjuna fears that if all his relatives are killed, he will be unable to share his opulence after victory.

Arjuna called Kṛṣṇa **Janārdana,** because if they are to be killed, then Kṛṣṇa, who descended to relieve the earth of its burden, should kill them. And Kṛṣṇa, being the Supreme Lord need not suffer the effects of sin in killing them also.

Kṛṣṇa had already killed them before their coming into the battlefield and Arjuna was only an instrument for Kṛṣṇa. A devotee doesn't retaliate against the wrongdoer, but the Lord does not tolerate any mischief done to the devotee by the miscreants.

36-38: Third reason – Fear of sinful reactions

36. If we slay such aggressors (*ātatāyinaḥ*), sin will overcome us. What should we gain, O Mādhava, and how could we be happy by killing our own kinsmen?

Six kinds of aggressors: One who – (1) gives poison, (2) sets fire to house, (3) attacks with weapons, (4) plunders riches, (5) occupies land, and (6) kidnaps wife. They should be killed at once, and there is no sin in doing so (*Manu Smṛti 8.350*).

Artha-śāstra Vs. Dharma-śāstra: The above statement of *artha śāstra* (politics and sociology) is inferior to that of *dharma śāstra* (religion and saintly behaviour), which says that one shouldn't afflict any living entity. Thus killing Bhīṣma and other worshipable people is certainly sin. So, Arjuna wanted to be saintly and forgive them. After all, kingdoms are not permanent.

---

[1] This shows Arjuna's **control** over his senses and mind (*śama* and *dama*).

[2] This shows Arjuna's **indifference** to enjoyment of this life and the next (*uparati*).

Arjuna called Kṛṣṇa as **Mādhava**, the husband (*dhava*) of Lakṣmī (*mā*), the goddess of fortune, because He wanted Him not to instigate a war that brings misfortune (Kṛṣṇa, however never brings misfortune to anyone, to say nothing of His devotees).

Although it's the obligation of a *kṣatriya* not to refuse to battle or gamble when he is so challenged by some rival party, Arjuna considered it better not to accept it.

37-38. These greedy men see no fault (*doṣam*) in killing the family (*kula-kṣaya*) or quarreling with friends (*mitra-droha*), as their hearts are overtaken by greed (*lobhopahata-cetasaḥ*). But, O Janārdana, why should we, who can see the crime in destroying a family, engage in these acts of sin (*pātakam*)?

Obligation is actually binding when the effect is good, but not when the effect is otherwise. Considering all these pros and cons, Arjuna decided not to fight.

39-43: Fourth reason – Harmful effects of destroying the family

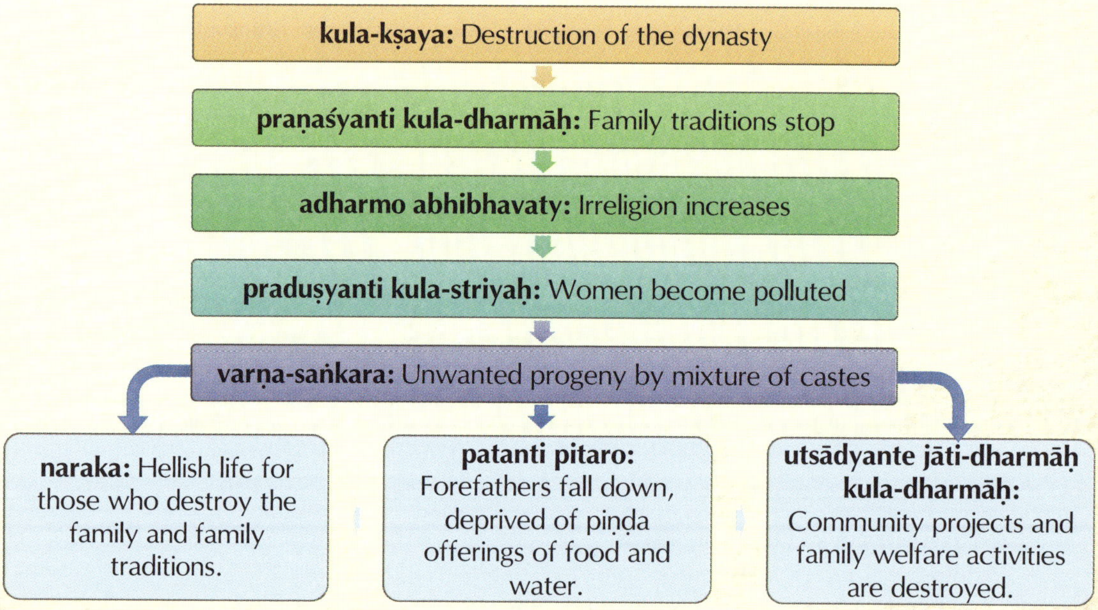

Elders in a family in the *varṇāśrama* system are responsible for the right conduct of younger family members. But upon their death, family traditions may stop, and others develop irreligious habits and thereby lose their chance for spiritual salvation.

Chaste women engaged in different family traditions of religious activities will give birth to a good population, which is the basis of peace, prosperity and spiritual progress in human society.

Forefathers, sometimes may suffer from some sinful reactions or may not acquire gross bodies, but remain in subtle bodies. When their descendants offer them *viṣṇu-prasāda* (remnants of food offered to Viṣṇu), they are delivered from sinful reactions. However, simply by performing devotional service unto the Supreme Lord, one can deliver thousands of forefathers from all kinds of misery.

Mixture of castes results in many faults that destroy both the principles of castes like *kṣatriya* (*jāti dharma*) and the principles of particular families (*kula-dharma*), which are designed for the ultimate salvation of a human being. Irresponsible leaders who break this tradition bring about chaos in that society.

44. Alas, how strange it is that we are preparing to commit greatly sinful acts (*mahat pāpaṁ*). Driven by the desire for royal enjoyment (*rājya-sukha-lobhena*), we are intent on killing our own kinsmen.

Even if Arjuna is disinclined to fight, the opposite party is inclined to fight and kill him. But Arjuna prefers to die in their hands without opposition, considering it as atonement (*prāyaścitta*) for the sin of thinking of killing relatives.

45. Better for me if the sons of Dhṛtarāṣṭra, weapons in hand, were to kill me unarmed (*aśastraṁ*) and unresisting (*apratīkāram*) on the battlefield.

46. Saying this, Arjuna cast aside his bow and arrows and sat down on the chariot, his mind overwhelmed with grief.

Qualification for enlightenment: Such a kind, soft-hearted and non-violent person like Arjuna, is fit to receive self-knowledge, by inquiring about *ātmā* (soul), and not one who is cruel and violent.

2. Contents of the Gīta Summarized

- **1-10:** Arjuna's indecision and accepting Lord Kṛṣṇa as his guru
  - 1-3: Lord Kṛṣṇa chastises Arjuna and disapproves his so-called compassion
  - 4-6: Arjuna's further doubts and confusion
  - 7-10: Arjuna surrenders to Kṛṣṇa and Kṛṣṇa begins to speak
- **11-30:** Jñāna/ Sāṅkhya – Analysis of body and soul (Matter and Spirit)
  - 11-13: Don't lament unnecessarily, all individuals exist eternally and changing bodies is natural.
  - 14-15: Tolerate dualities; equanimilty is eligibility for liberation
  - 16-22: The soul never dies and the body is perishable. Changing bodies is similar to changing clothes.
  - 23-25: The qualities of the eternal soul
  - 26-30: Birth and death are inevitable. No need to lament for the eternal soul.
- **31-37:** Sakāma-karma – Performing prescribed duty gives enjoyment
  - 31-32: Doing prescribed duty of fighting open doors for heaven.
  - 33-36: By avoiding fight, you wil incur sin, infamy and criticism
  - 37: Benefit of fight – kingdom in victory and heaven in defeat.
- **38-53:** Niṣkāma-karma-yoga / Buddhi-yoga – Detached work without reactions
  - 38: Dutifully fight with equanimity → no sin
  - 39-40: Buddhi yoga – no loss in this yoga
  - 41-46: Vyasāyātmika intelligence and vedic karma-kāṇḍa
  - 47-49: How to practice Niṣkāma-karma-yoga
  - 50-53: Benefits of acting in Buddhi-yoga

54-72: Sthita-prajña – The qualities of a liberated soul (Jīvan-mukta)

- 54. Arjuna's questions about a sthita-prajña (Q1-Q4)
- 55. [A1] Symptoms of a sthita-prajña
- 56-57: [A2] Sthita-prajña's response to dualities (speech)
- 58-63: [A3] Sthita-prajña's sense control (sitting) – He withdraws senses like a tortoise. Sense control is difficult even for the wise, and is possible only by kṛṣṇa-bhakti. One falls down in eight stages due to uncontrolled mind.
- 64-71: [A4] Sthita-prajña's sense engagement (walking) – By attaining the Lord's mercy, one's intelligence is established and one attains peace. Agitated senses carry away intelligence and a sthita-prajña is unagitated. Qualities & destination of sthita-prajña.

In the previous chapter, Sañjaya concluded that Arjuna was not inclined to fight. That made Dhṛtarāṣṭra joyful that Pāṇḍavas would be renouncing the kingdom.

In this chapter Sañjaya, seeing Dhṛtarāṣṭra hopeful of not losing the kingdom for his sons, began to describe how Kṛṣṇa inspires Arjuna to fight.

This chapter is entitled as "Contents of the *Gītā* summarized," because, it describes the subject matters of *karma-yoga, jñāna-yoga*, and also a glimpse of *bhakti-yoga*. These very topics are discussed in the entire *Gītā*. In this chapter Lord Kṛṣṇa presents an analytical study of the material body and the spirit soul (*jñāna or sānkhya*), working with and without attachment to results (*sakāma* and *niṣkāma karmas*), and the characteristics of a person fixed in the conception of the real self (*sthita prajña*).

1-10: Arjuna's Indecision and Accepting Lord Kṛṣṇa As Guru

1-3: Lord Kṛṣṇa chastises Arjuna

1. Seeing Arjuna full of compassion (*kṛpayāviṣṭam*), lamentation (*viṣīdantam*) and his eyes full of tears (*aśru-pūṛṇa akulekṣaṇam*), Lord Madhusūdana spoke the following words:

Kṛṣṇa is called Madhusūdana, because He killed the demon named Madhu. Now Arjuna wanted Kṛṣṇa to kill the demon of misunderstanding that had overtaken him in the discharge of his duty.

2-3. Lord Kṛṣṇa disapproves Arjuna's so-called compassion	
śrī-bhagavān uvāca	The Supreme Personality of Godhead, Kṛṣṇa said –
kutas tvā kaśmalam idaṁ viṣame samupasthitam	How have these impurities come upon you in this critical hour of crisis? They –
anārya-juṣṭam asvargyam akīrti-karam arjuna	(*i*) do not befit a civilized man who values liberation, (*ii*) do not lead to higher planets, but (*iii*) lead to infamy, O Arjuna!
klaibyaṁ mā sma gamaḥ pārtha	Do not yield to this degrading impotence (cowardice), O Pārtha (you are My friend),
naitat tvayy upapadyate	This is not suitable to you.
kṣudraṁ hṛdaya-daurbalyaṁ	This (so-called magnanimity and non-violence) is petty weakness of heart.
tyaktvottiṣṭha parantapa	Give it up and arise, O chastiser of the enemy.

Bhagavān means one who possesses all riches, all strength, all fame, all beauty, all knowledge and all renunciation in full. Only Kṛṣṇa can claim this. No living entity, including Brahmā and Śiva can possess opulences as fully as Kṛṣṇa. It is concluded in *Brahma-saṁhitā* and *Śrīmad-Bhāgavatam* that Kṛṣṇa is the Supreme Personality of Godhead.

Āryan is one who knows the value of life and has a civilization based on spiritual values and liberation from material bondage. Cowardice is befitting the non-Āryans.

4-6: Arjuna's further doubts and confusion

4. How can I counterattack in battle men like Bhīṣma and Droṇa, who are worthy of my worship, O killer of enemies (*ari-sūdana*), O Madhusūdana?

Superiors are always respectable and not to be offered even a verbal fight, even if they are sometimes harsh. It is general etiquette. Even Kṛṣṇa will injure only enemies (*ari-sūdana*), not His own grandfather, Ugrasena, or His teacher, Sāndīpani Muni!

5. Better to live by begging[1] (*bhaikṣyam*) than to kill such great souls (*mahā-anubhāvān*), my teachers and superiors (*gurūn*), though they desire worldly gain (*artha-kāmān*). If they are killed, everything we enjoy will be tainted with their blood (and the sin of killing *gurus*).

A teacher who does an abominable action and has lost discrimination is fit to be abandoned. Bhīṣma and Droṇa were obliged to take the side of Duryodhana because of his financial assistance, and thus lost their respectability. Yet Arjuna denied killing them because of his continued acceptance of them as *gurus*.

---

[1] This shows Arjuna's **tolerance** of dualities of nature (*titikṣa*)

6. I do not know which is better—conquering or being conquered. If we kill the sons of Dhṛtarāṣṭra, we should not care to live. Yet they are standing before us.

Arjuna is confused –

- "Should I dutifully fight and risk unnecessary violence?"
- "Should I refrain and live by begging?" (This shows his detachment)
- "Victory is anyways not certain!"
- "Victory is also defeat, as we can't live happily after killing relatives!"

Arjuna's intelligence got bewildered in trying to understand the implementation of *dharma*. Therefore he submits himself as a disciple of Kṛṣṇa seeking His guidance.

7-10: Arjuna surrenders to Lord Kṛṣṇa

7. Arjuna accepts Lord Kṛṣṇa as his guru	
kārpaṇya-doṣopahata-svabhāvaḥ	Due to miserly weakness, I am afflicted.
pṛcchāmi tvāṁ dharma-sammūḍha-cetāḥ	I ask You, being confused about my duty.
yac chreyaḥ syān niścitaṁ brūhi tan me	Tell me for certain what is best for me.
śiṣyas te 'haṁ śādhi māṁ tvāṁ prapannam	Now I am Your disciple, and a soul surrendered unto You[1]. Please instruct me.

8. I can find no means to drive away this grief, which is drying up my senses, even if I win a prosperous, unrivaled kingdom with sovereignty like that of the devatās.

A guru has to be approached to solve the perplexities of life and to understand the solution. Arjuna realized that so-called knowledge, wealth and material comforts are useless in solving his problems. Therefore, He wants to stop friendly talks with Kṛṣṇa and become a disciple of Kṛṣṇa, as he finds no one superior to Him.

Dhṛtarāṣṭra must have been very glad to know that Arjuna was not going to fight and his sons could get the kingdom. But Sañjaya disappointed him by speaking as follows:

9. Arjuna, the chastiser of enemies (*parantapa*), then told Hṛṣikeśa, Kṛṣṇa, "Govinda, I shall not fight," and fell silent.

Arjuna is called **Parantapa,** because although he was overwhelmed with false grief due to family affection, because he surrendered unto Kṛṣṇa, the supreme *guru*, he would soon be enlightened and surely fight.

Kṛṣṇa is called **Hṛṣikeśa** (controller of the senses), because Kṛṣṇa will now make Arjuna manifest intelligence to fight. Kṛṣṇa is called **Govinda** (knower of everything), because Kṛṣṇa will make Arjuna accept his *dharma* to fight.

[1] This shows Arjuna's **deep faith** in the words of his *guru* Lord Kṛṣṇa (*śraddhā*).

Arjuna's qualification to receive spiritual knowledge: As a devotee, he showed –

- *śama* and *dama*: complete control over his mind and senses (1.32)
- *uparati*: indifference to enjoyment (1.35)
- *titikṣa*: tolerance towards dualities (2.5)
- *śraddha*: faith in the instruction of Śrī Kṛṣṇa (2.7)

Thus Arjuna was quite fit for liberation.

10. Then Kṛṣṇa smiled and spoke to the grief-stricken Arjuna, in the midst of both the armies.

Lord Hṛṣīkeśa smiled slightly because his friend Guḍākeśa had chosen to become a disciple. Yet He supressed His smile and at once assumed the role of a *guru* and talked with gravity, chastising His student. Hṛṣīkeśa was previously controlled by the words of Arjuna out of love for him (1.24), and now He became the controller of Arjuna's mind, again out of love, for the benefit of Arjuna.

11-30: JÑĀNA/ SĀṄKHYA – ANALYSIS OF BODY AND SOUL (MATTER AND SPIRIT)

Gist of the section: Kṛṣṇa addresses the first concern of Arjuna due to which he didn't want to fight. Arjuna earlier felt '*compassionate*' towards the fighters of both parties (in 1.28-30). Lord Kṛṣṇa instructs Arjuna to '*give up unnecessary lamentation*' by understanding that '*the spirit soul is eternal*' and '*the material body is perishable*' and encourages him to '*fight.*'

11. Don't lament unnecessarily	
aśocyān anvaśocas tvaṁ prajñā-vādāṁś ca bhāṣase	You are mourning for what is not worthy of grief, while speaking learned words.
gatāsūn agatāsūṁś ca nānuśocanti paṇḍitāḥ	The wise lament neither for the living nor for the dead.

Arjuna was not wise because, he argued that *dharma-śāstra* (religious principles) is greater than *artha-śāstra* (politics or sociology), but he did not know that *jñāna-śāstra* (knowledge of matter, soul and the Supreme Controller of both) is even greater.

There should be no lamentation for the destruction of the –

- *gross body* – since it is inevitable.
- *subtle body* – since it is indestructible when the gross body changes.
- *soul* – since it is eternal.

12. All individuals exist eternally	
na tv evāhaṁ jātu nāsaṁ	Never was there a time when I (*paramātmā*) did not exist,
na tvaṁ neme janādhipāḥ	nor you (*jīvātmā*), nor all these kings (*jīvātmās*);

na caiva na bhaviṣyāmaḥ	nor in the future
sarve vayam ataḥ param	shall any of us cease to be.

Kṛṣṇa is the Supreme eternal amongst all the eternal beings and is the maintainer of all individual living entities both in their conditioned and liberated states.

Arjuna might argue, "Although the soul is eternal, body is related to the soul and thus becomes an object of affection. One's relatives who are connected to that body also become dear. So when their bodies perish, there will certainly be lamentation."

13. Change of body is natural	
dehino 'smin yathā dehe	As the embodied soul continuously passes, in this body,
kaumāraṁ yauvanaṁ jarā	from boyhood to youth to old age,
tathā dehāntara-prāptir	the soul similarly passes into another body at death.
dhīras tatra na muhyati	A sober person is not bewildered by such a change.

Dhīra is a sober person who has perfect knowledge of the constitution of the individual soul, the Supersoul, and nature—both material and spiritual.

One may rejoice the changes of the body, as one gets a new body with rejuvenated energy. Changes of body account for varieties of enjoyment or suffering, according to one's work in life. Bhīṣma and Droṇa, being noble souls, will surely get spiritual bodies or at least heavenly bodies. So, in either case, there was no need to lament.

Arjuna might argue, "But still, I am attached to their current bodies, and lament due to separation from them. Thus, my senses and mind are burning up."

14. Tolerate the temporary dualities	
mātrā-sparśās tu kaunteya	O son of Kuntī, senses experiencing the sense objects
śītoṣṇa-sukha-duḥkha-dāḥ	produce sensations of cold and heat (winter and summer) or happiness and distress.
āgamāpāyino 'nityās	Their appearance and disappearance are nonpermanent.
tāṁs titikṣasva bhārata	One must learn to tolerate them, O scion of Bharata.

One has to execute his duty despite climatic inconveniences; similarly a *kṣatriya* has to fight dutifully even if it is with some friend or relative.

Arjuna is called **Kaunteya** and **Bhārata** indicating the greatness of his heritage from his mother's side and father's side respectively. A great heritage brings responsibility in the matter of proper discharge of duties; therefore, he cannot avoid fighting.

15. Equanimity is the eligibility for liberation	
yaṁ hi na vyathayanty ete puruṣaṁ puruṣarṣabha	O best among men [Arjuna], a person who is not disturbed and is
sama-duḥkha-sukhaṁ dhīraṁ	equal in both happiness and distress and is patient,
so 'mṛtatvāya kalpate	is certainly eligible for liberation.

Following one's *dharma* (duty) leads to *jñāna* (knowledge), from which arises *mukti* (liberation), after which there is no compliance to follow those rules.

16. The seers of the truth (*tattva-darśibhiḥ*) realized the conclusion that there is –

i. no permanent existence for the material body (*asat*), and
ii. no change for the eternal soul (*asat*).

nāsato vidyate bhāvo nābhāvo vidyate sataḥ
ubhayor api dṛṣṭo 'ntas tv anayos tattva-darśibhiḥ

Matter Vs. spirit: The body changes every moment by the actions and reactions of different cells. But the soul remains the same despite all changes of body and mind. The soul actually does not have a relation with the subtle or gross material bodies and their products like lamentation and bewilderment. This relation is only due to ignorance or misidentification of the soul with the body.

17. The soul is indestructible (*avināśi*). The soul pervades the entire body (and is perceived as individual consciousness). No one can destroy that imperishable (*avyaya*) soul.

18. Material body Vs. Spirit soul	
antavanta ime dehā	The material body is perishable.
nityasyoktāḥ śarīriṇaḥ	The embodied soul is eternal.
anāśino aprameyasya	That soul is indestructible and immeasurable.
tasmād yudhyasva bhārata	Therefore, fight, O descendant of Bharata

19. The soul doesn't kill or get killed (*nāyaṁ hanti na hanyate*): Neither he who thinks the soul is the killer nor he who thinks it is killed is in knowledge.

The size of the soul is one ten-thousandth part of the tip of the hair (*Śvetāśvatara Upaniṣad* 5.9). It is a spiritual atom smaller than the material atoms. It is situated within the heart (*Muṇḍaka Upaniṣad* 3.1.9). It is beyond measurement and cannot even be seen by an enemy, to say nothing of being killed. What is killed is only the material body. Thus Arjuna, a soul is neither the killer nor is the object of killing.

20. Soul never dies	
na jāyate mriyate vā kadācin	The soul has neither birth nor death at any time.
nāyaṁ bhūtvā bhavitā vā na bhūyaḥ	He has not come into being, does not come into being, and will not come into being.
ajo nityaḥ śāśvato 'yaṁ purāṇo	He is unborn, eternal, ever-existing and primeval.
na hanyate hanyamāne śarīre	He is not killed when the body is killed.

The body undergoes six changes, namely – birth, existence, growth, producing by-products, dwindling and death. Soul doesn't undergo these changes.

21. No one can kill the soul: O Pārtha, how can a person who knows that the soul is indestructible, eternal, unborn and immutable kill anyone or cause anyone to kill?

22. Changing bodies is similar to changing clothes	
vāsāṁsi jīrṇāni yathā vihāya	As a person gives up old garments
navāni gṛhṇāti naro 'parāṇi	and accepts new garments,
tathā śarīrāṇi vihāya jīrṇāny	the soul similarly gives up old and useless bodies
anyāni saṁyāti navāni dehī	and attains new bodies.

23-25. The eternal soul –	
nainaṁ chindanti śastrāṇi	– cannot be cut by weapons.
nainaṁ dahati pāvakaḥ	– cannot be burnt by fire (weapon).
na cainaṁ kledayanty āpo	– cannot be moistened by water (weapon).
na śoṣayati mārutaḥ	– cannot be withered by wind (weapon).
acchedyo 'yam adāhyo 'yam	– is unbreakable and cannot be burnt.
akledyo 'śoṣya eva ca	– is insoluble and cannot be dried.
nityaḥ sarva-gataḥ sthāṇur	– is everlasting, exists everywhere[1] and unchangeable,
acalo 'yaṁ sanātanaḥ	– is immovable and eternally the same.
avyakto 'yam acintyo 'yam	– is imperceptible and inconceivable.
avikāryo 'yam ucyate	– is immutable or without changes.
tasmād evaṁ viditvainaṁ	Knowing it to be thus,
nānuśocitum arhasi	you should not grieve for the body.

[1] **Souls exist everywhere** throughout the God's creation – on the land, in the water, air, earth and even fire, and in all planets, accepting all types of bodies according to one's *karma*.

Lord Kṛṣṇa so far presented His own opinion and the scriptural conclusions on why one shouldn't lament for the soul. In 2.26, Kṛṣṇa will present other viewpoints according to material vision that rejects the existence of soul. Knowing them, one can appreciate Kṛṣṇa's viewpoint, which He reiterates in 2.27.

26. Other doctrines[1]**:** Even if you think that the soul is always born and dies forever, you still have no reason to lament, O mighty-armed.

27. The inevitable birth-death cycle	
jātasya hi dhruvo mṛtyur	One who is born is sure to die (due to *karma*).
dhruvaṁ janma mṛtasya ca	After death one is sure to take birth again.
tasmād aparihārye 'rthe	Both are unavoidable, therefore, in doing your duty,
na tvaṁ śocitum arhasi	you should not lament.

By avoiding his duty, Arjuna would not be able to stop the death of his relatives, but he would be degraded due to his selection of the wrong path of action.

Birth is combination of *ātmā* with previously non-existing senses and body.

Death is the separation of the *ātmā* from that body with its senses.

Birth and death arise from one's good and bad deeds.

28. All living beings are –

i. invisible in their beginning (before birth),

ii. manifest in their interim state (during the lifetime), and

iii. invisible again when destroyed (after death). So why lament?

This verse is explained form the perspective of two philosophies as follows –

Sāṅkhya: Even when the living entities are not visible, their subtle and gross bodies exist invisibly in a potential form (due to their *karmas*), as the elements (like earth) composing the bodies always exist (*sāṅkhya*). The law of conservation of energy remains, but in course of time things are manifested and unmanifested.

Dṛṣṭi-sṛṣṭi vāda: Even when the living entities are visible in their middle period, that visibility is also an illusion.

Thus, whether one believes in the existence of the soul or not, there is no need to lament for loss of the body.

---

[1] The *Lokāyatas* claim that the body is *ātmā*, or the self, which is continually born and continually dies. The *Vaibhāsikas* maintain that the *ātmā* is different from the body, but is still subject to destruction at every moment. In both of these philosophies, there is no next birth and thus no fear of sin continuing into next life, and there is unavoidable creation and destruction of the selves (body), whose very nature is change. Thus there is no need to lament.

29. The Amazing Soul	
āścarya-vat paśyati kaścid enam	Some see the soul as amazing.
āścarya-vad vadati tathaiva cānyaḥ	Some describe the soul as amazing.
āścarya-vac cainam anyaḥ śṛṇoti	Some hear of the soul as amazing.
śrutvāpy enaṁ veda na caiva kaścit	Others, even after hearing, cannot know it.

Astonishing soul: Though the soul is atomic it exists and spreads throughout the bodies of gigantic and microbic entities. Yet, it is untouched by the bodily changes. With many such contradictory qualities, the soul is truly astonishing.

30. Conclusion: The soul that dwells in the body can never be killed (*avadhyaḥ*), O descendant of Bharata. Therefore, you need not lament for any living being.

So far Kṛṣṇa explained the science of soul (*ātmā jñāna*) to induce Arjuna to fight. To produce steadiness in this knowledge, now Kṛṣṇa speaks lesser principles that promise material benefits by performing actions with personal desires (*sakāma karma*).

In the following section Kṛṣṇa elaborates on 2.2, in which He said that avoidance of prescribed duty leads not to higher planets but to infamy.

31-37: Sakāma-karma – Performing Prescribed Duty Gives Enjoyment

Gist of the section: Arjuna reasoned earlier that there would be no enjoyment even if he emerges victorious (1.31-35). So, Kṛṣṇa says that if Arjuna performs his *dharma* of fighting, there will be enjoyment both in victory or in loss, in earth or heaven respectively. He also discusses the problems in abandoning such duty to fight. This process is called *sakāma-karma* or *karma-kāṇḍa*, perfroming prescribed Vedic rituals for fruitive results.

31. Duty (sva-dharma): Considering your specific duty as a *kṣatriya*, there is no better engagement for you than fighting; So there is no need for hesitation or fear.

sva-dharmam api cāvekṣya na vikampitum arhasi
dharmyād dhi yuddhāc chreyo 'nyat kṣatriyasya na vidyate

32. Destination (svarga): O Pārtha, fortunate are the *kṣatriyas* to whom such religious fighting opportunities come unsought, opening the doors of heaven.

The immortality of soul described earlier doesn't recommend unnecessary violence. As a *kṛatriya,* Arjuna's dutiful fight for the noble cause of eliminating inimical kings is a religious violence approved by the Supreme Lord. Killing or being killed in a religious battle leads to heaven, and not hell.

33a. Sin (pāpa): If you do not fight, then you will incur sins (*pāpa*) for neglecting your duties.

33b-34. Infamy (akīrti): Thus you will lose your reputation (*kīrti*) as a fighter[1] and people will speak of your infamy. For a respectable person, dishonor is worse than death (better to die in the battle).

35-36. Criticism (ninda):

i. **The great warriors** who regarded you very highly will consider you insignificant thinking that you left the battlefield out of fear only.

ii. **Your enemies** will speak many unkind words about you criticizing your ability (*sāmarthyaṁ*). What could be more painful (*duḥkhataraṁ*) for you?

Here Kṛṣṇa points out that the warriors like Duryodhana and Karṇa will not think that Arjuna had left the battlefield out of compassion for brothers and grandfather, as he said earlier. They will only think that he fled out of fear of life.

37. Benefit either way: If you are killed, you will attain heaven. If victorious, you will enjoy the earth. So, rise and fight with determination (*kṛta-niścayaḥ*), O Arjuna.

Having described about working for material benefits (*sakāma-karma*), now Kṛṣṇa will explain woking in knowledge without attachment to results (*niṣkāma-karma-yoga*).

38-53: Buddhi-yoga/ Niṣkāma-karma-yoga – Detached Work Without Reactions

Gist of the section: Arjuna wanted to avoid war due to fear of sinful reactions (in 1.36-38). Kṛṣṇa already told him (in 2.33) that it is by avoiding one's duty of fighting, one will incur sin. Now in this section, Kṛṣṇa will explain how one can avoid all reactions by performing one's duty with detachment from the results.

To motivate Arjuna to fight, Kṛṣṇa first explained *jñāna* or knowledge (2.11-30) and then *karma* or work (2.31-37). Now He is asking Arjuna *work* with *knowledge* and *detachment*, as an offering to the Lord. This process is called *niṣkāma-karma-yoga* or *karma-yoga* in short.

38. Fight as a duty – Equanimity in duality	
sukha-duḥkhe same kṛtvā	Being equal in happiness or distress,
lābhālābhau jayājayau	gain or loss, victory or defeat,
tato yuddhāya yujyasva	fight for the sake of fighting (as a duty)
naivaṁ pāpam avāpsyasi	and thus you shall never incur sin.

[1] Arjuna was a famous fighter who pleased Lord Śiva and attained *pāśupata-astra*, got weapons from Droṇācārya and killed Nivātakavacas and helped Indra.

39. Buddhi-yoga: So far I have given an analytical description of the body and soul (*sāṅkhya-yoga* or *jñāna-yoga*). O son of Pṛthā, now hear about *buddhi-yoga*. When you engage (*yukta*) your intelligence in this *yoga*, you will become free from the bondage of work (*karma-bandham*).

eṣā te 'bhihitā sāṅkhye buddhir yoge tv imāṁ śṛṇu
buddhyā yukto yayā pārtha karma-bandhaṁ prahāsyasi

The *ācāryas* have explained that in this section, *buddhi-yoga* indicates both *karma-yoga* and *bhakti-yoga*. In verses like 10.10 and 18.57, the word *buddhi-yoga* indicates exclusively *bhakti-yoga* or devotional service to the Supreme Lord Kṛṣṇa.

40. No loss in this yoga[1]	
nehābhikrama-nāśo 'sti pratyavāyo na vidyate	In this endeavor, there is no loss or diminution (no destruction or decrease).
sv-alpam apy asya dharmasya	Even a little advancement on this path can
trāyate mahato bhayāt	protect one from the most dangerous type of fear.

41-46: Vyasāyātmikā intelligence and Vedic karma-kāṇḍa

41. Intelligence – one-pointed Vs. many-branched	
vyavasāyātmikā buddhir[2] *ekeha kuru-nandana*	Those who have one-pointed intelligence are resolute in purpose and their aim is one, O beloved child of Kurus!
bahu-śākhā hy anantāś ca buddhayo 'vyavasāyinām	The intelligence of those who are irresolute has many branches of action and unlimited desires.

42-43. The unintelligent followers of Vedas (*veda-vāda-ratāḥ*) are attached to the flowery words (*puṣpitāṁ vācaṁ*) of the Vedas, which recommend various fruitive activities for elevation to heaven, good birth, power and so forth. Being desirous of sense enjoyment (*bhoga*) and material opulence (*aiśvarya*), they say that there is nothing more than this.

---

[1] In the process of *bhakti-yoga*, or devotional service unto Lord Kṛṣṇa, there is *no loss* by incomplete performance, and *no sin* by imperfect performance. It saves one from the most dangerous type of fear of repeated birth and death.

[2] **Best intelligence:** To achieve success in any path, one should have one-pointed intelligence. Among all types of intelligence, that intelligence concentrated on *bhakti-yoga* is the best. Such *vyavasāyātmikā-buddhi* is the strong faith that *bhakti* unto Lord Kṛṣṇa (Kṛṣṇa consciousness) will elevate one to the highest perfection of life. If Kṛṣṇa is satisfied by one's actions, then everyone will be satisfied. *Bhakti* is best practiced under the guidance of a bona fode *guru*.

When one is attached to *bhoga* and *aiśvarya* he cannot have one-pointed intelligence.

44. Obstacles for one-pointed intelligence	
bhogaiśvarya-prasaktānāṁ tayāpahṛta-cetasām	For those who are too attached to (*i*) sense enjoyment and (*ii*) material opulence, and are bewildered by them (their consciousness being stolen by lust and greed),
vyavasāyātmikā buddhiḥ samādhau na vidhīyate	resolute or one-pointed intelligence (determination for *yoga*) and fixed mind do not take place.

45. So, rise above Vedic karma-kāṇḍa	
trai-guṇya-viṣayā vedā	The subject of the Vedas is mainly the three modes.
nistrai-guṇyo bhavārjuna	O Arjuna, become transcendental to these modes.
nirdvandvo nitya-sattva-stho	Be free from all dualities, in a pure spiritual state,
niryoga-kṣema ātmavān	freed from all anxieties for gain and safety, being established in the self (in spiritual consciousness).

The **Vedas** deal mostly with fruitive activities to *gradually elevate* the general public from sense gratification to the transcendental position.

Bhakti is beyond the three modes, and by performance of *bhakti-yoga,* a person transcends the modes. *Jñāna* and *karma* cannot be said to be *nistraiguṇya* because of the presence of *sattva* (goodness) in *jñāna*, and *rajas* (passion) in *karma.*

46. Knowing the purpose of Vedas: All purposes served by a small well are fulfilled by a great water body. Similarly, all the purposes of the Vedas (rituals, sacrifices and devatā worship mentioned in them) can be served to one who knows the purpose behind the Vedas[1] and is in complete knowledge (*vijānataḥ*).

47-49: How to practice Niṣkāma-karma-yoga

47. Dutiful work with detachment to results	
karmaṇy evādhikāras te	(*i*) You have a right to perform your prescribed duty.
mā phaleṣu kadācana	(*ii*) You are not entitled to the results of action.
mā karma-phala-hetur bhūr	(*iii*) Never consider yourself the cause of the results of your activities (by desiring the results).

[1] **The purpose of the Vedas** is to know and worship the one Supreme Lord Kṛṣṇa, who is the knower and compiler of the Vedas. This is confirmed in 15.15.

mā te saṅgo 'stv akarmaṇi	(*iv*) Never be attached to not doing your duty (by thinking that the results are not yours anyway *or* by fearing that the results cause bondage).

Karma: Prescribed activities enjoined as per one's nature. They are of three kinds – (*i*) *nitya-karmas* or routine duties (auspicious and inauspicious), (*ii*) *kāmya-karmas* or desired activities and (*iii*) emergency duties.

Vikarma: Capricious action or actions without the sanction of authority.

Akarma: Inaction or not performing one's prescribed duties.

Arjuna's not fighting is another side of attachment, which doesn't lead to liberation. Any attachment, positive or negative, is cause for bondage. *Vikarma* and *akarma* are sinful (2.33). So, fighting as a matter of duty was the only auspicious path of liberation.

48. Yoga is equanimity	
yoga-sthaḥ kuru karmāṇi	Perform your duty being situated in *yoga*.
saṅgaṁ tyaktvā dhanañjaya	O Arjuna, give up all attachment to results.
siddhy-asiddhyoḥ samo bhūtvā	Be equal to success and failure.
samatvaṁ yoga ucyate	Such equanimity is called *yoga*.

Real yoga means to concentrate the mind upon the Supreme by controlling the ever-disturbing senses. And because the Supreme Lord Kṛṣṇa Himself is telling Arjuna to fight, Arjuna has to just follow His dictation without worrying about the results.

49. Reject all abominable actions[1] (*avaraṁ-karma* or *sakāma-karma*) by *buddhi-yoga* (*niṣkāma-karma-yoga*), and surrender to this *yoga*, O conqueror of wealth! Those who want to enjoy the fruits of their work are misers (*kṛpaṇāḥ*).

dūreṇa hy avaraṁ karma buddhi-yogād dhanañjaya
buddhau śaraṇam anviccha kṛpaṇāḥ phala-hetavaḥ

50-53: Benefits of acting in Buddhi-yoga

50. No reactions: One gets rid of both good and bad reactions even in this life. Therefore, engage in this *yoga* without attachment, which is the real skill or art of all work (*yogaḥ karmasu kauśalam*).

51. No birth-death cycle: One becomes free from the cycle of birth and death (*janma-bandha-vinirmuktāḥ*) and attains the state or place beyond all miseries (*padaṁ gacchanty anāmayam*).

---

[1] Except for work in Kṛṣṇa consciousness, all activities are abominable because they continually bind the worker to the cycle of birth and death.

52. Indifference to Vedas: When your intelligence has crossed the dense forest of delusion (*moha-kalilaṁ*), you shall become indifferent (neutral) to all that has been heard and all that is to be heard about the fruits of action or Vedic rituals.

53. Fixed intelligence (acalā buddhi) & trance (samādhi): When your mind is no longer disturbed (*niścalā*) by the flowery words of the Vedas, and your intelligence is fixed in the trance of self-realization, then you will attain divine consciousness, the status of *jīvan-mukta*.

Hearing about intelligence fixed (*acalā-buddhi*) in *samādhi*, Arjuna now asks Kṛṣṇa about the characteristics of such a *yogī*, who is also called *sthita-prajña* (one with fixed intelligence). Work performed without craving for results produce steadiness in knowledge (*jñāna niṣṭhā*) also known as *sthita prajñatā*. This is realization of *ātmā*.

54-72: STHITA-PRAJÑA – THE QUALITIES OF A LIBERATED SOUL (JĪVAN-MUKTA)

54. **Arjuna's questions about a sthita-prajña** (a self-realized soul/ a jīvan-mukta/ one who is in samādhi or divine consciousness)		**Lord Kṛṣṇa answers in**
Q1	**Kā bhāṣā:** What are his general symptoms?	**A1** 2.55
Q2	**Kim prabhāṣeta** (How does he speak?): On receiving praise or blame, affection or hate, what will he say externally or internally?	**A2** 2.56-57
Q3	**Kim āsīta** (How does he sit?): How does he restrain his senses from the sense objects?	**A3** 2.58-63
Q4	**Kim vrajeta** (How does he walk?): How does he respond to the sense objects?	**A4** 2.64-71

55: [A1] Symptoms of a sthita-prajña	
prajahāti yadā kāmān	One who gives up all kinds of material desires
sarvān pārtha mano-gatān	that arise from the mind, O Pārtha,
ātmany evātmanā tuṣṭaḥ	and is satisfied in the self (as a servant of the Supreme),
sthita-prajñas tadocyate	is said to be a *sthita-prajña* (in pure consciousness).

With the mind withdrawn from the sense objects, he is satisfied by the soul whose very nature is bliss (*ātmanā tuṣṭaḥ*).

56-57: [A2] Sthita-prajña's response to dualities (speech)	
duḥkheṣv anudvigna-manāḥ	He is undisturbed in mind amidst threefold miseries.
sukheṣu vigata-spṛhaḥ	He is not elated when there is happiness.
vīta-rāga-bhaya-krodhaḥ	He is free from attachment, fear and anger.
sthita-dhīr munir[1] *ucyate*	Such a person is called a sage of steady mind.
yaḥ sarvatrānabhisnehas[2]	He is unaffected everywhere in this world,
tat tat prāpya śubhāśubham	by whatever good or evil he may obtain,
nābhinandati na dveṣṭi	neither praising it nor despising it.
tasya prajñā pratiṣṭhitā	Such a person is firmly fixed in perfect knowledge.

58-63: [A3] Sthita-prajña's sense control (sitting)

58. Withdraw senses like a tortoise	
yadā saṁharate cāyaṁ	One who is able to withdraw –
kūrmo 'ṅgānīva sarvaśaḥ	just as the tortoise draws its limbs within the shell,
indriyāṇīndriyārthebhyas	– his senses from the sense objects[3],
tasya prajñā pratiṣṭhitā	is firmly fixed in perfect consciousness (*prajñā*).

59. Experiencing a higher taste	
viṣayā vinivartante nirāhārasya dehinaḥ	Though the embodied soul may practice to restrict his senses from enjoying the sense objects,
rasa-varjaṁ raso 'py asya	the taste for sense objects (desire for enjoyment) remains.
paraṁ dṛṣṭvā nivartate	But one can cease from it by experiencing a higher taste[4].

---

[1] *Muni* means one who can speculate in various ways in his mind without coming to a factual conclusion. Every *muni* has a different angle of vision, and unless a *muni* differs from other *munis*, he cannot be called a *muni*. But the *sthita-dhīr muni* is always steady and fixed in Kṛṣṇa consciousness, for he has exhausted all his business of creative speculation.

[2] He is devoid of specific affection (*anabhisnehaḥ*) for any living entity (*sarvatra*). However, since he has the quality of compassion, he has a little general affection.

[3] Arjuna is being taught here to use his senses for the Lord's service, instead of for his own satisfaction.

[4] Sense control by substandard processes is meant for neophytes. But one who has tasted the beauty of the Supreme Lord Kṛṣṇa no longer has a taste for dead, material things.

Secret of sense control: Developing higher taste is the secret of success. One who is not in Kṛṣṇa consciousness, however powerful he may be in controlling the senses by artificial repression, is sure to fail ultimately, for the slightest thought of sense pleasure will agitate him to gratify his desires. In the next four verses, Kṛṣṇa explains how the senses distract and degrade a person if he doesn't develop a higher taste.

60. Even the wise are distracted by senses (Rarity of a sthita-prajña)	
yatato hy api kaunteya	O Arjuna, although endeavoring to control the senses,
puruṣasya vipaścitaḥ	even for a man of full discrimination,
indriyāṇi pramāthīni[1]	the senses are so strong and impetuous that
haranti prasabhaṁ manaḥ	they forcibly carry away his mind.

Kṛṣṇa indicates here that even a *jñānī* who can discriminate between matter and spirit will be distracted by the senses. So it is better to perform *buddhi-yoga* and not give up work. Kṛṣṇa is showing the defect in practicing *jñāna* to establish the superiority of *bhakti*. Thus, in the next verse, He directly refers to Himself as the object of devotion, for the first time.

61. Sense control is possible only by devotion to Lord Kṛṣṇa	
tāni sarvāṇi saṁyamya	One who restrains his senses,
yukta āsīta mat-paraḥ	and fixes his consciousness upon Me,
vaśe hi yasyendriyāṇi	keeping the senses under full control[2],
tasya prajñā pratiṣṭhitā	is known as a man of steady intelligence.

Mind control: The *sthita-prajña* not only controls the senses, but also controls the mind and focuses on Kṛṣṇa. That indeed is the cause of control of the senses. Without surrender to Kṛṣṇa, the senses join the weak mind to the respective sense objects.

2.60 spoke of the senses taking away the mind by force to sense objects. Verses 2.62-63 describe the effects coming from that uncontrolled mind.

---

[1] Because the senses are strong (*pramāthīni*) they can suppress one's knowledge. So, the *sthita prajña* carefully protects his steadiness in *jñāna* from the senses, like a treasure.

[2] The person whose senses have already been brought under control (*vase hi*) is the *sthita-prajña*. *Sādhaka* is a person who is *attempting* to do so.

62-63. The stages of fall down due to uncontrolled mind	
dhyāyato viṣayān puṁsaḥ	While contemplating sense objects,
saṅgas teṣūpajāyate	one develops attachment for them.
saṅgāt sañjāyate kāmaḥ	From such attachment lust develops.
kāmāt krodho 'bhijāyate	From lust anger arises.
krodhād bhavati sammohaḥ	From anger, complete delusion[1] arises.
sammohāt smṛti-vibhramaḥ	From delusion bewilderment of memory.
smṛti-bhraṁśād buddhi-nāśo	When memory is lost, intelligence is lost.
buddhi-nāśāt praṇaśyati	When intelligence is lost one falls down again into the material ocean.

So far Kṛṣṇa explained the dangers of accepting sense objects and how a *sthita-prajña* controls himself from being distracted by them. Now He says that it is not a fault to accept the sense objects, if it is done with *controlled* senses, without undue attachment in the mind.

64-72: [A4] Sthita-prajña's sense engagement (walking)

64. Attaining prasāda: One who is free from attachment (*raga*) and aversion (*dveṣa*) and engages his senses in the sense objects with a controlled mind or regulative principles of freedom (*vidheyātmā*), attains peace or mercy of the Lord (*prasāda*).

65. Result of attaining prasāda	
prasāde sarva-duḥkhānāṁ hānir asyopajāyate	By attaining the Lord's mercy or peace, all of one's distresses are destroyed.
prasanna-cetaso hy āśu	In such satisfied consciousness,
buddhiḥ paryavatiṣṭhate	one's intelligence is soon well established.

66. No happiness or peace without connecting to the Supreme	
nāsti buddhir ayuktasya na cāyuktasya bhāvanā	One who is not connected with the Supreme, can have neither fixed intelligence nor a steady mind,
na cābhāvayataḥ śāntir	Without steady mind, there is no peace.
aśāntasya kutaḥ sukham	Without peace, how can there be any happiness?

[1] *Saṁmohaḥ* is the loss of discrimination of what should and what should not be done.

67. Agitated senses carry away intelligence	
indriyāṇāṁ hi caratāṁ	Even *one* of the roaming senses
yan mano 'nuvidhīyate	on which the mind focuses
tad asya harati prajñāṁ	can carry away one's intelligence.
vāyur nāvam ivāmbhasi	just as a strong wind sweeps away a boat on the water.

68. Steady intelligence (*prajñā*) is therefore, to restrain the senses from their objects (by fixing the mind on Kṛṣṇa), O mighty-armed Arjuna.

A *sthita prajña* spontaneously conquers the senses by his perfection of absorbing his mind in *bhagavān*. But a person aspiring for the state of *sthita prajña* will practice to control the mind.

69. A sthita-prajña's day and night (metaphor)	
yā niśā sarva-bhūtānāṁ	What is night for all beings is
tasyāṁ jāgarti saṁyamī	the time of awakening for the self-controlled (*sthita-prajña*).
yasyāṁ jāgrati bhūtāni	The time of awakening for all beings is
sā niśā paśyato muneḥ	night for the introspective sage (*sthita-prajña*).

Two types of intelligence:

i. **Sthita-prajña's intelligence** fixed on the soul, that makes him experience bliss, i.e., he is awake (This is night for the materialists, who cannot see the things perceived by the intelligence fixed on the soul).

ii. **Materialist's intelligence** fixed on the sense objects, that makes him experience happiness, lamentation and bewilderment, i.e., he is awake (This is night for the *sthita-prajña* as he is disinterested in material objects).

70. A sthita-prajña is unagitated by desires	
āpūryamāṇam acala-pratiṣṭhaṁ *samudram āpaḥ praviśanti yadvat*	The ocean is always still, although it is being filled with many rivers that enter it.
tadvat kāmā yaṁ praviśanti sarve *sa śāntim āpnoti na kāma-kāmī*	Similarly, the *sthita prajña* remains peaceful and undisturbed by the incessant flow of desires. But one who strives to satisfy such desires is not.

The fruitive workers, the salvationists, and also the *yogīs* who are after mystic powers are all unhappy because of unfulfilled desires. But a Kṛṣṇa conscious person is happy in the service of the Lord, and he has no material desires to be fulfilled.

71. Qualities of a sthita-prajña –	
vihāya kāmān yaḥ sarvān	– he has given up all objects of sense enjoyment,
pumāṁś carati niḥspṛhaḥ	– he is without desires[1] (except for bodily maintenance),
nirmamo *nirahaṅkāraḥ*	– he has given up all sense of possessiveness, – he is devoid of false ego (false identity).
sa śāntim adhigacchati	Such a person alone can attain real peace.

72. Destination of a sthita-prajña: That is the way of the spiritual and godly life (*brāhmī sthitiḥ*), attaining which a person is not bewildered. If one is thus situated even at the hour of death, one can enter the kingdom of God and attain a deathless form (*brahma-nirvāṇam*).

[1] **Real desirelessness:** No one can be desireless, but one has to change the quality of one's desires. One who understands that everything belongs to the Supreme Lord Kṛṣṇa, doesn't falsely claim proprietorship over anything or desire anything for his selfish enjoyment. Such attitude is based on the understanding that every living entity, in his spiritual identity, is a part and parcel of Kṛṣṇa and thus His eternal servitor. This is Kṛṣṇa consciousness and is the basic principle of real peace. Thus real desirelessness is desire for the satisfaction of Kṛṣṇa, not an artificial attempt to abolish desires.

3. Karma-yoga

- **1-2:** Arjuna's Confusion – 'Renunciation or Action?'
  - Arjuna asked Kṛṣṇa, "If You think that buddhi is better than karma, why do you want me to fight?"
- **3-9:** Niṣkāma-Karma-Yoga is better for Arjuna than Jñāna-yoga
  - 3: Two types of people – jñāna-yogīs who renouce work and karma-yogīs who do prescribed work.
  - 4-5: Premature renunciation of work is not recommended, because inaction is unnatural
  - 6-9: A pretender externally renouces work but internally dwells on sense objects. Better perform prescribed work for Viṣṇu and avoid bondage.
- **10-16:** From Karma-kāṇḍa to Karma-yoga
  - 10-11: Attaining happiness by sacrifice (yajña) and cooperation between men and devatās.
  - 12-13: One should eat food which is first offered in sacrifce, otherwise he is a thief
  - 14-16: Cycle of sacrifice. Life becomes sinful without sacrifice.
- **17-35:** Niṣkāma-karma-yoga to set the Right Example
  - 17-19: A self-realized soul need not work, yet he works as an obligation with detachment
  - 20-24: Kings like Janaka and even Kṛṣṇa engage in work to set example, as common people follow a great person.
  - 25-29: A karma-yogī works with detachment and doesn't disturb the ignorant men who think themselves the doers.
  - 30-32: Working for Kṛṣṇa and the results of following and not following His orders
  - 33-35: One should do one's own duty according to one's nature for purification, instead of imitating others.
- **36-43:** Conquering Lust, the Greatest Enemy
  - 37-40: Insatiable lust causes material entanglement, covers knowledge and influences in three degrees.
  - 41-43: One can conquer lust by regulating the senses and making the mind steady by deliberate spiritual intelligence.

A summary chart on the flow of Chapter Three

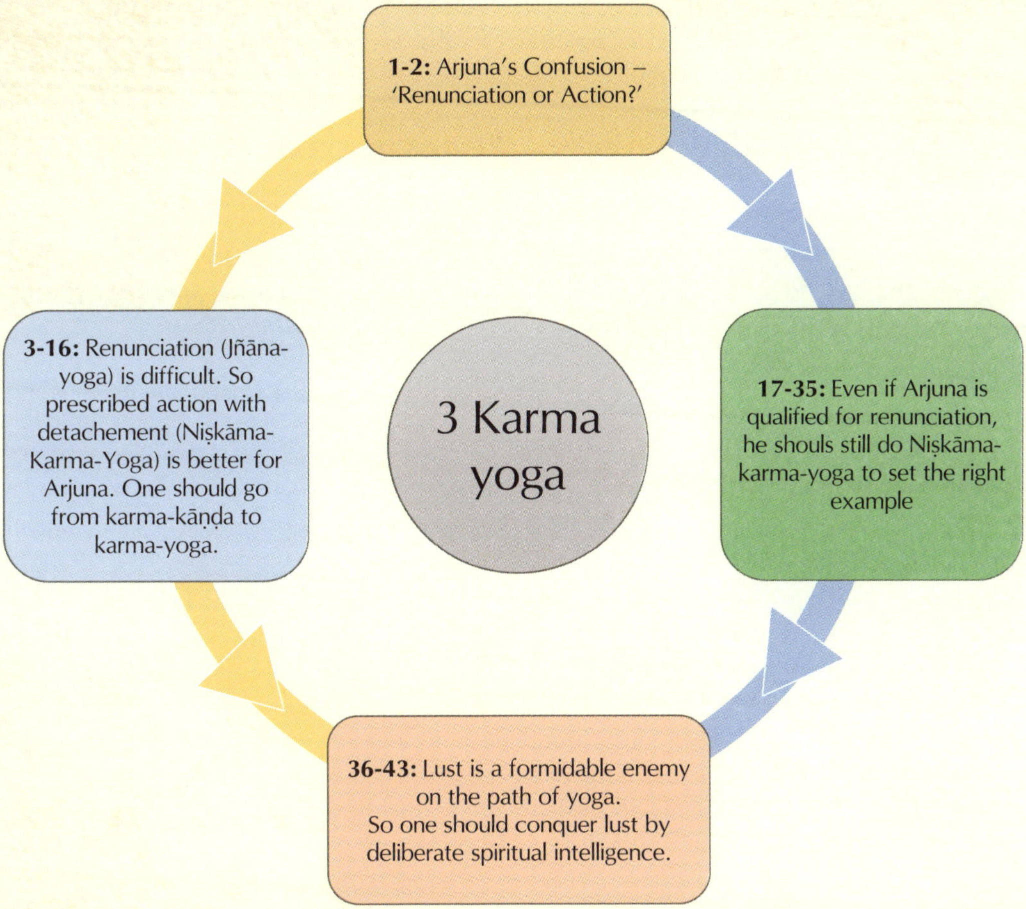

In the previous chapter, Kṛṣṇa gave a prelude to the *Bhagavad-gītā*, by presenting different topics such as *sāṅkhya-yoga, karma-kāṇḍa, buddhi-yoga, karma-yoga* and so on. But they were unsystematic. From this chapter, He gives a more organized outline of these paths.

In this chapter, Kṛṣṇa describes *niṣkāma-karma-yoga* or the great art of doing prescribed actions as an offering to the Supreme Lord Kṛṣṇa, without personal desire and thus avoiding the bondage in work. Kṛṣṇa also describes the discrimination necessary for a person desiring to conquer over lust (material desire) and anger.

The word '*karma*' could mean 'action' or 'reaction for an action (fate or destiny)' depending on the context. Sometimes it could also mean a 'fruitive action' which is intended to attain a specific result.

In 2.49, Kṛṣṇa told Arjuna to keep all abominable actions (*avaraṁ karma*) far away by *buddhi-yoga*. He meant to establish the superiority of *niṣkāma-karama-yoga* over *karma-kāṇḍa* there. However, Arjuna thought that fighting is an abominable action and that intelligence or *buddhi-yoga* means to renounce it. But Kṛṣṇa's urging him to fight seemed contradictory to Arjuna. So he asked Kṛṣṇa about this.

1-2: Arjuna's Confusion – 'Renunciation or Action?'

1-2. Arjuna asked Kṛṣṇa: "O Janārdana, O Keśava, if You think that intelligence (*buddhi*) is better than action (*karma*), why do You want to engage me in this ghastly warfare? I am bewildered by Your equivocal instructions. Therefore, please tell me decisively which is most beneficial for me."

Janārdana means one who is the object of entreaty for those desiring their ultimate benefit. **Keśava** refers to the Supreme Lord Kṛṣṇa, who is the source and controller of both Brahmā (*ka*) and Śiva (*īśa*). Arjuna requested Kṛṣṇa, whose instructions cannot be transgressed even by Brahmā and Śiva, to clearly tell him what is most beneficial.

In response to Arjuna's question whether to work or renounce work, Kṛṣṇa will now describe *niṣkāma-karma-yoga*, working with knowledge and detachment. Before that He points out the defects in Arjuna's desire to renounce his prescribed duty to fight.

3-9: Niṣkāma-Karma-Yoga (Is Better for Arjuna than Jñāna-yoga)

Gist of this section: Liberation or bondage is not determined by one's activities, but by one's consciousness in performing those activities. Thus, renunciation is not actually giving up action, but giving up attachment to the results of action. Renunciation of activities without necessary knowledge and purification will lead to destruction on the path of spiritual advancement. Without prescribed duties, an unfulfilled desire for activity will lead the premature renunciate to sinful action.

3. There are two types of people, distinguished based on their faith or *niṣṭhā* –

i. **Jñana-yoga** or *sāṅkhya-yoga* practitioners

ii. **Karma-yoga** or *buddhi-yoga* practitioners

O sinless (*anagha*) Arjuna, I have spoken of this earlier (in 2.39 etc).

Although Kṛṣṇa has described people of two types of *niṣṭhā*, the *karma-yogīs* who perform prescribed work and the *jñāna-yogīs* who renouce work, they are ultimately one in the sense that they aspire for the same goal (two rungs on same ladder). This will be more clear in 5.5. Both these *yogas* are interdependent, as philosophy and religion. Religion without philosophy is sentiment, and philosophy without religion is speculation.

One with an impure heart should perform prescribed duties for purification of the heart. This is explained in the next thirteen verses (2.4-16).

4. Premature renunciation discouraged: By merely abstaining from prescribed action (*karma*), one cannot achieve purity or freedom from reaction (*naiṣkarmya*). By renunciation of activities, one cannot attain perfection or liberation.

Purification: To purify the hearts of materialistic people, prescribed duties are laid down in the scriptures. One can accept renounced order of life (*sannyāsa*) after being purified by the discharge of such duties.

If a person with impure heart renounces prescribed activities, taking to Vedic *karma-sannyāsa*, he reverts to material action, for such a person cannot remain inactive.

5. Inaction is unnatural	
na hi kaścit kṣaṇam api *jātu tiṣṭhaty akarma-kṛt*	No one can refrain from doing something, not even for a moment.
kāryate hy avaśaḥ karma *sarvaḥ prakṛti-jair guṇaiḥ*	Everyone is forced to act helplessly according to the qualities he has acquired from the material modes.

But we sometimes see some *sannyāsīs*, who does not engage any of their senses and sometimes even speak philosophy! What about them?

6. A pretender (*mithyācāraḥ*) restrains his senses from action, but dwells on the sense objects in his mind. He certainly deludes himself.

karmendriyāṇi saṁyamya ya āste manasā smaran
indriyārthān vimūḍhātmā mithyācāraḥ sa ucyate

In contrast to such a renunciant (*sannyāsī*), a householder (*gṛhastha*) who performs scriptural actions (*karma-yoga*) without longing for results of one's actions is better.

7. A sincere person, on the other hand, tries to control the active senses by the mind and performs *karma-yoga* with his senses, without attachment. He is by far superior (to a pretender who adopts show-bottle spiritualism to cheat the innocent public).

8. So, do your prescribed duty (*niyatam karma*), for it is better than renunciation of action (*karma-sannyāsa*). One cannot even maintain one's body without work.

But by performing actions, one may become bound up by those activities!

9. Work for Viṣṇu and avoid bondage	
yajñārthāt karmaṇo 'nyatra *loko 'yaṁ karma-bandhanaḥ*	Without performing actions as a sacrifice for Viṣṇu, people are bound by their actions.
tad-arthaṁ karma kaunteya	So, do your prescribed duties for His satisfaction,
mukta-saṅgaḥ samācara	Thus you will always remain free from bondage.

Mukta-saṅgaḥ in this verse could also mean being detached from the results of actions.

Offering prescribed duties (*dharma*) to Lord Viṣṇu or Kṛṣṇa without personal desire is called *yajña* or sacrifice. The Vedas enjoin, '*yajño vai viṣṇuḥ*' – the same purpose is served whether one performs prescribed *yajñas* or directly serves Viṣṇu or Kṛṣṇa.

Kṛṣna thus suggested that working for the Lord without desire for results (*karma-yoga*), is better for Arjuna than premature renunciation of work (*jñāna-yoga*). Now Kṛṣṇa tells Arjuna, "But if you are not free from desire for the results of actions, then you should still perform actions with desire (*karma-kāṇḍa*), rather than giving up actions completely." By satisfying one's desires in a religious way, those who are attached will be purified.

10-16: From Karma-kāṇḍa to Karma-yoga

Gist of this section: Lord Kṛṣṇa has designed this material world to encourage *yajña* or sacrifice. He does this by making material advancement dependent upon sacrifice. By worshiping the Lord for material well-being, one becomes purified.

10. Happiness by yajña: Long ago, Viṣṇu, the Lord of all creatures (*prajāpatiḥ*), created population along with sacrifices (*yajñas*), and said, "May you get all desirable things by this *yajña* to live happily and achieve liberation."

11. Cooperation between men and devatās: "The devatās[1], being pleased by sacrifices, will supply all necessities to human beings. Thus, by cooperation between men and devatās, prosperity will reign for all."

12. Thief: "But one who enjoys such gifts (like food that comes through rain etc) without offering them to the devatās in return is certainly a thief (*stenaḥ*)."

13. Eating food offered in sacrifice	
yajña-śiṣṭāśinaḥ santo mucyante sarva-kilbiṣaiḥ	Those devotees, who eat food remnants of sacrifice (offered to Viṣṇu), are released from all kinds of sins.
bhuñjate te tv aghaṁ pāpā ye pacanty ātma-kāraṇāt	Others, who prepare food for personal sense enjoyment, verily eat only sin.

14-15. The cycle of sacrifice	
annād bhavanti bhūtāni	All living bodies subsist on food grains.
parjanyād anna-sambhavaḥ	Grains are produced from rains.

---

[1] **The devatās** like Indra, Varuṇa and Vāyu are authorized administrators assisting the Supreme Lord Viṣṇu in various affairs of this world. They supply rain, water, air and all other necessities to people. They are like the limbs of the Supreme Lord and are dependent on the performance of *yajñas* by the human beings. Some *yajñas* are meant to satisfy particular devatās; but Viṣṇu or Kṛṣṇa is the chief beneficiary of all *yajñas* (*bhoktāraṁ yajña-tapasām*).

yajñād bhavati parjanyo	Rains are produced by performance of *yajña*.
yajñaḥ karma-samudbhavaḥ	*Yajña* is born of prescribed duties.
karma brahmodbhavaṁ viddhi	Prescribed duties are mentioned in the Vedas.
brahmākṣara-samudbhavam	Vedas are directly manifested from the Lord.
tasmāt sarva-gataṁ brahma nityaṁ yajñe pratiṣṭhitam	Consequently the all-pervading Supreme Lord is eternally situated in acts of sacrifice.

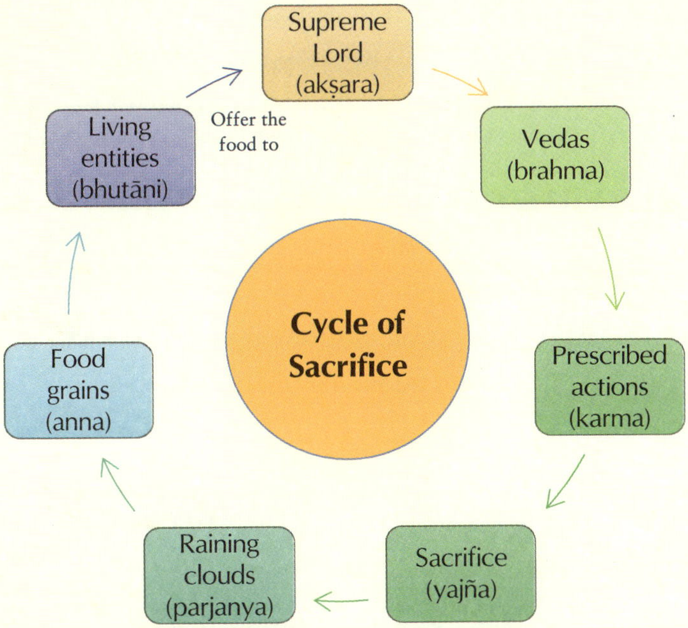

16. Sinful life without sacrifice: My dear Arjuna, a human being who does not follow the cycle of sacrifice established by the Vedas certainly leads a futile life full of sin (*agha-āyuḥ*), living only for the satisfaction of the senses (*indriya-ārāmaḥ*).

Kṛṣṇa explained so far that if one has desires, then he may work with desire in a religious way. Now He will explain that even if one has no desire, he should still work to set example for others. The previous section described "*indriya-ārāma*" person and the next section will describe "*ātmārāma* or *ātma-tṛpta*" person.

17-35: Niṣkāma-karma-yoga to Set the Right Example

Gist of this section: One who is in full knowledge doesn't have material desires or attachment. So, he does not need to do prescribed duties for his purification. Still he performs obligatory duties prescribed by the scriptures, setting the example for those who are less knowledgeable.

17-19: A self-realized soul need not work, yet he works

17-18. Self-realized person[1] has no duty: But for one who takes pleasure in the self (*ātma-ratiḥ*), who is satisfied in the self (*ātma-tṛptaḥ*), fully satiated in himself alone (*ātma-santuṣṭaḥ*) – there is

- no obligation to do any prescribed actions
- no taste for material pleasures
- no purpose or gain in performing such actions
- no reason for not performing such work too
- no need to depend on any other living being or devatās

One who has spiritual intelligence doesn't perform prescribed actions with desires, but does them without attachment to results to set the right example for others.

19. Obligatory work with detachment	
tasmād asaktaḥ satatam	Therefore, without being attached to the fruits of actions,
kāryam karma samācara	one should act as a matter of duty.
asakto hy ācaran karma	By working dutifully with detachment,
param āpnoti pūruṣaḥ	one can attain liberation or the Supreme Lord.

Arjuna wonders if there are any examples of persons who attained God consciousness by *karma-yoga*. Thus Kṛṣṇa next cites the examples of other warriors who attained success through action.

20-24: Setting right example of work

20. Setting example: Kings such as Janaka attained perfection (*saṁsiddhim*) solely by performance of prescribed duties (although they are self-realized and beyond doing any obligatory work). Therefore, just for the sake of teaching people in general, you should perform your work.

21. Common men follow a great person	
yad yad ācarati śreṣṭhas *tat tad evetaro janaḥ*	Whatever action a great man performs, common men follow.
sa yat pramāṇaṁ kurute *lokas tad anuvartate*	And whatever standards he sets by exemplary acts, the whole world pursues.

[1] Verses 3.17 and 5.24 are similar.

A leader has to teach the public by his own practical behavior. A leader cannot teach people to stop smoking if he himself smokes. And his teaching should be based on the scriptires. A leader who acts whimsically deriding the scriptures should be rejected.

22. Even Kṛṣṇa engages in work: O Pārthā, there is no work prescribed for Me within all the three worlds. Nor am I in want of anything or need to obtain anything. Yet I am engaged in prescribed duties.

23-24. If I ever failed to engage carefully in performing prescribed duties,

- all men would certainly follow My path
- all these worlds would be put to ruination
- I would be the cause of creating unwanted population[1]
- I would thereby destroy the peace of all living beings

Law maker is beyond law: Though Lord Kṛṣṇa teaches us by performing prescribed duties, we also see that He sometimes acts independent of the law, to please His devotees. Such actions, however, are not to be performed by those inferior to Him.

Following Vs. imitating: Lord Kṛṣṇa lifted Govardhana Hill. Lord Śiva drank poison. Great personalities are unaffected by their unconventional activities. But an ordinary human being cannot do such things. It is best, therefore, not to *imitate* the powerful, but simply *follow* their instructions.

Because even Lord Kṛṣṇa performs prescribed duties, a person who is established in knowledge (*jñāna*) also should work, to set right example. One can avoid sinful reactions in such a work by doing it with detachment.

25-29: Attached worker and Detached worker (Karma-kāṇḍī and Karma-yogī)

In this subsection, 3.25, 27 and 28 will describe the differences between an attached worker and a detached worker. 3.26 and 29 will describe how a detached worker deals with an attached worker.

25. Act without attachment, to set example: As the ignorant people work with attachment to results, the wise may similarly act, but without attachment, for the sake of leading people on the right path.

26, 29. Don't disturb the ignorant: Bewildered by the material modes (*guṇa-sammūḍhāḥ*), the ignorant perform material activities and become attached to their results. But the wise should not unsettle them. Rather, by personally working with detachment, they should engage them in activity.

---

[1] Here Kṛṣṇa addresses Arjuna's concern about *varṇa-saṅkara* that he raised in 1.39-43.

na buddhi-bhedaṁ janayed ajñānāṁ karma-saṅginām
joṣayet sarva-karmāṇi vidvān yuktaḥ samācaran

Inspiring even the ignorant: Ignorant people cannot appreciate activities in Kṛṣṇa consciousness, and therefore Lord Kṛṣṇa advises not to disturb them and simply waste valuable time. But the devotees understand the Lord's purpose and approach ignorant men to try to engage them in the acts of Kṛṣṇa consciousness, which are most beneficial for all.

Supreme purity of bhakti: *Jñāna* is dependent on purity of heart, and purity of heart is dependent on action without desire. But *bhakti* is by nature very strong, and is not dependent even on the purity of the heart. So, if it is possible to inspire people with faith in *bhakti*, then one can disturb the minds of those attached to action. Because, those who have faith in *bhakti* have no obligation for performing *karma*.

If both the person in knowledge (*vidvān*) and the ignorant person perform work in a similar way, how to distinguish between them?

27. Ignorant person thinks himself the doer	
prakṛteḥ kriyamāṇāni guṇaiḥ karmāṇi sarvaśaḥ	All activities are in actuality carried out by the three modes of material nature, but
ahaṅkāra-vimūḍhātmā	the spirit soul bewildered by false ego
kartāham iti manyate	thinks himself the doer of activities.

The free will and responsibility of the *jīva* will never disappear. However, the *jīva's* **doership** is made possible by the body, senses and life airs, and by the *paramātmā*, who is the activator of all things. The *jīva* is not the only factor (See 18.14-16 and 5.13-16 also). How the *jīva* can conquer over the influence of *karma* and *svabhāva* is discussed at the end of the chapter.

28-29. The person in knowledge of the Absolute Truth (*tattva-vit*) understands that he is separate from the senses and the sense objects and does not engage in sense gratification, knowing well the differences between work in devotion and work for fruitive results. He never disturbs the ignorant (See 3.26).

Having described about *karma-yoga,* Kṛṣṇa will now mention that ultimately He is the object of it and every activity needs to be done as an offering to Him. Such *karma-yoga* is actually *bhakti-yoga*.

30-32: Working for Kṛṣṇa and following Him

30. Do your duty depending on Me (Stage of Bhakti-yoga: Purpose of the Gīta)	
mayi sarvāṇi karmāṇi sannyasyādhyātma-cetasā	Offering all your activities unto Me, (*i*) with full knowledge and dependence on Me,
nirāśīr nirmamo bhūtvā	(*ii*) without personal desires, (*iii*) without a sense of proprietorship, and
yudhyasva vigata-jvaraḥ	(*iv*) free from lethargy, fight.

Working for the Lord: The cashier may count millions of dollars for his employer, but nothing belongs to him (*nirmama*) and thus he does not claim a cent for himself (*nirāśīr*). Similarly, one has to do his prescribed duty for the Lord, without reluctance (*vigata-jvaraḥ*), knowing that nothing in the world belongs to any individual person, but that everything belongs to the Supreme Lord (*mayi*). That will lead one to the path of liberation.

31. Result of following My teachings: Those who execute their duties according to My injunctions (the essence of all Vedic wisdom) faithfully (*śraddhāvanto*), without envy (*anasūyanto*), become free from the bondage of fruitive actions.

32. Result of disregarding My teachings: Out of envy (*abhyasūyantaḥ*) those who do not follow My teachings are devoid of all knowledge and discrimination, and are befooled and ruined.

Will a person, who is aware of the punishments for sinful actions, be afraid of committing them? – Not necessarily! Even such people are impelled to act sinfully due to strong past habits and impressions (*vāsanas* or *saṁskāras*). What then to speak of one who is unaware of the punishment?

33-35: Working according to one's nature

33. Deep-rooted conditioned nature: Even a man knowledgeable of scriptures, acts according to his own nature acquired from the three modes. What can repression or punishment accomplish (*nigrahaḥ kiṁ kariṣyati*)?

Limitations of karma and jñāna: The scriptural instructions (*nigrahaḥ*) of *niṣkāma-karma-yoga* can purify and enlighten the impure hearted. The scriptural instructions of *jñāna-yoga* can purify and enlighten the pure hearted. But neither can purify the extremely impure hearted people (*nigrahaḥ kiṁ kariṣyati*).

Glory of bhakti: *Bhakti-yoga* arising from 'the causeless mercy of Lord Kṛṣṇa' and 'the association of His saintly devotees' can deliver even such most sinful persons. Unless one is situated on the transcendental platform of Kṛṣṇa consciousness, he cannot get free from the influence of the modes of material nature (7.14).

34. Gradual purification: There are principles to regulate attachment (*rāga*) and aversion (*dveṣa*) pertaining to the senses and sense objects. One should not come under the control of these two obstacles on the path of self-realization.

Attachment means beinging one's senses in contact with their objects.

Aversion means hatred for those that obstruct one's sense enjoyment.

One should not fall under the control of such attachment and aversion.

Arjuna might ask, "What if one adopts to other's duties such as non-violence, rather than doing one's own duty of fighting the battle due to attachment and repulsion."

35. Do your duty; Don't imitate others	
śreyān sva-dharmo viguṇaḥ para-dharmāt sv-anuṣṭhitāt	It is far better to perform one's own duties, even in a faulty way, than doing another's duties perfectly.
sva-dharme nidhanaṁ śreyaḥ para-dharmo bhayāvahaḥ	Even death in the course of doing one's duty is beneficial, but to follow another's path is dangerous.

Obligation: Material duties are as per one's psychophysical condition, under the modes. Spiritual duties are as ordered by *guru* for the Lord's service. They may be different, but the authorized direction is always good for the performer, rather than whimsically adopting to others' duties. Everyone has to cleanse his heart by a gradual process, not abruptly, beyond the sanction of the Vedas. It causes misfortune.

Transcending: However, when one transcends the modes and is fully situated in Kṛṣṇa consciousness, he can perform anything and everything under the direction of a bona fide *guru*.

36-43: Conquering Lust, the Greatest Enemy

Gist of this section: The arch-enemy of spiritual advancement is lust. One can curb lust by following regulations of religious life (sense control) and by cultivating knowledge of the soul's real nature.

Refering to 3.34, about *rāga* and *dveṣa*, Arjuna now asks about the *jīva's* attachment to the sense objects, even though it is forbidden by scripture.

36. Arjuna's question: "O descendant of Vṛṣṇi, by what is one impelled to do sinful acts, even unwillingly (*anicchan*), as if by force (*balād iva*)?"

A living entity, as part and parcel of the Supreme, is originally spiritual, pure, and free from all material contaminations. Therefore, by nature he is not subject to the sins of the material world. So, Arjuna asked Kṛṣṇa about the perverted nature of the living entities who act in sin, as if instigated by someone. Now Kṛṣṇa explains (in 3.37-43) who is the instigator behind the *jīva's* sinful action?

37-40: Lust leads to degradation

37. Lust causes material entanglement	
kāma eṣa krodha eṣa rajo-guṇa-samudbhavaḥ	Lust, which is born of mode of passion and when unsatisfied, turn into anger (born of mode of ignorance),
mahāśano mahā-pāpmā viddhy enam iha vairiṇam	is the all-devouring sinful enemy of this world (that instigates one to commit sin). Please know that.

Misuse of minute independence: The Supreme Lord expanded Himself into many for His ever-increasing spiritual bliss, and the living entities are His parts and parcels (See 15.7). They also have little independence, but by misusing it, their service attitude is transformed into the propensity for sense enjoyment, and they come under the sway of lust. They love Kṛṣṇa eternally, but that love is transformed into lust, which when unsatisfied turns into anger and then illusion and so on (See 2.62-63).

Spiritualizing lust and anger: Lust can be transformed into love for the Lord by desiring everything for Kṛṣṇa. Anger can be employed in the service of the Lord by fighting against the miscreants. Therefore, lust and anger, when employed in Kṛṣṇa consciousness, become our friends instead of our enemies.

38. Three degrees of covering of lust	
dhūmenāvriyate vahnir	(*i*) As fire is covered by smoke [*slight*; in human beings]
yathādarśo malena ca	(*ii*) As a mirror is covered by dust [*medium*; in animals]
yatholbenāvṛto garbhas	(*iii*) As the embryo is covered by womb [*intense*; in trees]
tathā tenedam āvṛtam	– the conditioned *jīvas* in this world are covered by lust.

(*i*) **The fire,** though covered by smoke, still burns to some degree. Similarly, a human being is covered by lust slightly and can conquer it by *bhakti* under able guidance.

(*ii*) **The mirror** covered by dust does not reflect images properly, though it is known as a mirror. Similarly, birds and beasts who are covered by lust moderately.

(*iii*) **The fetus** covered by womb cannot even move. Similarly, the consciousness of the trees is covered very deeply.

Object	Covered by	Compared to consciousness of	Degree of lust	Chance of overcoming
Fire	Smoke	Humans	Slight	Maximum
Mirror	Dust	Animals	Medium	Medium
Embryo	Womb	Trees	Intense	Minimum

39. Lust is never satisfied: Thus, the wise person's pure consciousness is covered by his eternal enemy[1] (*nitya-vairiṇā*) in the form of lust (*kāma-rūpeṇa*), which is never satisfied (*duṣpūreṇa*) by any amount of sense enjoyment, just as fire is never extinguished by a constant supply of fuel.

40. Three locations of lust: The senses (*indriyāṇi*), the mind (*mana*) and the intelligence (*buddhi*) are the seats of this lust. Through them lust covers one's real knowledge (*jñānam āvṛtya*) and bewilders him (*vimohayaty*).

The enemy, lust, has captured strategic positions in the body. Lusty *intelligence* influences the soul to acquire the false ego and identify itself with matter, and thus with the material *mind* and *senses*.

41-43: How to conquer lust?

41. By first regulating the senses, one should curb this great symbol of sin, lust, in the very beginning, and slay this destroyer of knowledge and self-realization.

The enemy, lust, can be conquered by conquering its shelters, the senses, mind and intelligence, which are respectively increasingly difficult to conquer. The senses may be difficult to control, but they are easier to conquer than the other items (mind and intelligence). Therefore, first the senses should be conquered by regulation. By restricting the senses, after some time the mind will become freed of lust.

One should not try to conquer over the mind and intelligence first, because they are more powerful than the senses.

42. Matter < Senses < Mind < Intelligence < Soul	
indriyāṇi parāṇy āhur	*Senses* are superior to dull *matter*.
indriyebhyaḥ paraṁ manaḥ	*Mind* is higher than the senses.
manasas tu parā buddhir	*Intelligence* is higher than the mind.
yo buddheḥ paratas tu saḥ	*Soul* is higher than the intelligence.

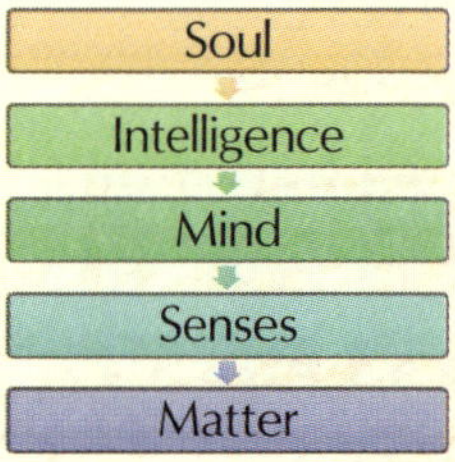

43. Steady the mind by deliberate spiritual intelligence [Kṛṣṇa consciousness], knowing oneself to be transcendental to the material senses, mind and intelligence. Thus by spiritual strength, conquer this formidable enemy known as lust.

evaṁ buddheḥ paraṁ buddhvā saṁstabhyātmānam ātmanā
jahi śatruṁ mahā-bāho kāma-rūpaṁ durāsadam

[1] The phrase "eternal enemy" indicates that lust must by all means be killed. Lust is indeed the ignorance of the *jīva*, for it covers the knowledge of the *jīva*.

4. Transcendental Knowledge

- **1-4:** The lineage of transcendental knowledge (Paramparā)
  - 1-3: Rājarṣīs understood this science in disciplic succession (Kṛṣṇa → Sun-god → Manu → Ikṣvāku), but it is broken. Kṛṣṇa explains it to Arjuna, His devotee and friend.
  - 4: Arjuna's question – "Sun-god is born before You! How did You speak to him?"
- **5-10:** The divine nature of Lord Kṛṣṇa's appearance
  - 5: Kṛṣṇa remembers all His previous appearances, but not Arjuna
  - 6-10: The uniqueness, time and purpose of Kṛṣṇa's appearance and the result of properly knowing about it
- **11-15:** Kṛṣṇa, the creator and culmination of all paths
  - 11: Kṛṣṇa reciprocates with the worshiper's mood
  - 12: People worship devatās for quick results
  - 13: Kṛṣṇa created the four varṇas
  - 14: Kṛṣṇa's work doesn't affect Him
  - 15: Liberated souls worked by understanding Kṛṣṇa
- **16-24:** Understanding karma on the platform of jñāna
  - 16-18: Intricacies of karma are difficult to understand
  - 19-24: Seeing inaction in action – Symptoms of detached worker
- **25-33:** Attaining jñāna through yajña (sacrifice)
  - 25-29: Different types of sacrifices – devatā worship, Brahman worship, sense enjoyment, self control and so on
  - 30-33: Purpose of sacrifices – development of jñāna, destruction of sins and attaining spiritual realm.
- **34-42:** Method, results and glories of attaining jñāna
  - 34: Attain jñāna from a guru, by surrender, inquiry and service
  - 35-38: Results and glories of jñāna – no bewilderment, pure vision, and destruction of sins
  - 39-42: Role of faith in acquiring jñāna – Who can and cannot attain jñāna?; Reaction free work; Rise and fight!

In the previous chapter, Kṛṣṇa described how lust causes material bondage and how one has to curb the lust by deliberate spiritual intelligence (3.36-43).

In this chapter, Kṛṣṇa presents transcendental knowledge by which one can be protected from the bondage of lust. Kṛṣṇa describes how He personally gave this spiritual knowledge to great kings who are meant to impart it to the citizens by education, culture and devotion, and thus help them utilize the opportunity of the human form of life.

In the previous chapter(s) Kṛṣṇa desribed *niṣkāma-karma*, dutiful detached work, which is said to be the means to attain *jñāna*. The goal of *niṣkāma-karma is jñāna.*

In this chapter, Kṛṣṇa presents *jñāna* or transcendental knowledge and the glories of such *jñāna*. He begins by describing the lineage in which that knowledge descends.

1-4: The Lineage of Transcendental Knowledge (Paramparā)

1-2. The saintly kings understood this imperishable (*avyaya*) science of *jñāna yoga* through the chain of disciplic succession (*paramparā*) originating from Me. But by the influence of time, the succession was broken, and the science as it is appears to be lost.

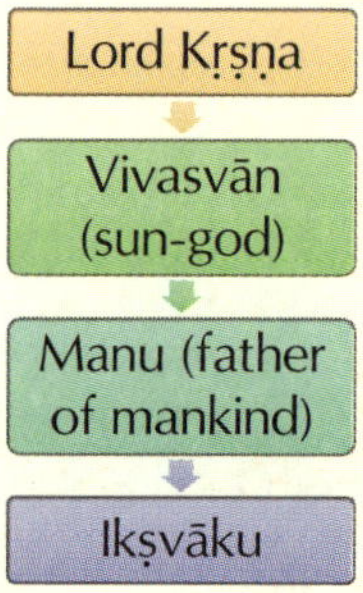

evaṁ paramparā-prāptam imaṁ rājarṣayo viduḥ
sa kāleneha mahatā yogo naṣṭaḥ parantapa [2]

When the original purpose of the *Gīta* was scattered by the motives of the unscrupulous commentators and their unauthorized interpretations, there arose the need to reestablish the bona fide disciplic succession. Therefore, Lord Kṛṣṇa spoke that science to Arjuna again 5000 years back.

3. Because you are My devotee and friend (*bhakta* and *sakha*), I am speaking to you that ancient and confidential science of the relationship with the Supreme.

sa evāyaṁ mayā te 'dya yogaḥ proktaḥ purātanaḥ
bhakto 'si me sakhā ceti rahasyaṁ hy etad uttamam

The qualification of a recipient of spiritual science is to be a devotee of Kṛṣṇa, for demons cannot understand it.

4. Arjuna's question: "The sun-god Vivasvān is born before You. How can I understand that You spoke this science to him?"

Being a devotee of Kṛṣṇa, Arjuna knew perfectly well that Kṛṣṇa, although appeared as son of Devakī on this earth, is the omniscient Supreme Lord. But atheistic people consider Kṛṣṇa an ordinary man and may not believe that He instructed the sun-god. So, Arjuna wanted Kṛṣṇa to authoritatively establish the truth about Himself. Now Kṛṣṇa answers:

5-10: The Divine Nature of Lord Kṛṣṇa's Appearance

5. Many births, both you and I have gone through. I can remember all of them, but you cannot, O subduer of the enemy!

(*i*) **The conditioned soul** who transmigrates from one material body to another forgets everything due to change of body. He is different from his body.

(*ii*) **Kṛṣṇa's eternal devotees** like Arjuna also appear with Him. But He covers their knowledge, by the influence of *yoga-māyā,* to fulfill the purpose of His pastimes.

(*iii*) **Supreme Lord Kṛṣṇa** appears in various incarnations (*avatāras*), but does not change His *sac-cid-ānanda* body, which is not different from Himself. Everything in relation to Him is spirit. Being omniscient He remembers all His past appearances.

6. Uniqueness of Kṛṣṇa's appearance	
ajo 'pi sann avyayātmā	Although I am unborn and My body is imperishable,
bhūtānām īśvaro 'pi san	and although I am the Lord of all living entities,
prakṛtiṁ svām adhiṣṭhāya	in My original transcendental form,
sambhavāmy ātma-māyayā	I still appear in every *yuga* by My own energy (mercy).

7. Time of Kṛṣṇa's appearance	
yadā yadā hi dharmasya *glānir bhavati bhārata*	Whenever and wherever there is – (*i*) a decline in *dharma*[1] or religious practice, O descendant of Bharata
abhyutthānam adharmasya *tadātmānaṁ sṛjāmy aham*	and (*ii*) a predominant rise of *adharma* or irreligion—at that time I descend Myself (to reverse the situation).

Kṛṣṇa's able devotees can rectify the destruction of *dharma* and the rise of *adharma.* Why is it necessary for Kṛṣṇa to personally appear? – Because Kṛṣṇa performs feats which are very difficult for others to do.

8. Purpose of Kṛṣṇa's appearance	
paritrāṇāya sādhūnāṁ	(*i*) To deliver the pious,
vināśāya ca duṣkṛtām	(*ii*) to annihilate the miscreants, and
dharma-saṁsthāpanārthāya	(*iii*) to reestablish the principles of religion,
sambhavāmi yuge yuge	I Myself appear, in every age.

[1] The principles of *dharma*, or religion, are taught by the Vedic scriptures, which are the direct orders of the Supreme Lord.

The primary reason for Kṛṣṇa's advent is to satisfy the longing of His pure devotees who desire to see Him and to protect them. Punishing demons is secondary. Devakī and Vasudeva were persecuted by cruel Kaṁsa, only because Kṛṣṇa was to be born of them. So Kṛṣṇa appeared primarily to deliver Devakī, rather than kill Kaṁsa, although both were performed simultaneously.

Punishment is also mercy: Kṛṣṇa's killing the evil persons is an act of mercy, because He bestows on them the bliss of liberation by killing them for their misdeeds.

Kṛṣṇa is the primeval Lord, the fountainhead of all *avatāras*, such as *puruṣāvatāras*, *guṇāvatāras*, *līlāvatāras*, *śakty-āveśa avatāras*, *manvantara-avatāras* and *yugāvatāras* —all appearing on schedule all over the universe.

9-10: Result of properly knowing Kṛṣṇa's appearance

9. Knowing Kṛṣṇa's appearance and activities	
janma karma ca me divyam *evaṁ yo vetti tattvataḥ*	One who understands in truth, the uncommon and spiritual nature of My appearance and activities,
tyaktvā dehaṁ punar janma *naiti mām eti so 'rjuna*	upon leaving the body, doesn't take his birth again in this world, but attains My eternal abode, O Arjuna.

10. Knowers of Kṛṣṇa love Kṛṣṇa	
vīta-rāga-bhaya-krodhā	Being freed from attachment, fear and anger,
man-mayā mām upāśritāḥ	being fully absorbed in Me and taking refuge in Me,
bahavo jñāna-tapasā	many persons in the past, by their true knowledge of Me and their austerity (tolerating opposition),
pūtā mad-bhāvam āgatāḥ	became purified—and attained love for Me (liberation).

Kṛṣṇa's dedicated devotees consider His birth and activities to be divine and eternal, but others who approach Him with different goals, do not consider so!

11-15: Kṛṣṇa, the Creator and Culmination of All Paths

11. Kṛṣṇa reciprocates with the worshiper's mood	
ye yathā māṁ prapadyante	In the manner and mood people surrender unto Me,
tāṁs tathaiva bhajāmy aham	I reciprocate with them accordingly.
mama vartmānuvartante *manuṣyāḥ pārtha sarvaśaḥ*	Everyone follows My path (paths leading to Me directly or indirectly) in all respects, O son of Pṛthā.

Degrees of realization: Kṛṣṇa rewards the devotees according to their different intensities of love for Him. People on different paths do not realize different things – they realize different degrees and aspects of Kṛṣṇa.

In the spiritual world, Kṛṣṇa reciprocates with His pure devotees just as the devotee wants Him – as a master, friend, son or lover. In the material world, He similarly reciprocates with different types of worshipers as per their approach.

If by worshiping Kṛṣṇa (path of *bhakti*) one is awarded with whatever he wants, why do people worship others with material desires?

12. People worship devatās desiring success in their material work[1] (path of *karma*) and they get the results (like attaining heaven) quickly.

The Supreme God is one—Kṛṣṇa—and the devatās, who are His parts and parcels and servants, are delegated with powers to manage this material world. All men, whose discrimination of temporary and eternal is eclipsed by their desire for quick material enjoyment, worship the *devatās*, Kṛṣṇa's servants. However, the boons of the devatās are material and temporary.

The paths of *bhakti* and *jñāna* give liberation, but the path of *karma* leads to bondage. Does it mean that there is some inequality in Kṛṣṇa, the creator of all paths? – No! Kṛṣṇa has created the four *varṇas* for people who have particular desires for enjoyment.

13. Kṛṣṇa created the four varṇas	
cātur-varṇyaṁ mayā sṛṣṭaṁ	I created the four divisions of human society,
guṇa-karma-vibhāgaśaḥ	according to their qualities (modes) and work,
tasya kartāram api māṁ	And although I am the creator of this system,
viddhy akartāram avyayam	know that I am yet the nondoer, being impartial.

Impartial creator: Kṛṣṇa is the creator of everything. Everything is born of Him, everything is sustained by Him, and everything, after annihilation, rests in Him. He creates through the agency of *guṇas* (modes) of *prakṛti* (material nature), but actually He is not the creator, since His *svarūpa* is beyond the *guṇas* and *prakṛti*. Therefore, He is indestructible (*avyayam*).

The suffix *ya* in the word *cātur-varṇya* indicates self-interest in the four orders.

See 18.41-48 for more details on the four *varṇas*, their *guṇas* and *karmas*.

Kṛṣṇa has appeared in a *kṣatriya* family, and performs activities obligatory to the *kṣatriya*! How to understand His activities? In the next verse, Kṛṣṇa will further explain how He is the non-doer, and the result of thoroughly understanding this.

---

[1] Desire for enjoyment of results of one's actions, is an obstacle for *niṣkāma karma*.

14. Kṛṣṇa's work doesn't affect Him	
na māṁ karmāṇi limpanti	There is no work that contaminates Me.
na me karma-phale spṛhā	I do not aspire for the fruits of work (like heaven).
iti māṁ yo 'bhijānāti	One who understands this truth about Me,
karmabhir na sa badhyate	does not become bound in the reactions of work[1].

Work without attachment: Being full of eternal bliss as the Supreme Lord, the only reason for Kṛṣṇa's work is to encourage the mankind. Kṛṣṇa's activities of creation, maintenance and destruction are in response to the *karmas* of the *jīva*. He has no desire for results of His actions. He who knows this is not bound, but he who does not know it is bound by *karma*.

The Lord is never partial to any living entity. The living entity is responsible for his own acts. The Lord only gives him facilities, through the agency of material nature. The rain pours water on all seeds, and according to the type of seed, they all sprout into different plants. Similarly the Lord inspires the *jīvas* to act, but they act differently according to their past desires.

15. By understanding this about Me, all the liberated souls in ancient times did their work without desire. So, you also do your duty, following in their footsteps.

Having said that one has to work according to the examples of previous bona fide devotees, Kṛṣṇa will now explain why one's action should not be independent:

16-24: Understanding Karma on the Platform of Jñāna

16-17. The intricacies of karma are difficult to understand. Even the wise get bewildered. Now I shall explain *karma* (action), *akarma* (inaction) and *vikarma* (forbidden action), knowing which you shall be liberated from all misfortune.

18. One who sees inaction in action, and action in inaction, is intelligent among men. He is in transcendental position, although engaged in all sorts of actions.

19-24: Inaction in action – Symptoms of detached worker (karma-yogī)

This section describes the qualities of a person who is in the state of inaction (*akarma*) or having no reactions to work, although performing actions (*karma*).

[1] This is similar to verse 4.9. He who knows that Kṛṣṇa is transcendental to this material world attains liberation.

19. His knowledge (jñāna) burns up his actions (karma)	
yasya sarve samārambhāḥ	One who engages in all activities,
kāma-saṅkalpa-varjitāḥ	but being devoid of desire for sense enjoyment, has
jñānāgni-dagdha-karmāṇaṁ	burned up all reactions of work by fire of knowledge.
tam āhuḥ paṇḍitaṁ budhāḥ	The sages say that such a person is most learned.

20. Stage of practice (sādhana or āruruksu)	
tyaktvā karma-phalāsaṅgaṁ	Giving up attachment to the results of his activities,
nitya-tṛpto nirāśrayaḥ	being ever satisfied and independent,
karmaṇy abhipravṛtto 'pi	although engaged in all kinds of activities,
naiva kiñcit karoti saḥ	he performs no fruitive action.

21-23: Stage of perfection (siddha or ārudha)	
nirāśīr yata-cittātmā	(*i*) free from desires, (*ii*) self-controlled
tyakta-sarva-parigrahaḥ	(*iii*) free from sense of proprietorship,
śārīraṁ kevalaṁ karma	(*iv*) acts only for the bare necessities of life,
kurvan nāpnoti kilbiṣam	(*v*) he doesn't incur any sin.
yadṛcchā-lābha-santuṣṭo	(*i*) satisfied with what comes of its own accord,
dvandvātīto vimatsaraḥ	(*ii*) tolerant of dualities, (*iii*) free from envy,
samaḥ siddhāv asiddhau ca	(*iv*) steady in both success and failure,
kṛtvāpi na nibadhyate	(*v*) never entangled, although performing actions.
gata-saṅgasya muktasya	(*i*) unattached to the modes of material nature,
jñānāvasthita-cetasaḥ	(*ii*) fully situated in transcendental knowledge,
yajñāyācarataḥ karma	(*iii*) acts for the sake of Yajña (Kṛṣṇa),
samagraṁ pravilīyate	(*iv*) doesn't incur reactions, merges into transcendence.

If one should perform actions for the purpose of *yajña* (*yajñāya ācarataḥ karma*) what type of *yajña* is this? Kṛṣṇa will explain it in 4.24-33.

24. Yajña in spiritual consciousness leads to spiritual goal	
brahmārpaṇaṁ brahma havir	By spiritual oblations with spiritual instruments,
brahmāgnau brahmaṇā hutam	offered into spiritual fire, by the spiritual person,
brahmaiva tena gantavyaṁ	one surely attains the spiritual kingdom,
brahma-karma-samādhinā	by being absorbed in spiritual activities.

Brahma: The word *brahma* (Brahman) means "spiritual." The Lord is spiritual, and the rays of His transcendental body are called *brahma-jyoti*, His spiritual effulgence.

Yajña is not just fire sacrifice, but any activity performed to attain certain goal. Ultimately an activity or sacrifice is meant to be done in spiritual consciousness for the satisfaction of Lord Viṣṇu, or Kṛṣṇa (who is also called Yajña).

Having explained that sacrifice uncovers Brahman, Kṛṣṇa will now list different types of sacrifices.

25-33: Attaining Jñāna Through Yajña (Sacrifice)

25-29: Different types of sacrifices	
25a	**Devatā worship:** *Karma-yogīs* worship the devatās by different sacrifices.
25b	**Brahman worship:** *Jñāna-yogīs* offer sacrifices into the fire of Brahman.
26a	**Mind control:** *Brahmacārīs* offer senses in the fire of mind control.
26b	**Sense enjoyment:** *Gṛhasthas* offer sense objects in the fire of senses.
27	**Self-control:** Followers of *Patañjali yoga* system offer the functions of their senses and life airs (*prāṇa-vāyus*) in the fire of self-control.
28a	**Charity:** *Dravya-yajña* or sacrificing one's possessions.
28b	**Austerity:** *Tapo-yajñā* or sacrifices by performing severe austerities.
28c	**Mysticism:** *Yoga-yajña* or practice the *yoga* of eightfold mysticism.
28d	**Scriptural study:** *Svādhyāya-jñāna-yajña or* studying the Vedas to advance in transcendental knowledge.
29	**Prāṇāyāma:** Controlling the breathing process and the airs circulating within the body by reversing their directions; Curtailing the eating process to control the senses. **Breath control involves** *pūraka* (prolonged inhalation), *recaka* (prolonged exhalation), *kumbhaka* (stopping the breath after inhaling or exhaling) and stopping the movement of both upward going *prāṇa* and downward going *apāna* airs. Some make the *prāṇa* merge with the *apāna* through *pūraka*. Some make the *apāna* merge with the *prāṇa* through *recaka*.

30-33: Purpose of sacrifices

30. All sinful reactions are destroyed (*yajña-kṣapita-kalmaṣāḥ*) by performing such sacrifices. Having tasted the nectar of results, the knowers and performers of sacrifices attain the eternal spiritual realm (*brahma sanātanam*).

The common aim of all sacrifices is to control the senses. Sense gratification is the root cause of material existence; therefore, unless and until one rises above it, there is no chance of being elevated to the eternal spiritual platform of full knowledge and bliss. This platform is in the eternal atmosphere, or Brahman atmosphere.

31. Without sacrifice, one can never live happily in this life (or planet) or the next.

32. Thus many types of sacrifice are described in the Vedas (*brahmaṇaḥ*). They are born of different types of work (*karma-jān*) of the body, mind and words (to suit different workers). Knowing and practicing them, you will be liberated (*vimokṣyase*).

33. Yajñas culminate in jñāna: The sacrifice performed in knowledge (*jñāna-yajña*) is better than the mere sacrifice of material possessions (*dravya-yajña*). After all, O Pārtha, all sacrifices of work culminate in transcendental knowledge.

With the elevation of transcendental knowledge, all sacrifices are on spiritual platform, otherwise they are simply material activities. Depending on differences in consciousness, sacrifices are sometimes called *karma-kāṇḍa* (fruitive activities) and sometimes *jñāna-kāṇḍa* (knowledge in the pursuit of truth). But real knowledge culminates in Kṛṣṇa consciousness, the highest stage of transcendental knowledge.

Mental speculation, dry arguments or independent study of books cannot help one attain perfect knowledge. One has to approach a bona fide spiritual master (*guru*).

34-42: Method, Results and Glories of Attaining Jñāna

34. Process of attaining jñāna – from a guru, by surrender, inquiry and service	
tad viddhi praṇipātena	Just try to learn the truth by approaching a *guru*.
paripraśnena sevayā	Inquire from him submissively and serve him.
upadekṣyanti te jñānaṁ	He can impart knowledge unto you, because
jñāninas tattva-darśinaḥ	such self-realized souls are seers of truth.

Blind following and absurd inquiries – both are condemned. Not only should one *hear* submissively from the *guru*, but one must *inquire* to get a clear understanding from him, and render service unto him. Then one gets perfect knowledge.

35-38: Results and glories of jñāna	
35a	**No bewilderment:** You will never fall again into such illusion.
35b	**Bestows pure vision** of seeing all living beings as parts of Me[1], the Supreme.
36	**Destroys sins:** The *boat* of knowledge (*jñāna-plava*) makes even the most sinful among sinners cross over the ocean of sins and miseries.
37	**Destroys all reactions:** The *fire* of knowledge (*jñānāgniḥ*) burns to ashes all reactions to material activities (even piety also).
38	**Purest (pavitram):** In due course of time, it is attained of itself from within, by mature practice of *niṣkāma-karma-yoga* (*yoga-saṁsiddhaḥ*)[2].

39-42: Role of faith in acquiring jñāna

39. Who can attain jñāna?	
śraddhāvāl labhate jñānaṁ tat-paraḥ saṁyatendriyaḥ	Knowledge is attained by one who has – (*i*) faith in scripture, (*ii*) dedication to the process (of *niṣkāma-karma-yoga*) and (*iii*) sense control.
jñānaṁ labdhvā parāṁ śāntim acireṇādhigacchati	Having achieved such knowledge, he quickly attains the supreme spiritual peace (or liberation).

40. Who cannot attain jñāna?	
ajñaś cāśraddadhānaś ca	(*i*) The ignorant, (*ii*) the faithless and
saṁśayātmā vinaśyati	(*iii*) those who doubt the scriptures, fall down.
nāyaṁ loko 'sti na paro na sukhaṁ saṁśayātmanaḥ	For the doubting soul there is happiness neither in this world nor in the next.

(*i*) *ajña* (the ignorant) is foolish like the animals, with no knowledge and faith.

(*ii*) *aśraddadhāna* (the faithless) has knowledge of *śāstra*, but having seen the mutual disagreements of proponents of various theories, he has no trust in any of them.

(*iii*) *saṁśayātmā* (the doubter) has both knowledge and faith, but is doubtful whether the process will be effective for him.

[1] A living being, as Lord Kṛṣṇa's part and parcel and eternal servitor, cannot be separated from Kṛṣṇa. His sense of being an identity apart from Kṛṣṇa is called *māyā* (*mā*-not, *yā*-this).

[2] Ignorance is the cause of our bondage, and knowledge is the cause of our liberation.

41. Reaction-free work	
yoga-sannyasta-karmāṇaṁ	One– (*i*) who renounces fruitive actions by *karma-yoga*
jñāna-sañchinna-saṁśayam	(*ii*) whose doubts have been destroyed by knowledge,
ātmavantaṁ na karmāṇi *nibadhnanti dhanañjaya*	(*iii*) who has realized the self – is not bound by reactions of work, O conqueror of riches.

42. Rise and fight: Therefore, cutting all doubts, which have arisen from ignorance, with the sword of knowledge, armed with *yoga*, rise and fight, O Bhārata.

tasmād ajñāna-sambhūtaṁ hṛt-sthaṁ jñānāsinātmanaḥ
chittvainaṁ saṁśayaṁ yogam ātiṣṭhottiṣṭha bhārata

The word "*karma*" in the first line of 4.41 could lietrally mean "action," but the spirit in which Kṛṣṇa says is "results of actions." So, Kṛnṣa is not recommending renouncing work, but renouncing the fruits of work. Thus, in 4.42, He told Arjuna to work (fight). However, Arjuna found these two verses contradictory and thus questioned Kṛṣṇa in the beginning of the next chapter.

5. Karma-yoga – Action In Kṛṣṇa Consciousness

1: Arjuna's question – 'Sannyāsa or Karma-yoga?'	Which is better – Renunciation of work or working with detachment?
2-6: Karma-yoga is equal to, but easier than Sannyāsa	Renunciation and working in the spirit of renunciation are same. But for Arjuna, working is better, because premature renunciation is distressful.
7-16: Performing Niṣkāma-karma-yoga that frees one from bondage	7-12: Characteristics of a Yoga-yukta – never entangled; self controlled; doer yet non-doer; works for the Supreme with detachment, seeking purification → attains peace.
	13-16: Knowledge of the three doers – the soul, the material nature and the Lord; Ignorance bewilders the soul while knowledge enlightens.
17-29: Liberation by focusing on the Supreme	17-21: Symptoms of a self-realized person – focusing on the Supreme makes him equipoised and attain Brahman platform.
	22-25: Sense enjoyment is distressful, so, tolerate agitations till the end of life by delighting inwards (brahma-bhūta stage)
	25-26: How to attain liberation
	27-28: Liberation through Aṣṭāṅga-yoga – a preview
	29: The peace formula – knowing Kṛṣṇa (bhakti-yoga)

In the previous chapter, Kṛṣṇa spoke of attaining peace by *jñāna* (4.39) and renouncing *karma* by *jñāna* (in 4.41), but again asked Arjuna to take up *karma-yoga* (in 4.42). Arjuna found it impossible to perform both 'renunciation of work (*karma-sannyāsa*) in knowledge (*jñāna*)' and 'working with detachment (*karma-yoga*)' simultaneously.

In this chapter, Arjuna asks Kṛṣṇa about the above contradiction and Kṛṣṇa explains how renunciation and work are not opposite, but could be integrated. Kṛṣṇa will explain the process of achieving liberation through *karma-yoga*.

1: Arjuna's Question – 'Sannyāsa or Karma-yoga?'

1. Arjuna asked: "O Kṛṣṇa, You ask me to renounce work (*sannyāsa*[1]), and then You recommend working with detachment (*karma-yoga*[2]). Please tell me definitely which is better?"

This question by Arjuna is similar to his question in 3.1-2. Arjuna thought that *sannyāsa* should be altogether free from all kinds of activity, because work and renunciation appear to be mutually incompatible to him.

However, 'detached work in full knowledge' and 'renunciation' are not contradictory and are thus same as inaction. Kṛṣṇa actually recommends the spirit of *renunciation in work* (*sannyāsa* in *karma*) but not *renunciation of work* (*sannyāsa* of *karma*). Performing work with renunciation is superior to inaction with knowledge. Thus *karma* is superior to *jñāna*. Kṛṣṇa will explain this deeply in this chapter.

2-6: Karma-yoga Is Equal to, But Easier Than Sannyāsa

2. Karma-yoga is better: Renunciation of work (*karma-sannyāsa*) and working with detachment (*karma-yoga*) are both good for liberation. But, of the two, *karma-yoga* is better.

sannyāsaḥ karma-yogaś ca niḥśreyasa-karāv ubhau
tayos tu karma-sannyāsāt karma-yogo viśiṣyate

As long as the heart is not purified, one has to work on the fruitive platform. But action in Kṛṣṇa consciousness automatically helps one escape the result of fruitive

---

[1] **Sannyāsa:** In this chapter, the word "*sannyāsa*" is used to indicate "*karma-sannyāsa*" which means "renunciation" or "giving up work."

[2] **Yoga:** In this chapter, the word "*yoga*" at several places is used to indicate "*karma-yoga*" or "*niṣkāma-karma-yoga*," i.e., working with devotion, without attachment to results.

"*Yoga-yukta*" or "*karma-yogī*" means one who is engaged in such *karma-yoga*.

"*Ayoga*" or "*ayukta*" means a fruitive worker, one who is not engaged in *karma-yoga*.

action so that one need not descend to the material platform. Therefore action in Kṛṣṇa consciousness is superior to renunciation, which entails a risk of falling.

3. A karma-yogī can be a true sannyāsī	
jñeyaḥ sa nitya-sannyāsī	A constant *sannyāsī* or renunciant is one who –
yo na dveṣṭi na kāṅkṣati	neither hates nor desires the fruits of his actions.
nirdvandvo hi mahā-bāho	He is free from dualities, O mighty armed Arjuna.
sukhaṁ bandhāt pramucyate	He can easily overcome bondage and be liberated.

One should understand that, factually, nothing belongs to anyone. Then where is the question of renunciation?

4-5. Karma-yoga and sannyāsa are same: Only the ignorant say that *sāṅkhya* (analytical study of material world or *jñāna or karma-sannyāsa*) and *yoga* (*karma-yoga*) are different. Performing one of these completely, one attains the results of both. One who sees both of them on the same level is the **actual seer.**

Sānkhya-yoga / Jñāna-yoga / Karma-sannyāsa: *Sāṅkhya* means to analytically study the material world, the material body and the soul. Analysis of the temporary material world leads to detachment from matter and material action (*sannyāsa* or renunciation). Such knowledge (*jñāna*) ultimately leads one to find the root of all existence, which is the Supreme Lord, Viṣṇu or Kṛṣṇa.

Niṣkāma-karma-yoga: In such perfect knowledge that one is not this material body but spirit soul, a part and parcel of the Supreme Lord, one wants to render service unto Him (watering the root). That is acting on the status of spirit soul with detachment, *niṣkāma-karma-yoga* or work in Kṛṣṇa consciousness. Knowledge or renunciation alone are not sufficient for liberation.

Similarity: In Chapter 3, Kṛṣṇa established the superiority of *jñāna-yoga* over *karma-yoga,* but recommended that *karma-yoga* is more suitable for Arjuna's situation. However, in essence, the aim of both these *yogas* is Lord Viṣṇu. Because 'detachment from matter' or *sannyāsa* is complete only when one gets 'attachment to the Spirit,' through *karma-yoga.* Thus both processes are the same in the sense that they aim for the same goal, although superficially one involves detachment and the other involves attachment. But *karma-yoga* is more relevant in Arjuna's context.

6. Mere renunciation is difficult and distressful, without performing *niṣkāma-karma-yoga* (*ayogataḥ*). A thoughtful person (*jñānī*) engaged in *karma-yoga* (*yoga yuktaḥ*) quickly attains the Supreme.

Jñāna-yoga that involves stopping the activities of the senses (*sannyāsa*), brings about sorrow without also practicing *karma-yoga.* By performing *niṣkāma-karma*, a *jñānī*, purifies his heart and his *jñāna* becomes fixed.

7-16: Performing Niṣkāma-karma-yoga Frees One From Bondage

Gist of the section: One who is in knowledge understands his incompatibility with material nature and thus acts only for purification, unattached to material results.

7-12: Characteristics of a Yoga-yukta

7. Never entangled	
yoga-yukto viśuddhātmā	One who works in devotion, who is a pure soul,
vijitātmā jitendriyaḥ	and who controls his mind and senses
sarva-bhūtātma-bhūtātmā	is dear to everyone, and everyone is dear to him.
kurvann api na lipyate	Though always working, he is never entangled.

A *yoga-yukta* (*karma-yogī*) cannot think of any living being as separate from Lord Kṛṣṇa, just as the leaves and branches of a tree are not separate from the tree. He knows very well that by pouring water on the root of the tree, the water will be distributed to all the leaves and branches. Thus he is very dear to everyone.

In the next two verses Kṛṣṇa describes *jitendriya*, the detached, sense-controlled worker.

8-9. Doer, yet non-doer: A knower of truth (*tatva-vit*) or *niṣkāma-karma-yogī*, although seeing, hearing, touching, smelling, eating, moving about, sleeping and breathing, always knows that only the material senses are interacting with their objects and that he is aloof from them.

The soul is not the independent doer of actions. The other doers who work in coordination with the soul are described in the next section.

Having said that the *karma-yogī* is not the *doer* of actions, yet does actions, Kṛṣṇa will now explain that such a *yogī* acts for the sake of the Supreme Lord.

10. Works for the Supreme with detachment	
brahmaṇy ādhāya karmāṇi	One who offers results of his actions to the Supreme,
saṅgaṁ tyaktvā karoti yaḥ	while performing his duties without attachment,
lipyate na sa pāpena	is unaffected by sins in his actions,
padma-patram ivāmbhasā	just as the lotus leaf is untouched by water.

Why does a person who knows that he is a spirit soul and not the body, and is thus detached, still perform work?

11. Seeks purification: The *karma-yogīs* act with body, mind, intelligence and the senses, without attachment, only for the purpose of purification (*ātma-śuddhaye*).

12. Summary: A *karma-yogī* attains unadulterated peace (*naiṣṭhikīm śāntim*) by giving up results of all activities (*karma-phalam tyaktvā*), whereas a *karmī* or one who works with desires, being greedy for the results, becomes entangled.

yuktaḥ karma-phalaṁ tyaktvā śāntim āpnoti naiṣṭhikīm
ayuktaḥ kāma-kāreṇa phale sakto nibadhyate

Karma-yoga Vs. karma: Performing action without attachment leads to liberation and performing action with attachment leads to bondage. So it is not the action that causes bondage or liberation, but it is the the consciousness in which that action is performed.

Kṛṣṇa will now explain how the pure soul is the doer, yet non-doer – knowing which one can be detached, understand the Supreme and attain liberation.

13-16: Knowledge of the three doers

13. Role of the soul: When the embodied soul works by mentally renouncing (*manasā-sannyāsa*) all actions, he resides happily in the city of nine gates (material body[1]), neither working nor causing work to be done[2].

14. Role of material nature: The *jīva*, master of his body, does not act, nor does he induce people to act, nor does he create the fruits of action. All this is enacted by his *svabhāva* (i.e., the particular nature acquired by the *jīva* under the influence of the modes of material nature).

Svabhāva indicates the beginningless material impressions (*vāsanā*) arising from the beginningless identification of the *jīva* with the material body and senses, that impel one to act. Thus the *jīva* may alternately be said to be impelled by material nature. In this verse and section, Kṛṣṇa reiterates His instruction in 3.27.

15a. Role of the Lord: Nor does the Supreme Lord (*vibhu*) assume anyone's sinful or pious activities (He is just the witness and the sanctioner).

15b. Ignorance bewilders: Because the *jīvas'* knowledge is covered by ignorance (*ajñānenāvṛtaṁ jñānaṁ*), they are bewildered (*muhyanti*).

The Supersoul can understand the desires of the soul, as one can smell the flavor of a flower by being near it. Thus man proposes and God disposes, without interfering with the desires of the minute independent living entities. But under the spell of ignorance, the living entity claims that the Lord is responsible for his conditional existence.

---

[1] The material body has 9 holes – 2 eyes, 2 ears, 2 nostrils, mouth, anus and genitals.

[2] However, one cannot claim that there is no doership at all for the soul, because soul itself is defined by its power of ascertainment and contemplation (implies doership). This subject of doership of an activity is elaborated more in 18.13-18.

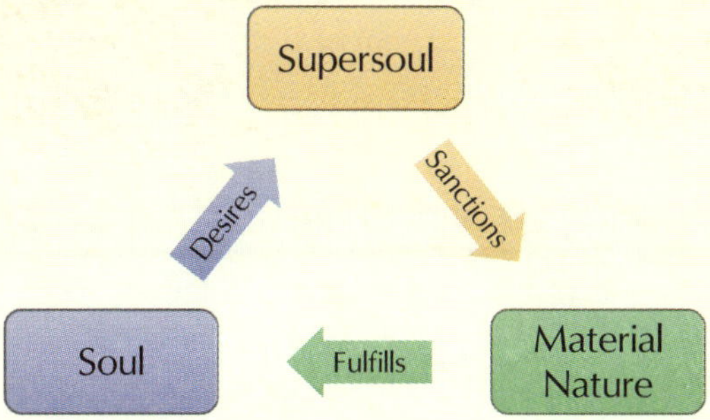

16. Knowledge enlightens: When one's ignorance is destroyed by knowledge (*jñāna*), that spiritual knowledge reveals everything, as the sun illuminates everything.

When one's ignorace is removed by knowledge about the living entity, material nature and the Supreme Lord, one will take shelter of the Lord and attain liberation.

17-29: LIBERATION BY FOCUSING ON THE SUPREME

Gist of the section: A *yogī* can attain liberation by fixing his mind on the Supreme Lord. That involves tolerating temptations of the material senses and redirecting one's pleasure seeking propensity from matter to spirit, or from outwards to inwards.

17. Focus on the Supreme leads to liberation	
tad-buddhayas tad-ātmānas *tan-niṣṭhās tat-parāyaṇāḥ*	When one's intelligence, mind, faith and refuge are all fixed in Me, the Supreme, then
gacchanty apunar-āvṛttiṁ *jñāna-nirdhūta-kalmaṣāḥ*	one becomes cleansed of misgivings through knowledge and thus proceeds on the path of liberation.

When one focuses on the Supreme, what would be his vision of people and objects in this world? Kṛṣṇa explains:

18. Equal vision of a self-realized person	
vidyā-vinaya-sampanne	The humble sages, by virtue of true knowledge, see
brāhmaṇe gavi hastini	a learned *brāhmaṇa*, a cow, an elephant,
śuni caiva śva-pāke ca	a dog and a dog-eater [outcaste]
paṇḍitāḥ sama-darśinaḥ	with equal vision. Such people are wise.

Spiritual vision: *Brāhmaṇas* and cows are in mode of goodness, elephant is in passion, and dogs and dog-eaters are in ignorance. But those who are beyond the modes do not see such external differences, but they see them equally as spirit souls and that the Lord as Paramātma is present in all.

19. Brahman platform: People with equal vision conquer birth and death. They are flawless like Brahman, and thus they are situated in Brahman[1].

20-21. Symptoms of a self-realized person –

i. doesn't rejoice something pleasant
ii. doesn't lament for something unpleasant
iii. fixed intelligence (*sthira-buddhi*)
iv. unbewildered (*asammūḍho*)
v. knows the science of God (*brahma-vid*)
vi. situated in transcendence
vii. unattracted to material pleasure (*asaktātmā*)
viii. enjoys pleasure within (*akṣayam sukham*), realizing Paramātma

Detachment from external pleasures and focusing inwards requires an understanding that material enjoyment is insubstantial and foolish.

22. Sense enjoyment is ultimately distressful	
ye hi saṁsparśa-jā bhogā duḥkha-yonaya eva te	The enjoyment arising from the contact of the senses with sense objects is the source of distress.
ādy-antavantaḥ kaunteya	Such pleasures have a beginning and an end, O Arjuna.
na teṣu ramate budhaḥ	So the wise man does not delight in them.

Even if one knows that sense enjoyment brings distress, the urges of the senses continue to exist. So, Kṛṣṇa will now advise to tolerate the urges.

23. Tolerate agitations till the end of life	
śaknotīhaiva yaḥ soḍhuṁ	If one is able to tolerate,
prāk śarīra-vimokṣaṇāt	till the time of giving up his present body,
kāma-krodhodbhavaṁ vegaṁ	the urges of senses arising from desire and anger,
sa yuktaḥ sa sukhī naraḥ	he is well situated and is happy in this world.

Tolerating agitations and retiring from external engagements that give superficial happiness are possible when one has a higher taste or relishes happiness within.

24. Delighting inwards (brahma-bhūta stage): One whose happiness is inwards (*antah-sukha*), relish is inwards (*antar-ārāma*) and sight is inwards (*antar-jyoti*) is actually the perfect mystic (*yogī*). He is self-realized, liberated and attains the Supreme (*brahma-nirvāṇaṁ*).

[1] Because these people are convinced and absorbed in the quality of impartiality displayed by the Brahman (the Lord) they easily attain liberation.

25. Sādhana for attaining liberation (*brahma-nirvāṇam*)

i. freedom from sins (*kṣīṇa-kalmaṣāḥ*)

ii. freedom from dualities and doubts (*chinna-dvaidhā*)

iii. minds being engaged within (*yatātmānaḥ*)

iv. working for everyone's welfare (*sarva-bhūta-hite ratāḥ*)

The qualifications mentioned in the last two verses seem to be very rare and difficult to achieve. Now Kṛṣṇa reassures in the next verse.

26. One can attain liberation soon by being free from anger and material desires (*kāma-krodha-vimuktānāṁ*), controlling mind (*yata-cetasām*), sincerely endeavoring for perfection with self-discipline and being self-realized (*vidita-ātma*).

So far, Kṛṣṇa explained how to attain liberation by working in complete knowledge of the Supreme. In the next two verses, Kṛṣṇa will give a brief explanation on how to attain liberation by *aṣṭānga yoga*, thus introducing us to the next chapter.

27-28. Liberation through Aṣṭāṅga-yoga: Shutting out all external sense objects, focussing the eyes between the eyebrows, suspending the inward and outward breaths, and thus controlling the mind, senses and intelligence, the transcendentalist aiming at liberation becomes free from desire, fear and anger and will certainly be liberated.

A Kṛṣṇa conscious person, however, being always engaged in devotional service, does not risk losing his senses to some other engagement. This is a better way of controlling the senses than by the *aṣṭāṅga-yoga*. This will be elaborately explained in the next chapter.

29. The peace formula – Knowing Kṛṣṇa (Bhakti-yoga)	
bhoktāraṁ yajña-tapasāṁ	(*i*) I am the **Supreme Enjoyer,** the ultimate beneficiary of all sacrifices and austerities (object of worship of *karma-yogīs* and *jñānīs* respectively)
sarva-loka-maheśvaram	(*ii*) I am the **Supreme Proprietor** of all planets and devatās (object of worship of *aṣṭāṅga-yogīs* as Paramātmā)
suhṛdaṁ sarva-bhūtānāṁ	(*iii*) I am the **Supreme well-wisher** of all living entities, by instructing on *bhakti* (object of worship of *bhaktas*)
jñātvā māṁ śāntim ṛcchati	One who knows this attains peace (liberation) from the pangs of material miseries.

Unless one understands that Lord Kṛṣṇa is the master of material nature, and the conditioned souls are under the stringent rules of material nature, it is not possible to achieve peace in the world either individually or collectively. Kṛṣṇa consciousness brings one into spiritual life even while one is within the jurisdiction of matter, for it is an arousing of spiritual existence by practice in the material world.

6. Dhyāna-yoga

- **1-9:** Advancing in Aṣṭāṅga-yoga (Āruruksa to Ārūḍha Stage)
  - 1-2: Yoga and sannyāsa are the same
  - 3-4: Two levels of Aṣṭāṅga-yoga – beginning stage (āruruksa) and advanced stage (ārūḍha)
  - 5-6: Mind is both friend and enemy
  - 7-9: Symptoms of a person in Yogārūḍha stage
- **10-32:** The Stages of Aṣṭāṅga-yoga Practice
  - 10-17: Practicing stage of Aṣṭāṅga-yoga – basic practices, recommendation and goal of Aṣṭāṅga-yoga
  - 18-23: Perfectional stage of Aṣṭāṅga-yoga – various aspects and realizations of perfection
  - 24-32: Attaining perfection in Aṣṭāṅga-yoga (Realizing the Supersoul)
    - 24-26: Methods to attain Yogārūḍha stage and the success formula of bringing the mind back
    - 27-30: The platforms of Brahma-bhūta (realizing ātma) and Brahma-saṁsparśa (realizing paramātma), and seing Kṛṣṇa everywhere
    - 31-32: Actions of a perfect yogī
- **33-36:** Necessity of controlling the mind
  - 33-34. Arjuna's concern: Aṣṭāṅga-yoga is impractical due to fickle mind
  - 35. Kṛṣṇa's solution: Control the mind by practice and detachment
  - 36. Kṛṣṇa's conclusion: Mind control is must for yoga
- **37-45:** The destination of an unsuccessful yogī
  - 37-39: Arjuna's inquiry about the fate of a fallen yogī
  - 40-45: Kṛṣṇa's reply – For a yogī there is no misfortune even in failure; fate of fallen yogī after short and long practice; he resumes yoga and attains perfection
- **46-47:** Bhakti-yogī, the topmost yogī
  - 46: A yogī is greater than tapasvī, jñānī and karmī
  - 47: Bhakti-yogī who serves Kṛṣṇa is the best of all yogīs

In the previous chapter, Kṛṣṇa described how to attain liberation by *niṣkāma-karma-yoga* and also by *aṣṭāṅga-yoga* briefly (in 5.27-28).

In this chapter, Kṛṣṇa describes *aṣṭāṅga-yoga* in greater detail, as a means to control the mind and the senses. Before practicing the advanced stages of *aṣṭāṅga-yoga,* one must be purified by the practice of *niṣāma-karma-yoga.*

However, *aṣṭāṅga-yoga* is very difficult for people in general to perform, especially in this age of Kali. Thus before teaching *aṣṭaṅga yoga*, the culmination of *karma-yoga*, Kṛṣṇa first praises *niṣkāma-karma-yoga* in 6.1-2, because of its practicality.

1-9: Advancing In Aṣṭāṅga-yoga (Ārurukṣa to Ārūḍha Stage)

The beginning stage of *aṣṭāṅga-yoga* is called *ārurukṣa*, and the advanced stage is called *ārūḍha*.

1. A real sannyāsī and yogī[1]	
anāśritaḥ karma-phalaṁ	One who is unattached to the fruits of his work and
kāryaṁ karma karoti yaḥ	dutifully performs his prescribed work (as per scriptures)
sa sannyāsī ca yogī ca	is a real *sannyāsī*, and a true *yogī*,
na niragnir *na cākriyaḥ*	not he who lights no fire (for performing sacrifice) and not he who performs no work (for bodily maintenance).

One who desires practicing *aṣṭāṅga-yoga*, should not suddenly give up prescribed duties (*karma-yoga*) that purify his heart. Although working, since a *karma-yogī* renounces the results of his actions, he is called a *sannyāsī*. And because his mind doesn't dwell on the enjoyment of sense objects, he is called a *yogī*.

2. Yoga and sannyāsa are same, i.e, detached action is same as renunciation, for one can never become a *yogī* unless he renounces the desire for sense gratification.

Sannyāsa means to be fixed in *jñāna* characterized by stopping the functions of the senses or renouncing the results of actions. *Yoga* means to have a mind which is not agitated by the thirst to enjoy sense objects. Therefore, both could mean the same.

In the first two verses, Kṛṣṇa told that an *aṣṭāṅga-yogī* should not give up *niṣkāma-karma-yoga*, and that *sannyāsa* and *yoga* are same. So, should the *aṣṭāṅga-yogī* practice *niṣkāma-karma-yoga* for his whole life? Kṛṣṇa explains:

---

[1] Constitutionally every living entity is a part and parcel of the Supreme Lord Kṛṣṇa. The parts of the body work for the satisfaction of the whole body, and not for their individual sactifaction. Similarly, the living entity who acts for satisfaction of the supreme whole Kṛṣṇa and not for personal satisfaction is the perfect *sannyāsī*, the perfect *yogi*.

3-4. Two levels of aṣṭāṅga-yoga –

i. **Yoga-āruruksa, beginning stage:** Performing prescribed duties (*niṣkāma-karma-yoga*) is the cause of elevation. One should cultivate detachment and also practice *aṣṭāṅga-yoga*, doing *āsanas* etc. That gradually purifies the heart from fruitive desires.

ii. **Yoga-ārūḍha, advanced stage:** When one is completely purified of material desires, he can give up *niṣkāma-karma-yoga* and practice *aṣṭāṅga-yoga* exclusively. Then one neither acts for sense gratification nor engages in fruitive activities. This is the stage of steady meditation (*dhyāna*).

The eight limbs of Aṣṭāṅga-yoga are depicted in the flow chart.

1. Yama
Don'ts - Regulations or prohibitions

2. Niyama
Do's - Rules or prescriptions

3. Āsana
Bodily exercises

4. Prāṇāyāma
Breathing exercises

5. Pratyāhāra
Withdrawing the senses from sense objects

6. Dhāraṇa
Fixing the mind on the Lord's form

7. Dhyāna
Intensified meditation on the Lord

8. Samādhi
Complete absorption/ trance

Mind control and detachment from sense objects are the requirements to come to the *Yogārūḍha* stage. So in the next two verses, Kṛṣṇa describes the importance of mind control and thus discourages Arjuna indicating the impracticality of the path.

5-6. Mind is both friend and enemy	
uddhared ātmanātmānaṁ	One must deliver himself (soul) by the mind.
nātmānam avasādayet	One shouldn't degrade himself (by distracted senses).
ātmaiva hy ātmano bandhur	The (**controlled**) mind is the friend of the soul.
ātmaiva ripur ātmanaḥ	The (**uncontrolled**) mind is the enemy of the soul.
bandhur ātmātmanas tasya yenātmaivātmanā jitaḥ	The mind is the best of friends, for one who has conquered it.
anātmanas tu śatrutve vartetātmaiva śatru-vat	The mind is the greatest enemy for one who has failed to conquer it.

7-9: Symptoms of a person in Yogārūḍha stage	
jitātmanaḥ praśāntasya	(*i*) Controlled mind, (*ii*) Attained tranquility
paramātmā samāhitaḥ	(*iii*) Completely approached the Supersoul.
śītoṣṇa-sukha-duḥkheṣu tathā mānāpamānayoḥ	(*iv*) Neutral to all dualities – heat and cold (physical level), happiness and distress (mental level), honor and dishonor (egoistic level).
jñāna-vijñāna-tṛptātmā	(*v*) Satisfied in sastric knowledge and realization
kūṭa-stho vijitendriyaḥ	(*vi*) Situated in transcendence, (*vii*) Self-controlled.
yukta ity ucyate yogī	(*viii*) Self-realized, and is called a *yogī* [or mystic]
sama-loṣṭrāśma-kāñcanaḥ	(*ix*) Equal vision of pebbles, stones or gold.
suhṛn-mitrāry-udāsīna-madhyastha-dveṣya-bandhuṣu sādhuṣv api ca pāpeṣu sama-buddhir viśiṣyate	(*x*) A further advanced person[1] is equipoised to all people – well-wishers, benefactors, the neutral, mediators, the envious, friends and enemies, the pious and the sinners.

Having described the perfectional stage of *aṣṭāṅga-yoga,* Kṛṣṇa will now describe the activities in the practice stage, i.e., the method to achieve the goal of perfection.

10-32: The Stages of Aṣṭāṅga-yoga Practice

10-17: Practicing stage of Aṣṭāṅga-yoga

10. Practices in the Yogārūḍha stage

- Always engaging body, mind and self in *samādhi* (*yogī yuñjīta satatam*)
- Living alone in a secluded place (*rahasi sthitaḥ, ekākī*)
- Always carefully controlling mind (*yata-cittātmā*)
- Free from all desires and possessiveness (*nirāśīr, aparigrahaḥ*)

11-14. Basic practices of Aṣṭāṅga-yoga

- **Sitting firmly** in a clean, sacred and secluded place, not too high, not too low, on *kuśa* grass, with a deerskin and a soft cloth on top.
- **Fixing the mind** on one point, controlling the mind and senses, one should do *yoga* for purification of the consciousness (*ātma-visuddhaye*).

[1] This verse presents a more advanced level of equipoised vision than the previous verse, because it involves persons rather than objects.

- **Being erect** by keeping the body, neck and head straight, being motionless and firm, staring steadily at the tip of the nose.
- **Meditating on My form** (*mat-citta*), withdrawing the mind from sense objects, being fearless, with a vow of celibacy, making Me the ultimate goal of life (*mat-para*).

15. Goal of Aṣṭāṅga-yoga: Thus by practicing control of body, mind and activities, with regulated mind (*niyata-mānasaḥ*), the *yogī* attains –

- Cessation of material existence (*nirvāṇa-paramāṁ*) and
- Lord Kṛṣṇa's kingdom (*mat-saṁsthām*)

16-17. Recommendations in Aṣṭāṅga-yoga

- **Diet:** Don't eat too much or too little
- **Sleep:** Don't sleep too much or too little
- **Regulation** in habits of eating, sleeping, recreation and work in *yoga* mitigates all material suffering.

yuktāhāra-vihārasya yukta-ceṣṭasya karmasu
yukta-svapnāvabodhasya yogo bhavati duḥkha-hā [17]

18-23: Perfectional stage of Aṣṭāṅga-yoga

18-19. Perfection in Aṣṭāṅga-yoga (yukta) involves

- Disciplining mental activities or consciousness (*viniyataṁ cittam*)
- Being fixed in the self or transcendence (*ātmany evāvatiṣṭhate*)
- Devoid of all material desires (*nispṛhaḥ sarva-kāmebhyo*)
- *Example:* Just as a lamp in a windless place does not waver, so the *yogī* whose mind is controlled (*yata-cittasya*) remains steady in his meditation on the Self.

yathā dīpo nivāta-stho neṅgate sopamā smṛtā
yogino yata-cittasya yuñjato yogam ātmanaḥ [19]

20-23. Realizations in perfection (samādhi) of Aṣṭāṅga-yoga

- Consciousness completely restrained from material mental activities.
- One can see the Self by pure mind and be satisfied with it.
- One gets boundless spiritual bliss by spiritual intelligence, not material senses.
- One is never deviated from the truth of one's spiritual nature.
- Having obtained this, he thinks there is no greater gain.
- Situated in full determination, one is never shaken, even in greatest difficulty.

yaṁ labdhvā cāparaṁ lābhaṁ manyate nādhikaṁ tataḥ
yasmin sthito na duḥkhena guruṇāpi vicālyate [22]

This state of *samādhi* or trance (called as *asamprajñāta-samādhi*) is the real freedom from all material miseries.

Two types of *samādhi* –

- *samprajñāta-samādhi:* It involves meditation on various gross or subtle objects. One comes to transcendental position by various philosophical researches.
- *asamprajñāta-samādhi:* It involves meditation with no object. One becomes transcendental to all sorts of happiness derived from the senses.

24-32: Attaining perfection in Aṣṭāṅga-yoga (Realizing the Supersoul)

24-25. Methods to attain Yogārūḍha stage

- Practice with determination[1] (*niścayena*), without deviation (*anirviṇṇa-cetasā*)
- Giving up all material desires born of mental speculation (*kāmāṁs tyaktvā*)
- Controlling all the senses on all sides by the mind
- *Final stage:* Gradually coming to trance through intelligence sustained by full conviction, and thus fix the mind on the Self alone, thinking of nothing else.

śanaiḥ śanair uparamed buddhyā dhṛti-gṛhītayā
ātma-saṁsthaṁ manaḥ kṛtvā na kiñcid api cintayet [25]

26. Success formula in yoga: Bringing the mind back	
yato yato niścalati manaś cañcalam asthiram	From wherever the mind wanders due to its flickering and unsteady nature (due to passion or past attachments)
tatas tato niyamyaitad	one must certainly withdraw the mind and
ātmany eva vaśaṁ nayet	bring it back under the control of the Self.

Endeavoring to bring back the mind in this way, the *yogī* will again experience the bliss of *samādhi* and comes to the stage of *brahma-bhūta* or realizing *ātma* and *paramātma*.

27. Brahma-bhūta platform (Realizing ātma): The *yogī* whose mind is peaceful (*praśānta-manasaṁ*) by being fixed on Me, attains supreme bliss (*sukham uttamam*). He is devoid of passion (*śānta-rajasaṁ*), free of sin (*akalmaṣam*) and realizes his qualitative identity with the Brahman (*brahma-bhūtam*).

28. Brahma-saṁsparśa platform (Realizing paramātma): Thus, by constant practice, the self-controlled *yogī* is freed of all sin (*vigata-kalmaṣaḥ*), contacts the

---

[1] In *yoga*, one should have determination like the bird who attempted to dry up the ocean which stole her eggs. Inspired by Nārada, eventually Garuḍa, the Supreme Lord's eagle carrier came to help the bird. Being afraid of Garuḍa, the ocean retuned the eggs.

Supreme spirit (*brahma-saṁsparśa*) and attains supreme bliss. (He is called *jīvan-mukta*, liberated even in this life.)

29-30. Vision of a perfect yogī: Sees Paramātma or Kṛṣṇa everywhere	
sarva-bhūta-stham ātmānaṁ	A true *yogī* observes Me, the Supersoul, in all beings
sarva-bhūtāni cātmani	and also sees every being in Me.
īkṣate yoga-yuktātmā	Indeed, the self-realized person sees Me,
sarvatra sama-darśanaḥ	the same Supreme Lord, everywhere.
yo māṁ paśyati sarvatra *sarvaṁ ca mayi paśyati*	For one who sees Me everywhere and sees everything in Me,
tasyāhaṁ na praṇaśyāmi *sa ca me na praṇaśyati*	I am never lost to him, nor is he ever lost to Me.

31-32. Actions of a perfect yogī –

- **Worships Me** as one, though situated in all entities as Supersoul (Paramātmā), and thus exists in Me in all circumstances.
- **Sees all beings equally** by comparison to one's own self, and considers others' happiness and distress one's own.

Arjuna felt that such equal vision cannot be long-lasting. One can maintain such equal vision for friends or neutral persons, but not for enemies. So, Arjuna now speaks to Kṛṣṇa that the practice of *aṣṭāṅga-yoga* is difficult.

33-36: Necessity of Controlling the Mind

33-34. Arjuna's concern: Aṣṭāṅga-yoga is impractical due to fickle mind	
O Madhusūdana, the system of *yoga,* which You have described, appears impractical and unendurable to me, for the mind is restless and unsteady.	
cañcalaṁ hi manaḥ kṛṣṇa	O Kṛṣṇa, the mind is flickering,
pramāthi balavad dṛḍham	turbulent, obstinate and very strong.
tasyāhaṁ nigrahaṁ manye	To subdue the mind, I think,
vāyor iva su-duṣkaram	is more difficult than controlling the wind.

Fickle mind's strength: Although the discriminating intelligence is supposed to direct the mind, the obstinate mind attached to enjoyment, often overcomes the intellect.

Such a strong mind is supposed to be controlled by the practice of *yoga*, but Arjuna found it impractical for an ordinary person. So in the next two verses Kṛṣṇa gives solution for dealing with the mind.

35. Kṛṣṇa's solution: Control the mind by practice and detachment	
asaṁśayaṁ mahā-bāho	O mighty-armed one, it is undoubtedly
mano durnigrahaṁ calam	very difficult to curb the restless mind.
abhyāsena tu kaunteya	But O Arjuna, by suitable and repeated practice,
vairāgyeṇa ca gṛhyate	and by detachment, one can control the mind.

36. Kṛṣṇa's conclusion: Mind control is must for yoga
For one whose mind is uncontrolled, self-realization is difficult. But it is possible for one whose mind is controlled and who endeavors by appropriate means.

Yoga practice without controlling mind from material enjoyment is a waste of time, like trying to ignite a fire while pouring water on it. The *yogīs* who control their minds and give up their propensities for material enjoyment, perfect their *yoga* and finally attain liberation.

Having heard from Kṛṣṇa that one should endeavor to control the mind in the practice of *yoga*, Arjuna became inquisitive to know what happens to someone who fails to continue his endeavor in the *yoga* practice.

37-45: The Destination of An Unsuccessful Yogī

37-39. Arjuna's inquiry about the fate of a fallen yogī: "O Kṛṣṇa, if one takes up to *yoga* with faith, but fails to continue on the path due to his unsteady mind and thus does not attain perfection, what would be his destination? Doesn't he fall away from both spiritual and material success[1] and perish like a riven cloud? I see no one but You, who can dispel this doubt.[2]"

Three paths: Self-realization is sought by the path of knowledge (*jñana-yoga*), by the practice of the eightfold system (*aṣṭāṅga-yoga*) or by devotional service unto Lord Kṛṣṇa (*bhakti-yoga*). In each of these processes one has to realize the constitutional position of the living entity, his relationship with God (*sambandha*), and the activities whereby he can reestablish the lost link (*abhidheya*) and achieve the highest stage of love of God or Kṛṣṇa consciousness (*prayojana*).

---

[1] Material success is to attain higher planets like heavens for better enjoyment. Spiritual success is to attain the Supreme spiritual realm.

[2] Because, Lord Kṛṣṇa is the perfect knower of past, present and future.

Out of these three, *bhakti-yoga* is the best path, because it is the most direct method of God realization as Kṛṣṇa will describe in the further chapters of the *Gīta*. All other paths ultimately have to culminate in *bhakti-yoga*.

Following any of these methods, one is sure to reach the supreme goal sooner or later. Lord Kṛṣṇa asserted this in 2.40: even a little endeavor on the transcendental path offers a great hope for deliverance. Here Arjuna's question is meant to reconfirm Kṛṣṇa's statement in 2.40. Now Kṛṣṇa explains:

40. No misfortune: O Arjuna, one who is engaged in auspicious activities (*kalyāṇa-kṛt*) does not meet with destruction or misfortune (*durgatim*) either in attaining spiritual goals or in material goals.

41. An unsuccessful yogī who falls after a short practice attains the planets of the pious and enjoys there for many years. Then he takes birth in the house of righteous or wealthy people.

prāpya puṇya-kṛtāṁ lokān uṣitvā śāśvatīḥ samāḥ
śucīnāṁ śrīmatāṁ gehe yoga-bhraṣṭo 'bhijāyate

Some *yogīs*, even though perfected their practice, by fate, develop a desire to enjoy, and then accept such enjoyment (Example: Saubhari Muni).

42. An unsuccessful yogī who falls after a long practice takes his birth in a family of greatly wise *yogīs*. Certainly, such a birth is rare in this world.

43-44. Resuming the yoga: In both cases, one revives the divine consciousness of his previous life, and strives again (even harder) for complete perfection. He naturally becomes attracted to *yogic* principles, even without seeking them. Such an inquisitive *yogī* surpasses the ritualistic principles of the scriptures.

Examples: King Bharata who took birth as a deer and then as a *brahmaṇa* (Jaḍa Bharata) and perfected his *yoga*.

45. Attaining perfection: When such a *yogī* sincerely endeavors for perfection, being washed of all contaminations, he ultimately achieves the supreme goal of liberation, after many births of practice (See 7.28 also).

46-47: Bhakti-yogī, The Topmost Yogī

46. A yogī is greater than tapasvī, jñānī and karmī	
tapasvibhyo 'dhiko yogī	A *yogī* is greater than the ascetic.
jñānibhyo 'pi mato 'dhikaḥ	A *yogī* is greater than the empiricist.
karmibhyaś cādhiko yogī	A *yogī* is greater than the fruitive worker.
tasmād yogī bhavārjuna	Therefore, O Arjuna, in all circumstances, be a *yogī*.

Yoga: The word "*yoga*" means linking with the Supreme. When the linking process is predominantly in fruitive activities it is called *karma-yoga*, when it is predominantly empirical and analytical it is called *jñāna-yoga*, and when it is predominantly in a devotional relationship with the Supreme Lord and service to Him it is called *bhakti-yoga*. *Bhakti-yoga*, or Kṛṣṇa consciousness, is the ultimate perfection of all *yogas*, as will be explained in the next verse.

47. Bhakti-yogī who serves Kṛṣṇa is the best of all yogīs	
yoginām api sarveṣāṁ	Of all *yogīs*, the one who
mad-gatenāntar-ātmanā	always abides in Me, thinks of Me within himself, and
śraddhāvān bhajate yo māṁ	worships and renders service unto Me with great faith
sa me yuktatamo mataḥ	is most intimately united with Me in *yoga*.

This verse, a concise statement of *bhakti,* the process of direct surrender to Bhagavān Kṛṣṇa, which will be defined and elaborated in the middle six chapters (7-12) of the *Bhagavad-gīta*, is the thread-like ornament on the neck of the devotees or *bhaktas*. The *bhakta* is like a golden mountain while the others are just high and low mountains.

PART II
BHAKTI-YOGA
CHAPTERS 7-12

7. Knowledge of the Absolute

- **1-3:** The glory of knowledge about Lord Kṛṣṇa
  - Hearing reveals phenomenal and numinous knowledge (jñāna and vijñāna) about Kṛṣṇa. Realized knowledge is very rare.
- **4-12:** Knowledge of Lord Kṛṣṇa's energies
  - 4-5: Material energy constitutes of earth, water, air etc., and spiritual energy comprises the living entities.
  - 6-7: Kṛṣṇa is the creator, maintainer and destroyer
  - 8-12: Kṛṣṇa is all-pervasive, the essence of everything and is beyond the material modes
- **13-19:** Surrendering unto Lord Kṛṣṇa
  - 13-14: The jīva deluded by the modes can transcend them by surrender to Kṛṣṇa
  - 15-16: Four types of people who do and do not worship Kṛṣṇa
  - 17-19: Those who surrender to Kṛṣṇa are magnanimous and jñāni is the best of them. A pure devotee is extremely rare.
- **20-25: Devatā** worship and Impersonalism
  - 20-23: Devatā worshipers are less intelligent and their faith is given by Kṛṣṇa. They get quick material results that are perishable.
  - 24-25: Impersonalists are unintelligent and Kṛṣṇa is not obliged to reveal Himself to them
- **26-30:** From 'Delusion by Māyā' to 'Devotion to Kṛṣṇa'
  - 26. Kṛṣṇa knows past, present and future
  - 27-28: All jīvas are born into delusion and one who is sinless can do bhakti with determination
  - 29: A mokṣa-kāmī-bhakti takes shelter of Kṛṣṇa for liberation
  - 30: Knowing Kṛṣṇa as adhibhūta, adhidaiva and adhiyajña

In the first six chapters, the living entity has been described as nonmaterial spirit soul capable of elevating himself to self-realization by different types of *yogas*. At the end of Chapter Six, it has been clearly stated that the steady concentration of the mind upon Kṛṣṇa (*mad-gatenāntar-ātmanā*) or Kṛṣṇa consciousness is the highest form of all *yoga*, called the *bhakti-yoga* (6.47).

From this chapter, Kṛṣṇa begins to explain the process of *bhakti-yoga* elaborately. Earlier Kṛṣṇa spoke of attaining liberation by working with detachment 'renunciation in action,' now He will speak about 'devotion in action.' Of all the limbs of *bhakti-yoga, sravaṇam* or hearing about the Supreme Lord is foremost, by which one can know in full—the Absolute Truth, the living entities, the material nature and their manifestations. Now, in the Seventh Chapter, Kṛṣṇa asks Arjuna to hear about Him.

1-3: The Glory of Knowledge About Lord Kṛṣṇa

1. Hearing reveals knowledge about Kṛṣṇa: O Arjuna, now please hear (*śṛṇu*), how by taking shelter of Me (*mad-āśrayaḥ*) and practicing *bhakti-yoga* (*yogaṁ yuñjan*) with mind attached to Me (*mayy āsakta-manāḥ*), you can know Me in full (*jñāsyasi samagraṁ*), free from all doubts (*asaṁśayaṁ*).

mayy āsakta-manāḥ pārtha yogaṁ yuñjan mad-āśrayaḥ
asaṁśayaṁ samagraṁ māṁ yathā jñāsyasi tac chṛṇu

Complete knowledge of the Lord includes knowledge of matter, spirit and the source and controller of both, God. Actually it is not possible to know Kṛṣṇa in full. Here Kṛṣṇa is going to give knowledge of the essential principles or facts about Himself, the Supreme God and His diverse energies, but the details are unlimited.

2. Jñāna and Vijñāna about Kṛṣṇa	
jñānaṁ te 'haṁ sa-vijñānam idaṁ vakṣyāmy aśeṣataḥ	I will explain to you in full this knowledge, both phenomenal (about My material and spiritual energies) and numinous (about My personality and sweetness).
yaj jñātvā neha bhūyo 'nyaj jñātavyam avaśiṣyate	Knowing this, nothing further shall remain for you to know.

Greatness and sweetness of Kṛṣṇa: Generally *jñāna* refers to theoritical knowledge and *vijñāna* refers to realized knowledge. Realizing Kṛṣṇa's sweetness (*vijñāna*) is greater than knowing His energies (*jñāna*). Kṛṣṇa describes *jñāna* in Chapters 7-8, *vijñāna* in Chapter 9 and both in Chapters 10-11.

3. Rarity of realized knowledge (vijñāna)	
manuṣyāṇāṁ sahasreṣu	Out of many thousands among men,
kaścid yatati siddhaye	one may endeavor for perfection and attains it.
yatatām api siddhānāṁ	Of those who have achieved perfection,
kaścin māṁ vetti tattvataḥ	hardly anyone knows Me in truth.

In knowing Kṛṣṇa as He is (*tattvataḥ*), one realizes Kṛṣṇa as the possessor of unlimited, inconceivable energies, the cause of everything, as the jewel of unlimited auspicious qualities such as omniscience, omnipotence and affection for His devotees.

4-12: Knowledge of Lord Kṛṣṇa's Energies

Gist of the section: Kṛṣṇa is the source of both the material and spiritual energies. Everything within our experience is a combination of these two energies.

4. Kṛṣṇa's material energy (aparā prakṛti / māyā-śakti – nature)	
bhūmir āpo 'nalo vāyuḥ	Earth, water, fire, air,
khaṁ mano buddhir eva ca	ether (sky), mind, intelligence and
ahaṅkāra itīyaṁ me	false ego—all together these eight (5 gross + 3 subtle)
bhinnā prakṛtir aṣṭadhā	constitute My 'separated' material energies.

5 gross elements: earth, water, fire, air, and ether including their respective sense objects, their causes—smell, taste, form, touch and sound.

3 subtle elements: mind, intelligence and false ego (the soul's misidentification with matter and his illusory conception of 'I and mine'). False ego also includes its effects, the ten senses: nose, tongue, eye, skin, ear, hands, feet, voice, anus and genital.

5. Kṛṣṇa's spiritual energy (parā-prakṛti / jīva-śakti – living entity)	
apareyam itas tv anyāṁ *prakṛtiṁ viddhi me parām*	Besides this inferior and unconscious energy, know that there is another, superior (conscious) energy of Mine,
jīva-bhūtāṁ mahā-bāho *yayedaṁ dhāryate jagat*	O mighty-armed Arjuna, which comprises the living entities who exploit material nature for their enjoyment.

The jīva is also called *tataṣṭha-śakti* or marginal energy of the Lord. Because, although spiritual and can control the material energy, the *jīva* sometimes comes under its influence and becomes conditioned, forgetting his real spiritual position.

6. Kṛṣṇa is the creator and destroyer: All created beings have their source in these two energies (Everything that exists in this world is a combination of unconscious matter and the conscious spirit). And I am both the origin and the end of everything.

7. Kṛṣṇa is the maintainer and the Supreme Personality	
mattaḥ parataraṁ nānyat *kiñcid asti dhanañjaya*	There is no truth (and no one) superior to Me, O conqueror of wealth,
mayi sarvam idaṁ protaṁ *sūtre maṇi-gaṇā iva*	Everything rests upon Me (the Supreme shelter), as pearls are strung on a thread (i.e., Kṛṣṇa is the supreme maintainer of the whole universe).

Kṛṣṇa explains how He maintains this world in the next four verses. Kṛṣṇa is not only the source, cause and basis of everything, He is also the essence of everything. For instance, Kṛṣṇa said in 7.4 that the element water came from Him, now in 7.8, He says that He is the taste of that water, that quenches our thirst and is the active principle or essence of water. That taste is Kṛṣṇa's power (*vibhūti*).

8-11: Kṛṣṇa is all-pervasive and the essence of everything		
i	*raso 'ham apsu kaunteya*	I am the taste of water, O son of Kuntī.
ii	*prabhāsmi śaśi-sūryayoḥ*	I am the light of the sun and the moon.
iii	*praṇavaḥ sarva-vedeṣu*	I am the syllable *oṁ* in Vedic *mantras*.
iv *v*	*śabdaḥ khe* *pauruṣaṁ nṛṣu*	I am the sound in ether. I am the ability in man.
vi	*puṇyo gandhaḥ pṛthivyāṁ ca*	I am the natural fragrance of the earth.
vii	*tejaś cāsmi vibhāvasau*	I am the heat in fire.
viii	*jīvanaṁ sarva-bhūteṣu*	I am the life of all that lives.
ix	*tapaś cāsmi tapasviṣu*	I am the austerity of all ascetics.
x	*bījaṁ māṁ sarva-bhūtānāṁ* *viddhi pārtha sanātanam*	I am the original seed of all existences/ living beings, know that, O son of Pṛthā.
xi	*buddhir buddhimatām asmi*	I am the intelligence of the intelligent.
xii	*tejas tejasvinām aham*	I am the prowess of all-powerful men.
xiii	*balaṁ balavatāṁ cāhaṁ* *kāma-rāga-vivarjitam*	I am the strength of the strong, which is free from selfish desire and attachment.
xiv	*dharmāviruddho bhūteṣu* *kāmo 'smi bharatarṣabha*	I am sex life, which is not contrary to religious principles, O lord of the Bhāratas (Arjuna).

All the above 14 examples are present within the three modes of material nature, which are the aspects of Kṛṣṇa's material energy (*māyā*), and Kṛṣṇa is beyond them. Having said that He is both the cause and the essence of everything, Kṛṣṇa summarizes that even the three modes of material nature that control this world are under His control.

12. Kṛṣṇa is beyond the modes: All states of being or the modes of material nature—goodness (*sattva*), passion (*rajas*) and ignorance (*tamas*)—are manifested by My energy (*mayā*), but I am not under their influence.

Knowledge about Kṛṣṇa should lead to surrender unto Kṛṣṇa. But ignorance of His greatness, caused due to attachment to His inferior material energy, is an obstacle to such a surrender. Having said about Himself being distinct from His two energies (inferior and superior), Lord Kṛṣṇa will now explain the importance of taking His shelter, along with those who do and do not seek His shelter.

13-19: Surrendering Unto Lord Kṛṣṇa

13. The jīvas are deluded by the modes, and thus cannot understand Me, who am untouched by the modes and inexhaustible.

tribhir guṇa-mayair bhāvair ebhiḥ sarvam idaṁ jagat
mohitaṁ nābhijānāti mām ebhyaḥ param avyayam

14. Transcending māyā by surrendering to Kṛṣṇa	
daivī hy eṣā guṇa-mayī mama māyā duratyayā	This divine energy of Mine, the *māyā*, consisting of the three material modes, is difficult to overcome.
mām eva ye prapadyante	But those who have surrendered unto Me
māyām etāṁ taranti te	can easily cross over this *māyā*.

Release from bondage: Another meaning of *guṇa* is rope; the conditioned soul is tightly tied by the ropes of illusion in this world. A man bound by the hands and feet cannot free himself—he must be helped by someone who is not bound. *Bhakti-yoga* can help one gain such release. Kṛṣṇa, being the Lord of the illusory energy, can release the conditioned soul from bondage.

If surrendering to Kṛṣṇa is the solution to cross all the entangling material laws, then why don't all people surrender unto Kṛṣṇa?

15. Four types of duṣkṛtinas, impious people who do not surrender to Kṛṣṇa:

na māṁ duṣkṛtino mūḍhāḥ prapadyante narādhamāḥ
māyayāpahṛta-jñānā āsuraṁ bhāvam āśritāḥ

i. **Mūḍhāḥ:** Animalistic fools – who work hard solely for material sense pleasure, which is available for animals too.

ii. **Nara-adhamāḥ:** Lowest of mankind – humans who lose their chance to revive their lost relation with God. They give up *bhakti* even after practicing it.

iii. **Māyayā apahṛta jñānāḥ:** Deluded speculators – despite having studied the scriptures, their knowledge is stolen by *māyā* and they think of the God to be ordinary human.

iv. **Āsuram bhāvam āśritāḥ:** Demoniac atheists – envious of God.

16. Four types of sukṛtinas, pious people who worship (*bhajante*) Kṛṣṇa and eventually surrender (*prapadyante*) unto Kṛṣṇa.

catur-vidhā bhajante māṁ janāḥ sukṛtino 'rjuna
ārto jijñāsur arthārthī jñānī ca bharatarṣabha

i. **Ārta:** The distressed. *Eg:* Gajendra.

ii. **Jijñāsu:** The inquisitive. *Eg:* Śaunakādi Ṛṣis.

iii. **Arthārthī:** The seekers of wealth. *Eg:* Dhruva.

iv. **Jñāni:** The seekers of knowledge of Lord Kṛṣṇa. *Eg:* Śukadeva Gosvāmī.

Sukṛtinas are pious people who follow the scriptural principles, social and moral codes, the rules of *varṇāśrama* and worship Kṛṣṇa.

Types of bhakti (Kṛṣṇa describes the first two types in Chapters 7-12).

i. **Kevala bhakti** is unalloyed devotional service performed only to please Lord Kṛṣṇa, without any selfish motives (described in 7.1, 8.14, 9.13, 9.22 etc.). It is also called *ananyā bhakti, akiñcanā bhakti* or *uttamā bhakti* that results in the devotee becoming an associate of the Lord with *dāsya, sākhya*, and other *rasas*.

ii. **Pradhānī-bhūta-bhakti** is *bhakti* mixed with tendencies for *karma, jñāna* or *yoga,* but *bhakti* is more prominent than one's other desires. The four *sukṛtinas* are of this category. The first three types of *sukṛtinas* have *karma-miśra-bhakti.* And the last one has *jñāna-miśra-bhakti.* Later, *yoga-miśra-bhakti* will also be described in 8.12.

iii. **Guṇī bhūtā bhakti** is *bhakti* mixed with tendencies for *karma, jñāna, yoga* and so on, with *bhakti* as secondary element. It is seen in the *karmīs, jñānīs* and *yogīs*, who predominantly desire results for their actions (*bhukti* and *mukti*).

17. Jñānī is the best of the four *sukṛtinas*, because he constantly (*nitya-yukta*) thinks of Me and serves Me alone (*eka-bhakti*)[1]. I am very dear to him and he is dear to Me.

While the first three types of *sukṛtinas* serve Kṛṣṇa because Kṛṣṇa fulfills their desires, a *jñānī* serves Kṛṣṇa wanting to know about Him and without material desires. So, *jñāni* is the best. A *jñāni,* searching after knowledge, realizes that he is different from his

[1] He is not that type of *jñāni* who desires to merge in the impersonal Brahman.

material body. Upon further advancement, he knows the Brahman and Paramātmā. When fully purified, he realizes that his constitutional position is to be the eternal servant of Supreme God Kṛṣṇa.

Although Kṛṣṇa said that *jñāni* is dear to Him, He loves all the four types of *sukṛtina* devotees; after all they approach Kṛṣṇa, though they have material desires.

18. All of them are magnanimous (*udāraḥ*) in giving Me love[1]. But *jñānī,* who is in knowledge on Me, is exceedingly dear to Me, and like My own self[2]. Being engaged in My service (*yuktātmā*), he is sure to attain Me, the highest and most perfect goal.

Kṛṣṇa said that the *jñāni bhakta* is fixed in Him as the supreme goal and thus he attains Him. But how long does a *jñānī* take to beocme qualified as a pure devotee? – Echoing the 7.3, Kṛṣṇa now describes how rare it is for a *jñāni* to attain such a high level of devotion.

19. The rarity of a pure devotee (kevala-bhakta)	
bahūnāṁ janmanāṁ ante	After many many births and deaths,
jñānavān māṁ prapadyate	he who is actually in knowledge surrenders unto Me,
vāsudevaḥ sarvam iti	knowing Me, to be the cause of all causes and all-pervading (and surrenders to Me by devotee association).
sa mahātmā su-durlabhaḥ	Such a great surrendered soul (*mahātma*) is very rare.

Destination of sukṛtinas: The *ārtas*, *arthārtis* and *jijñāsus*, after experiencing material pleasures for many lives, finally in one birth find these pleasures distasteful, and by association with pure devotees, gain knowledge of Kṛṣṇa's *svarūpa* (become *jñānavān*) and surrender to Kṛṣṇa. And they ultimately attain Kṛṣṇa.

If worshiping Kṛṣṇa makes the *sakāma-bhaktas* successful in this way, what happens if they worship the *devatās* (devatās) to remove their distress or fulfill their desires? Kṛṣṇa explains this in the next four verses.

20-25: Devatā Worship and Impersonalism

Having described the four types of people who do and do not surrender unto Him, Kṛṣṇa now describes the position of those who surrender to someone else instead of Him. In 7.20-23, He describes surrender to devatās, and in 7.24-25, He describes the improper surrender of the impersonalists.

---

[1] Lord Kṛṣṇa is hungry for the love of His devotees. Therefore He describes His devotees as *udāra* (magnanimous or generous or charitable) in giving Him that love.

[2] Kṛṣṇa described *jñānī bhakti* to be His ownself. But He considers *kevala-bhakta* (pure devotee) more dear to Him than Himself. Thus pure devotee is the highest.

20-23: Devatā worshipers

20. Who does devatā worship? Those whose intelligence is stolen by material desires (*kāmais tais tair hṛta-jñānāḥ*) surrender unto devatās (*prapadyante anya-devatāḥ*) adopting various rules (mentioned in the scriptures) under the control of their own low natures or desires.

Those who worship Kṛṣṇa with material desires (*sakāma-bhaktas*) get liberated by the power of devotion to Kṛṣṇa. But those who worship *devatās* desiring immediate happiness continue to take birth, being averse to taking shelter of Kṛṣṇa.

21-22. I give faith and results to them: I make their faith steady in the worship of the particular devatā and thus they attain their respective desires. But in actuality, it is I who bestow those benefits.

God gave independence to everyone and doesn't interfere with it. As the Supersoul in everyone's heart He undertsands their desires, facilitates and directs them to particular devatās for fulfilment of their desires. Devatās are powerful, but their power comes from Kṛṣṇa; they cannot independently bestow boons without Kṛṣṇa's sanction.

23. Results of devatā worship are perishable	
antavat tu phalaṁ teṣāṁ tad bhavaty alpa-medhasām	Men of small intelligence worship the devatās, and the results they obtain are limited and temporary.
devān deva-yajo yānti	Those who worship the devatās go to their planets.
mad-bhaktā yānti mām api	But My devotees ultimately reach My supreme planet.

Diverse destinations: One cannot attain the same destination by worshiping anyone. It is very logical that a person attains what he worships. The positions of devatās are temporary, so how can the results of their worship be permanent? Thus it is said here that the devotees of *devatās* are less intelligent (*alpa-medhasām*). The Supreme Lord Kṛṣṇa is eternal, and therefore the results of *bhakti* unto Him are also eternal.

The devatās are Kṛṣṇa's limbs, so worshipping them should yield the same result as worshipping Kṛṣṇa directly! But it is often not so, because, the less intelligent devatā worshipers do not see the relationship between the devatās and the Supreme Lord, and worship them as independent lords who fulfill material desires. But those who worship the devatās with the understanding that they are the limbs of the Supreme Lord's body obtain infinite, eternal results.

24-25: Impersonalists

Impersonalists are those who think that the ultimate Absolute Truth is impersonal, devoid of any form and attributes, and that it temporarily takes a personal form as Kṛṣṇa (See also 9.11). Thus they consider the form and activities of Kṛṣṇa, the Supreme

Lord, to be illusory (*māyā*) and hence they are called Māyāvādīs. So, although they are detached from matter, and adopt to various spiritual practices, they do not understand Lord Kṛṣṇa.

But from the Gīta, it is clear that neither the devatās nor Kṛṣṇa are impersonal. They are all persons; Lord Kṛṣṇa is the Supreme Personality of Godhead, and He has His own planet, and the devatās have theirs.

24. Impersonalists are unintelligent	
avyaktaṁ vyaktim āpannaṁ manyante mām abuddhayaḥ	The foolish think that I, the Supreme Person, was impersonal before and have now assumed this personality (they think that the impersonal, formless Brahman has manifested an illusory form as Myself).
paraṁ bhāvam ajānanto mamāvyayam anuttamam[1]	They do not know My true nature (form, qualities and activities), which is imperishable and the finest.

In the previous verse, Kṛṣṇa called the devatā worshipers "*alpa-medhasaḥ*" or less intelligent. In this verse, Kṛṣṇa calls the impersonalists "*abuddhayaḥ*" or unintelligent. They are more worse.

If Kṛṣṇa has eternal form, qualities and pastimes, then why do we not see these things at all times? And why can't the impersonalists, who are detached from matter and are therefore also called transcendentalists, see Krsna?

25. Kṛṣṇa reserves the right of not revealing Himself to all	
nāhaṁ prakāśaḥ sarvasya	I am not manifest to everyone always (like the sun).
yoga-māyā-samāvṛtaḥ	I am covered by My internal potency (like the cloud).
mūḍho 'yaṁ nābhijānāti	Therefore the foolish people do not know that
loko mām ajam avyayam	I am unborn and infallible.

Even when Kṛṣṇa was personally present on this planet, only a few people could understand Him to be the Supreme Lord. Therefore, Kṛṣṇa says that but for His pure devotees, all men consider Him to be like themselves.

The Lord is not covered by *māyā*, but our vision of the Lord is covered by *māyā*. The Lord's knowledge is never covered, and He knows the past, present and future of everything and everyone.

[1] *Tama* means darkness or ignorance. *Uttama* means one who is beyond ignorance.

26-30: From 'Delusion by Māyā' to 'Devotion to Kṛṣṇa'

26. Kṛṣṇa knows past, present and future	
vedāhaṁ samatītāni	I know everything that has happened in the past,
vartamānāni cārjuna	all that is happening in the present, O Arjuna,
bhaviṣyāṇi ca bhūtāni	and all things in the future. I know all living entities;
māṁ tu veda na kaścana	but no one knows Me.

Why no one knows Kṛṣṇa? – Because of delusion and dualities of dishonor and honor, misery and happiness, woman and man, good and bad, pleasure and pain etc.

27. Delusion of the jīvas: All living entities are born into delusion (*sammohaṁ*), at the beginning of creation, and are bewildered by dualities (*dvandva-mohena*) arisen from desire (*icchā*) and hatred (*dveṣa*) continuing from previous life.

icchā-dveṣa-samutthena dvandva-mohena bhārata
sarva-bhūtāni sammohaṁ sarge yānti parantapa

Is there anyone who is free from this delusion of dualities and is qualified to manifest devotion to Kṛṣṇa at all? – Kṛṣṇa answers now:

28. Who can do determined bhakti?	
yeṣāṁ tv anta-gataṁ pāpaṁ	(*i*) One whose sins are eradicated
janānāṁ puṇya-karmaṇām	(*ii*) One who acted piously in previous and present lives
te dvandva-moha-nirmuktā	(*iii*) One who is freed from the dualities of delusion
bhajante māṁ dṛḍha-vratāḥ	– engages in My service with determination.

In 7.16, Kṛṣṇa spoke of three types of *sakāma-bhaktas* who worship Him. Now He describes a fourth type of *sakāma-bhakta* who desires liberation.

29. Mokṣa-kāmī-bhakta: Intelligent persons striving for liberation from old age and death (*jarā-maraṇa-mokṣāya*) take My shelter (*mām āśritya*) in devotional service. They are actually *Brahman*, because they know all about *Brahman*, the self and transcendental activities (*adhyātmaṁ, karma*).

30. Those who know Me as *adhibhūta* (governing principle of material manifestation), *adhidaiva* (controller of devatās) and *adhiyajña* (Lord of sacrifices), and are in full consciousness of Me, can understand Me even at the time of death (*prayāṇa-kāle*).

In these two verses (7.29-30), Lord Kṛṣṇa mentioned seven specific things: *brahma, adhyāma, karma, adhibhūta, adhidaiva, adhiyajña* and remembering Him at the time of death (*prayāṇa-kāle*). Arjuna will ask Kṛṣṇa about them in the next chapter (8.1-2).

Six types of devotees: In this chapter, Kṛṣṇa described six types of devotees: four types of *sakāma-bhaktas* in 7.16 (*ārta, arthārthi*, and *jijñāsu*) and 7.29 (*mokṣa-kāma*), *jñānī* in 7.16-18, and *kevala-bhakta* (7.1, 19).

8. Attaining the Supreme

- **1-4:** Lord Kṛṣṇa answers Arjuna's questions
  - Arjuna asks about brahma, adhyātma, karma, adhibhūta, adhidaiva, adhiyajña and prayāṇa-kāla. Kṛṣṇa answers all of them and elaborates the last topic in the rest of this chapter.
- **5-8:** Remembering Kṛṣṇa at the time of death
  - Whatever one remembers at the time of death, he attains that destination. So one should practice remembering Kṛṣṇa throughout life and while leaving body, and attain Him easily after death.
- **9-13:** Remembering Kṛṣṇa by Yoga-miśra-bhakti
  - 9: Different ways of remembering Kṛṣṇa – kaviṁ, purāṇam and so on.
  - 10-13: The process and results of Ṣaṭ-cakra-yoga.
- **14-16:** Remembering Kṛṣṇa by pure bhakti
  - One can attain Kṛṣṇa's abode easily by kevala-bhakti. For such devotees there is no rebirth which is there in all planets.
- **17-22:** Material world Vs. Spiritual world
  - 17-19: Material world and the conditioned living entities manifest at the beginning of Brahmā's day and unmanifest as the night falls.
  - 20-22: One attains Kṛṣṇa's abode, the eternal and indsutructible spiritual world, by ananya-bhakti and never returns to this world.
- **23-28:** Supremacy of pure bhakti in attaining Kṛṣṇa
  - 23-26: A yogī or jñānī who leaves body by the path of light attains liberation. A karmī who leaves body by the path of darkness returns back to this world.
  - 27-28: A devotee of Kṛṣṇa (bhakti-yogī) attains Kṛṣṇa's supreme abode and never returns back.

In the previous chapter, Kṛṣṇa mentioned several terms starting with Brahman (in 7.29-30).

In this chapter, Arjuna inquires about them in 8.1-2. Lord Kṛṣṇa answers seven of them in 8.3-4 and the last question in the rest of the chapter. Kṛṣṇa also speaks about *kevala-bhakti* and *yoga-miśra-bhakti*, and describes the two destinations of the *yogīs*.

1-4: Lord Kṛṣṇa Answers Arjuna's Questions

1-2. Arjuna's questions	3-4. Kṛṣṇa's answers
Q1. What is *brahma*?	**Jīva:** The indestructible (*akṣaraṁ*), transcendental living entity separate from the material body[1].
Q2. What is *adhyātma*?	**Svabhāva:** The eternal nature or the impressions that accompany the *jīva* and govern the body.
Q3. What is *karma*?	**The fruitive activities** of the *jīva* that lead to transmigration from one material body to another[2].
Q4. What is *adhibhūta*?	**Prakṛti:** The constantly changing (*kṣara*) physical world or material body, consisting of material elements.
Q5. What is *adhidaiva*?	**Virāṭ-puruṣa:** The gigantic universal form, which includes all the devatās and their planets.
Q6. Who is the *adhiyajña*?	**Paramātma:** I, the enjoyer of all sacrifices, the Supreme Lord represented as the Supersoul.
Q7. How is *adhiyajña* known in the body?	**In the heart** of every embodied being. As the regulator, I inspire performance of sacrifice and other acts.
Q8. How to know You at the point of death (*prayāṇa-kāle*)?	This is the main subject of the rest of this chapter.

By service to Kṛṣṇa, one attains the real meaning of these words and understands that *brahma* (*jīva*) and *adhiyajña* (the Lord) are worthy of realizing, and the other items (impressions, *karma*, gross body and universal form) as worthy of rejection.

Now Kṛṣṇa answers the last question (Q8) of Arjuna about remembering Him at the time of quitting the material body.

---

[1] **Brahma** refers to the living entity (*ahaṁ brahmāsmi*), and *Para-brahma* refers to the Supreme Personality of Godhead, Kṛṣṇa. Both are not the same, although the word '*Brahma*' is also sometimes used to refer to the Supreme Lord in certain contexts.

[2] **Karma** thus refers to the creative force that gives rise to various bodies through the material elements due to material consciousness.

5-8: Remembering Kṛṣṇa at the Time of Death

5. Remembering Kṛṣṇa at death	
anta-kāle ca mām eva smaran muktvā kalevaram	And whoever, at the end of his life, quits his body remembering Me alone
yaḥ prayāti sa mad-bhāvaṁ yāti nāsty atra saṁśayaḥ	at once attains My nature (the Supreme destination). Of this there is no doubt.

Just as by remembering Kṛṣṇa, one attains Kṛṣṇa, by remembering something else, one attains that object.

6. General law of 'destination after death'	
yaṁ yaṁ vāpi smaran bhāvaṁ	Whatever one remembers
tyajaty ante kalevaram	when leaving the body,
taṁ tam evaiti kaunteya	O son of Kuntī, he will surely attain
sadā tad-bhāva-bhāvitaḥ	a state similar to that object of constant thought.

Since previous thoughts are the cause of thoughts at death, one should practice (*abhyāsa*) remembering Kṛṣṇa throughout life while doing his duties. Then remembring Kṛṣṇa at the time of death is possible.

7. Thinking of Kṛṣṇa always	
tasmāt sarveṣu kāleṣu	Therefore, at all times, you should
mām anusmara yudhya ca	think of Me and do your prescribed duty of fighting[1].
mayy arpita-mano-buddhir	By offering your mind and intelligence unto Me (with your activities dedicated to Me),
mām evaiṣyasy asaṁśayaḥ	you will attain Me without doubt.

8. Attaining Kṛṣṇa by remembering Him	
abhyāsa-yoga-yuktena	He who practices to meditate,
cetasā nānya-gāminā	with undeviated mind and consciousness,
paramaṁ puruṣaṁ divyaṁ	upon Me, the Supreme transcendental Person,
yāti pārthānucintayan	attains Me by such constant thinking of Me.

Kṛṣṇa will now tell Arjuna different ways of remembering Him.

[1] Arjuna might consider thinking of Kṛṣṇa is easier and better than fighting, but Kṛṣṇa immediately told him to do his duty of fighting while thinking of Kṛṣṇa.

9-13: Remembering Kṛṣṇa by Yoga-miśra-bhakti

9. Ways of remembering Kṛṣṇa

i. *Kavim:* omniscient (knower of past, present and future)
ii. *Purāṇam:* beginningless or the oldest
iii. *Anuśāsitāram*: the controller of everything
iv. *Aṇoḥ aṇīyāṁsam:* smaller than the smallest
v. *Sarvasya dhātāram:* the maintainer of everything
vi. *Acintya*: inconceivable
vii. *Rūpam*: with a beautiful personal form
viii. *Āditya-varṇam*: luminous like the sun and self-revealing
ix. *Tamasaḥ parastāt:* transcendental to material nature full of ignorance

10. Ṣaṭ-cakra-yoga: One who, at the time of death, fixes his life air (*prāṇa*) between the eyebrows (*ājñā-cakra*) and by the strength of *yoga,* with an undeviating mind, remembers the Supreme Lord (with the qualities mentioned in 8.9) in full devotion (*bhaktyā*), will certainly attain Him.

Arjuna didn't understand the method of fixing the *prāṇa* in the *ājñā cakra*, as a part of *ṣaṭ-cakra-yoga* practice. So, Kṛṣṇa will now explain the process of performing it and the goal achieved by it.

11a. Requirements for ṣaṭ-cakra-yoga: (*i*) renunciation or no attachments (*vīta-rāga*), (*ii*) celibacy (*brahmacarya*), (*iii*) knowledge of Vedas (*veda-vidaḥ*), (*iv*) uttering '*oṁ.*'

11b. Result of ṣaṭ-cakra-yoga: Liberation or entrance into Brahman.

12. Process of ṣaṭ-cakra-yoga: (*i*) Closing all the doors of senses, i.e., withdrawing all senses from sense objects (*pratyāhāra*), (*ii*) fixing the mind on the heart, (*iii*) fixing the *prāṇa* on the top of head, (*iv*) taking shelter of Me completely (*yoga-dhāraṇām*).

13. Destination: Vibrating sacred syllable *oṁ*, if one thinks of Me (*mām anusmaran*) and quits his body, he will certainly reach spiritual planets (*paramāṁ gatim*).

14-16: Remembering Kṛṣṇa by Pure Bhakti

14. Attaining Kṛṣṇa is easy by Kevala-bhakti	
ananya-cetāḥ satataṁ	Without deviation of mind (to other processes or goals),
yo māṁ smarati nityaśaḥ	the devotee who always remembers Me exclusively,
tasyāhaṁ sulabhaḥ pārtha	for him, I am very easy to obtain, O Pārtha,
nitya-yuktasya yoginaḥ	because of his constant engagement in devotional service.

Bhakti Vs. other paths: The practitioners of *karma-yoga, jñāna-yoga* and *haṭha-yoga,* although have some *bhakti* added, have their own self-interests, but a pure *bhakti-yogī* is selfless and desires nothing but Kṛṣṇa's service; thus he is *niṣkāma*. Therefore, He can attain Kṛṣṇa very easily (*sulabhaḥ*).

15. No rebirth for pure devotees	
mām upetya punar janma	After attaining Me, they never take birth again
duḥkhālayam aśāśvatam	in this temporary world, which is full of miseries.
nāpnuvanti mahātmānaḥ	Such great souls never return to this world,
saṁsiddhiṁ paramāṁ gatāḥ	having attained the highest goal of personal service to Me.

Having said that there is no rebirth for one who has entered the eternal spiritual world, Kṛṣṇa will now contrast it with the temporary material world where there is repeated birth and death.

16. Rebirth is in all planets except Kṛṣṇa's abode	
ā-brahma-bhuvanāl lokāḥ	Everyone in all planets upto Brahmaloka
punar āvartino 'rjuna	take repeated birth and death (even if they are pious).
mām upetya tu kaunteya	But one who attains My abode, O son of Kuntī,
punar janma na vidyate	never takes birth again.

The rebirth of everyone (under the control of *karma* or fruitive actions and reactions) stated in the first two lines of verse 16 will be elaborated in verses 17-19. The Lord's abode described in the last two lines of verse 16 will be elaborated in verses 20-22.

17-22: Material World Vs. Spiritual World

17. Brahmā's one day (called one *kalpa*) is 1000 *yuga* cycles by human calculation; same is the duration of his night (In such a calculation, Brahmā lives for 100 years).

One yuga cycle (*divya-yuga* or *catur-yuga*) is the combination of the four Ages of Satya, Tretā, Dvāpara and Kali. One year of humans is a day and night of the devatās. 12,000 such devatā years make one *catur-yuga* (360 human years x 12,000 = 4,320,000 human years). 1000 such *catur-yugas* make one day of Brahmā, whose lifespan is 100 years according to that calculation. After that, even Brahmā's planet along with Brahmā and other residents is destroyed.

18-19. Manifest and unmanifest states of material world: At the beginning of Brahmā's day, all living entities become manifest (*vyakta*), and when the night falls, they become unmanifest (*avyakta*) again. In this way, the *jīvas* appear and disappear again and again (*bhūtvā bhūtvā pralīyate*) as the days and nights of Brahmā arrive.

Superior to the unmanifest state of Brahmā's night in this material world, there is another unmanifest nature which is the eternal spiritual world.

20-21. Eternal spiritual world, the abode of Kṛṣṇa	
Eternal spiritual world: There is another unmanifest nature, which is eternal (*sanātanaḥ*), supreme, indestructible and is transcendental to this manifested and unmanifested matter. When all in this material world is annihilated, it remains as it is.	
avyakto 'kṣara ity uktas *tam āhuḥ paramāṁ gatim*	That which is described as unmanifest and infallible (indestructible / eternal) and the supreme destination,
yaṁ prāpya na nivartante *tad dhāma paramaṁ mama*	that place from which, having attained it, one never returns—that is My supreme abode.

Having described about His supreme abode, Kṛṣṇa will now describe the process of attaining that abode.

22. Kṛṣṇa's abode is attainable by ananya-bhakti (pure bhakti)	
puruṣaḥ sa paraḥ pārtha	O Pārtha, the Supreme Person, who is greater than all,
bhaktyā labhyas tv ananyayā	is attainable by unalloyed and undeviating devotion.
yasyāntaḥ-sthāni bhūtāni	Everything is situated within Him.
yena sarvam idaṁ tatam	He is all-pervading, although He is present in His abode.

23-28: Supremacy of Pure Bhakti in Attaining Kṛṣṇa

23. Different times of death: I shall now explain the different times at which, passing away from this world, the *yogī* does or does not return to this world.

24-26: Two ways of leaving the body	Candidates	Destination
Path of light: At an auspicious moment, in light and fire (by the influence of sun-god, fire-god)[1], during the day, in *śukla-pakṣa* (fortnight of waxing moon), in *uttarāyaṇa* (six months when sun travels to north)	For *jñānīs* and *yogīs*	Brahma-jyoti (Liberation: path of no return)

[1] There are presiding deities of light, fire, day, waxing fortnight and *uttarāyaṇa* who make arrangements for the departure of the soul.

Path of darkness: In darkness (night), during smoke, in *kṛṣṇa-pakṣa* (fortnight of waning moon), in *dakṣiṇāyana* (six months when sun travels to south).	For *karmīs*	Heaven (Rebirth: path of return)

At the time of death, the mind carries one to a new life. People in general must leave the body at a suitable time, to be assured whether or not to return to this material world. But for the pure devotees in Kṛṣṇa consciousness, there is no fear of returning to this world, whether they leave their bodies at an auspicious or inauspicious moment, by accident or arrangement. Being fully surrendered souls, they leave everything in Kṛṣṇa's hands and easily go to the spiritual world.

27. Path of devotees: Although the devotees know these two paths, they are never bewildered. Therefore be always fixed in devotion, O Arjuna (*tasmāt sarveṣu kāleṣu yoga-yukto bhavārjuna*).

28. The supreme position of a bhakti-yogī	
vedeṣu yajñeṣu tapaḥsu caiva	By studying the Vedas, performing sacrifices, undergoing austerities and
dāneṣu yat puṇya-phalaṁ pradiṣṭam	giving charity, whatever pious results may be obtained,
atyeti tat sarvam idaṁ viditvā	one can surpass all of them by knowing Me and My glories (from chapters 7 and 8)
yogī paraṁ sthānam upaiti cādyam	and performing devotional service. Such a devotee attains the supreme eternal abode.

The beauty of Kṛṣṇa consciousness, however, is that by one stroke, by engaging in devotional service, one can surpass all the rituals of the different orders of life.

9. The Most Confidential Knowledge

1-3: Kṛṣṇa glorifies the knowledge He is about to reveal

- 1: One has to be non-envious to know or realize Kṛṣṇa.
- 2: Bhakti is the king of all knowledge, most confidential and is joyfully performed.
- 3: The faithless cannot attain Kṛṣṇa

4-10: Aiśvarya-jñāna – Kṛṣṇa's relationship with this world

- 4-6: Kṛṣṇa pervades and maintains the entire material world by His energies, yet He is not in everything.
- 7-9: The material world is created and destroyed periodically by Kṛṣṇa's energies and His will, but all this work cannot bind Him.
- 10: Kṛṣṇa is the Supreme Director

11-25: Different types of worshipers of Lord Kṛṣṇa

- 11-12: Fools consider Kṛṣṇa as an ordinary human
- 13-14: Mahātmas or ananya-bhaktas worship Kṛṣṇa constantly with devotion
- 15: Three kinds of jñānīs who worship Kṛṣṇa
  - 16-19: Worshiping Kṛṣṇa in His universal form (viśvarūpa upāsana) – Kṛṣṇa is all-pervading, ultimate shelter and cause of all causes
  - 20-25: Devatā worship (pratīkopāsanā) – is a wrong way of worshiping Kṛṣṇa; by piety one attains heaven, but comes back to earth. One's destination depends on one's worship. Better worship Kṛṣṇa.

26-34: The glories of Kṛṣṇa-bhakti

- 26: Bhakti is simple. Kṛṣṇa accepts anything offered with devotion
- 27-28: Do everything as an offering to Kṛṣṇa and thus be freed from bondage.
- 29-31: Kṛṣṇa is equal to all, but specially inclined to a devotee. He forgives and purifies an imperfect devotee.
- 32-34: People of sinful birth also can attain Kṛṣṇa. What to speak of qualified people? So worship Kṛṣṇa directly.

In the previous chapter, Lord Kṛṣṇa mentioned that a pure devotee solely fixed on performing *ananya-bhakti* unto Him surpasses the paths of light and darkness.

In this chapter, Kṛṣṇa explains how to become such a pure devotee or *ananya-bhakta.*

Confidentiality of knowledge in *Bhagavad-gīta* –

- *Chapters 2-6*: Knowledge of matter and spirit, confidential (*guhya*)
- *Chapters 7-8*: Knowledge of *bhakti*, more confidential (*guhyatara*)
- *Chapter 9*: Knowledge of *kevala-bhakti*, most confidential (*guhyatama*) – describes the majestic aspect of Kṛṣṇa (*aiśvarya*), and excellence of a pure devotee.

The *Gīta* is considered the essence of all scriptures, and essence of the *Gītā* is the middle six chapters. And Chapters 9-10, that appear exactly at the center of the *Gīta,* are the further essence of these six chapters.

Similarity between Chapters 7 and 9: The flow of thought and concepts discussed in both chapters are similar, but Chapter 9 describes them in a deeper manner.

- 7.1-2 and 9.1-2 → Hearing about Kṛṣṇa
- 7.4-7, 12 and 9.4-10 → Kṛṣṇa's energies and His relationship with material world
- 7.8-11 and 9.16-19 → Kṛṇṣa's all-pervasiveness within this world
- 7.20-23 and 9.20-28 → Devatā worship Vs. Kṛṣṇa worship
- 7.24-26 and 9.11-15 → Impersonalists Vs. devotees in understanding Kṛṣṇa

Just as Kṛṣṇa described *karma-yoga* in Chapter 3 and later elaborated it deeply in Chapter 5, Kṛṣṇa has described *bhakti-yoga* in Chapter 7 and elaborated it in Chapter 9.

1-3: Kṛṣṇa Glorifies the Knowledge He Is About to Reveal

Gist of this section: Kṛṣṇa explains that non-enviousness (*anasūya*) and faith (*śraddha*) are the real qualifications to receive the knowledge (*jñānaṁ*) of pure *bhakti* and thus the realization (*vijñānaṁ*) of the Supreme Lord Kṛṣṇa.

1. 'Knowledge of bhakti' and 'realization of Kṛṇṣa' by non-enviousness	
idaṁ tu te guhyatamaṁ pravakṣyāmy anasūyave	My dear Arjuna, because you are never envious of Me, I shall speak to you this most confidential
jñānaṁ vijñāna-sahitaṁ	knowledge of pure *bhakti* (hearing about Kṛṣṇa, chanting His glories, remembering and serving Him etc.) that culminates in direct realization of Me,
yaj jñātvā mokṣyase 'śubhāt	knowing which you shall be relieved of all miseries.

Anasūyave: Arjuna is not envious, selfish or hostile, and doesn't see any faults in Kṛṣṇa. Thus he can undersand Kṛṣṇa. Envious and selfish people cannot understand Kṛṣṇa or the knowledge of His devotional service.

2. Eight characteristics of the knowledge of pure bhakti		
i	*rāja-vidyā*	King of all education (essence of all philosophies)
ii	*rāja-guhyaṁ*	King of all secrets (about the eternal activities of soul)
iii	*pavitram idam*	Purest of all; purifies one of all material contamination
iv	*uttamam*	Transcendental to the darkness or ignorance of this world
v	*pratyakṣāvagamaṁ*	Gives direct experience of the self by realization.
vi	*dharmyaṁ*	Perfection of religion i.e., service to the Supreme Lord.
vii	*su-sukhaṁ kartum*	Easily and joyfully performed
viii	*avyayam*	Everlasting, eternal, indestructible i.e, beyond the modes

The process of pure *bhakti* and the knowledge of pure *bhakti* are transcendental. Just as pure *bhakti* is beyond the material modes, the knowledge of pure *bhakti* is also beyond the modes. The knowledge that is described earlier is in mode of goodness.

Although *bhakti* is so joyful, the faithless and envious people do not perform bhakti and are thus deprived of the supreme goal of attaining Kṛṣṇa.

3. The faithless cannot attain Kṛṣṇa	
aśraddadhānāḥ puruṣā	Those who are not faithful
dharmasyāsya parantapa	in this process of devotional service, O Arjuna,
aprāpya māṁ nivartante	cannot attain Me. They remain in the path of
mṛtyu-saṁsāra-vartmani	repeated birth and death in this material world.

Real faith is the complete conviction that simply by serving the Supreme Lord, Śrī Kṛṣṇa, one can achieve all perfection. Such faith is created by association of devotees.

Kṛṣṇa next speaks about His remarkable powers (*aiśvarya*) by which He sustains this material world. Knowing this can stimulate devotion to Him.

4-10: Aiśvarya-jñāna – Kṛṣṇa's Relationship With This World

4-6: Maintenance of material world by Kṛṣṇa's energies

4. Kṛṣṇa is in everything	
mayā tatam idaṁ sarvaṁ	I pervade this entire universe (I am in everything),
jagad avyakta-mūrtinā	in an unmanifested form (invisible to material senses).
mat-sthāni sarva-bhūtāni	All living beings are in Me (their existence is dependent on Me, as I am their cause),
na cāhaṁ teṣv avasthitaḥ	but I am not in them (I am not dependent on them, I am aloof and detached).

Kṛṣna is present everywhere by His personal representation, the diffusion of His different energies. As the Supersoul or *paramātmā* (*antaryāmī* of the universe), which is Kṛṣṇa's expansion, Kṛṣṇa controls and supports the universe by entering within it.

Though everything is situated in Kṛṣṇa, they are not situated in Him, since He is completely aloof and independent of everything.

5. Yet Kṛṣṇa is not in everything: Behold My mystic opulence (*yogam aiśvaram*). Everything that is created doesn't rest in Me (i.e., Kṛṣṇa is aloof). Although I maintain everything (*bhūta-bhṛt*), I am not a part of this creation (*na bhūta-sthaḥ*), for My Self is the very source of creation (*bhūta-bhāvanaḥ*).

Kṛṣṇa's yogam-aiśvaram, inconceivable mystic power: Kṛṣṇa said in 9.4 that everything is resting on Him and He is the mantainer, sustainer and shelter of whole universe. But in 9.5, Kṛṣṇa says the opposite. Kṛṣṇa is not contradicting Himself, but actually, He is not *directly* concerned with the maintenance of this universe. His inconceivable energies will maintain the universe while He stays aloof. For instance, the planets are floating in space, and this space is the Supreme Lord's energy. But He is different from space. Ultimately the continued existence and functioning of all moving and non-moving entities depends on Kṛṣṇa's will. Kṛṣṇa gives an example in the next verse:

6. An example: Just as the wind, blowing everywhere, rests always in the sky, all created beings rest in Me.

This material world is created, maintained for some time and is destroyed. The above verses describe how maintenance of this world takes place by Kṛṣṇa's will and energies. The following verses describe the creation and desctuction of this world, by His energies.

7-8: Creation and Destruction of material world by Kṛṣṇa's energies

7. Periodic creation and destruction: At the time of destruction (at the end of Brahmā's life) all beings enter into My energy (*prakṛti*) composed of the three modes, and at the beginning of another creation, by My potency, I create them again.

8. Kṛṣṇa's will: Under My will, with My energy, the whole cosmic order is manifested again and again (*visṛjāmi punaḥ punaḥ*), and is destroyed at the end.

Although Kṛṣṇa creates, maintains and destroys this material world (through His energies), all this work doesn't bind Him. So, He is not directly responsible for any good or evil that happens in this world.

9. All this work cannot bind Me, O Dhanañjaya. I am – (*i*) almost neutral (*udāsīna-vat*) and (*ii*) detached (*asaktaṁ*) from all these material activities.

Bondage arises from desire and attachment to action and its results. Because all of Kṛṣṇa's desires are automatically fulfilled, He need not act, and thus no bondage.

10. Kṛṣṇa is the Supreme Director	
mayādhyakṣeṇa prakṛtiḥ	By My direction (glance), this material nature,
sūyate sa-carācaram	is producing all moving and non-moving beings.
hetunānena kaunteya	Under its rule, O son of Kuntī,
jagad viparivartate	this universe is created and annihilated again and again.

Incarnations for creation: The Supreme Lord Kṛṣṇa has unlimited incarnations (*avatāras*) of which one category is called *puruṣa-avatāras* who are involved in the creation this material world. The first *puruṣa* called Mahā-viṣṇu or Kāraṇodakaśāyī Viṣṇu, lies within the Causal Ocean and breathes out innumerable universes. By His glance, He injects the living entities into the material universe, just as a father impregnates a mother. Into each universe the Lord again enters as Garbhodakaśāyī Viṣṇu, the second *puruṣa*. He still further manifests Himself as Kṣīrodakaśāyī Viṣṇu, the third *puruṣa* and enters into everything—even into the minute atom.

Superintendent: Although the living entities are born under the Lord's glance in the eniverse, they take birth in different forms and species, according to their own past desires and activities. So the Lord is not directly attached to this creation. Being the superintendent, He is the efficient cause (*nimitta*) and *prakṛti* is the material cause (*upādāna*). Being the *doer* and being *neutral* are not contradictory for the Lord, because He rules by proximity only.

Though Kṛṣṇa is the source of the three *puruṣas* who create and maintain this material world, still when Kṛṣṇa descends as the son of Vasudeva and Devakī into this world, some people misunderstand Him to be an ordinary human being or just an *aṁśa* of the *puruṣa-avatāras*.

11-25: Different Types of Worshipers of Lord Kṛṣṇa

11-12. Fools or impersonalists consider Kṛṣṇa as an ordinary human	
avajānanti māṁ mūḍhā	Fools deride Me
mānuṣīṁ tanum āśritam	when I descend in the human form.
paraṁ bhāvam ajānanto	They do not know My transcendental nature
mama bhūta-maheśvaram	as the Supreme Lord and proprietor of all that be.
Fate of such fools:	
moghāśā	Baffled in their hopes for attaining the Lord's abode or *sālokya-mukti* (if they are *bhaktas*),
mogha-karmāṇo	Baffled in their fruitive activities and results of attaining heaven or *svarga* (if they are *karmīs*),

mogha-jñānā	Do not attain the results of culturing knowledge, which is liberation (if they are *jñānīs*).
vicetasaḥ	They all are deluded by *māyā* (and lost discriminating power by the sin of rejecting Me).
rākṣasīm āsurīṁ caiva	They are attracted by demonic and atheistic views.
prakṛtiṁ mohinīṁ śritāḥ	Having taken shelter of the illusory material energy.

13-14. Mahātmas or ananya-bhaktas worship Kṛṣṇa constantly with devotion	
mahātmānas tu māṁ pārtha daivīṁ prakṛtim āśritāḥ	O Pātha, those who are not deluded, the great souls, are under the protection of the divine spiritual nature (not under the control of material nature).
bhajanty ananya-manaso	They do My devotional service without distractions
jñātvā bhūtādim avyayam	knowing Me (My human-like body) as the cause of everything and inexhaustible, being fully spiritual.
satataṁ kīrtayanto māṁ	Always chanting My glories,
yatantaś ca dṛḍha-vratāḥ	endeavoring with great determination,
namasyantaś ca māṁ bhaktyā	bowing down before Me, with great devotion
nitya-yuktā upāsate	these great souls perpetually worship Me.

Kṛṣṇa will explain more about the pure devoees (*ananya-bhakta*) and pure devotional service (*ananya-bhakti*) in 9.29-34 and 10.1-11.

15. Three kinds of jñānīs worship Kṛṣṇa by cultivating knowledge (jñāna-yajña)			
i	**Ekatvena** *(ahangrahopāsanā)*	They worship Me 'in oneness,' thinking themselves as God.	12.1-5 will elaborate on this
ii	**Pṛthakvena** *(pratīkopāsanā)*	They worship Me 'in diversity,' in many forms as the devatās.	9.20-25 will elaborate on this
iii	**Viśvato-mukham** *(viśvarūpa upāsanā)*	They worship Me 'in the Universal form,' that I am everything.	9.16-19 & Chapter 11 will elaborate on this

16-19: Worshiping Kṛṣṇa in His universal form (viśvarūpa upāsana)

16. Kṛṣṇa is the various elements of all sacrifices: I am the –

- *Kratu:* rituals mentioned in the *śruti* scriptures
- *Yajña:* sacrifices mentioned in *smṛti* scriptures
- *Svadhā*: oblation offering to the ancestors
- *Auṣadham*: the healing herbs

- *Mantraḥ*: transcendental chant
- *Ājyam*: the ghee (melted butter)
- *Agniḥ*: fire
- *Hutam:* the act of offering.

17-19. Kṛṣṇa is all-pervading, ultimate shelter and cause of all causes	
pitāham asya jagato	I am the father of the whole universe.
mātā dhātā pitāmahaḥ	I am the mother, the maintainer and the grandsire.
vedyaṁ pavitram oṁkāra	I am object of knowledge, the purifier, syllable *oṁ*.
ṛk sāma yajur eva ca	I am also the Ṛg, the Sāma and the Yajur Vedas.
gatir bhartā prabhuḥ sākṣī	I am the goal, the sustainer, the master and witness.
nivāsaḥ śaraṇaṁ suhṛt	I am the abode, the shelter, and the dearest friend.
prabhavaḥ pralayaḥ sthānaṁ	I am the creation, destruction and maintenance of all.
nidhānaṁ bījam avyayam	I am resting place, eternal seed (indestructible cause).
tapāmy aham ahaṁ varṣaṁ	I give heat, and I cause rain.
nigṛhṇāmy utsṛjāmi ca	I withhold and send forth that rain.
amṛtaṁ caiva mṛtyuś ca	I am immortality (liberation), and I am also death.
sad asac cāham arjuna	I am both spirit and matter (subtle and gross), Arjuna.

20-25: Devatā Worship (pratīkopāsanā)

20. Attaining heaven by piety: The knowers of the three Vedas, drinking the *soma* juice, purified of sins, worship Me indirectly through sacrifices, praying to enter heaven. Attaining piety (*puṇya*), they enter the heaven and enjoy celestial delights.

21. Coming back to earth: By enjoying the heavenly sense pleasures, the results of their pious acts get exhausted and they return to this mortal planet again (*kṣīṇe puṇye martya-lokaṁ viśanti*). Thus such pleasure seekers who follow Vedic rites achieve only repeated birth and death.

In contrast to the *devatā* worshipers, the pure devotees of Kṛṣṇa attain unfallible protection directly from Kṛṣṇa, which is not obtained by pious acts.

22. Kṛṣṇa's complete protection for an ananya-bhakta: But those who always worship Me with exclusive devotion, meditating on Me, desiring My association—to them I supply what they lack (*yoga*), and I preserve what they have (*kṣemaṁ*). Thus I personally take the responsibility to carry (*vahāmi*) the burden of their maintenance (their spiritual and material welfare).

ananyāś cintayanto māṁ ye janāḥ paryupāsate
teṣāṁ nityābhiyuktānāṁ yoga-kṣemaṁ vahāmy aham

Yoga-kṣemaṁ: *Yoga* refers to a devotee's approach towards Kṛṣṇa. *Kṣema* refers to Kṛṣṇa's merciful protection. Kṛṣṇa helps the devotee to achieve Kṛṣṇa consciousness by *yoga*, and when he becomes fully Kṛṣṇa conscious, He protects him from falling down to a miserable conditioned life.

23. Devatā worship – a wrong way of worshiping Kṛṣṇa	
ye 'py anya-devatā-bhaktā	Those who are devotees of other gods
yajante śraddhayānvitāḥ	and who worship them with faith
te 'pi mām eva kaunteya	actually worship only Me, O son of Kuntī,
yajanty avidhi-pūrvakam	but they do so in a wrong way.

Avidhi-pūrvakam: The right way of growing a plant is by watering its root, and not the leaves and branches. The right way of nourishing the body is to feed food to the stomach, not the other limbs. Similarly, the right way of worshiping the Supreme Lord is to serve Him directly, and not the devatās, who are His representtaives in managing the affairs of this world in the Lord's government. It is illegal to bribe the government representatives, without following the rules of the government. So worshiping the devatās is the wrong way of worshiping Kṛṣṇa (*avidhi-pūrvakam*) and thus they return to take birth in this material world.

24. All acts are meant for satisfying Kṛṣṇa	
ahaṁ hi sarva-yajñānāṁ bhoktā ca prabhur eva ca	I am the only enjoyer and master of all sacrifices (and also the giver of all results, through the devatās).
na tu mām abhijānanti tattvenātaś cyavanti te	Therefore, those who do not recognize My true transcendental nature fall down.

25. Different types of worship → different destinations	
yānti deva-vratā devān	Those who worship devatās go to devatās' planets.
pitṝn yānti pitṛ-vratāḥ	Those who worship ancestors go to the ancestors.
bhūtāni yānti bhūtejyā	Those who worship ghosts will take birth among ghosts.
yānti mad-yājino 'pi mām	Those who worship Me will come to Me (no rebirth).

Our destination thus depends on our choice to accept certain object of worship. The best choice, however, is to worship Kṛṣṇa. Now in the next section, Kṛṣṇa elaborates on exclusive worship of Himself. Having established that He is the only enjoyer of all sacrificial offerings, Kṛṣṇa first reveals what types of offerings He desires.

26-34: The Glories of Kṛṣṇa-bhakti

26. The simplicity of bhakti: Kṛṣṇa accepts anything offered with devotion	
patraṁ puṣpaṁ phalaṁ toyaṁ yo me bhaktyā prayacchati	If an unmotivated devotee offers Me with love and devotion a leaf, a flower, a fruit or water,
tad ahaṁ bhakty-upahṛtam aśnāmi prayatātmanaḥ	I accept that loving offering from that genuine devotee in pure consciousness.

Love is the only qualification to serve Kṛṣṇa. Kṛṣṇa is self-sufficient and not in need of anything from anyone, yet He accepts the offering of His devotee in an exchange of love and affection. No one is barred from *bhakti* because it is so easy and universal. Even the poorest of the poor, can attempt to do *kṛṣṇa-bhakti.* The sign of purity in one's *bhakti* is that he has no motivations in his service to Kṛṣṇa and he can never give up such service any time.

Bhakti is mentioned twice in this verse in order to declare emphatically that *bhakti*, or devotional service, is the only means to approach Kṛṣṇa. No other condition, such as becoming a scholar, rich man or a philosopher, can induce Kṛṣṇa to accept some offering. This also indicates that Kṛṣṇa is a person who reciprocates with pure love. He is not impersonal as some people imagine.

Kṛṣṇa described the process of pure *bhakti* in 9.14, 22 and 26 that involves complete dedication to Him. For those who are not able to perfrom *bhakti* at that level, Kṛṣṇa will now describe the process of doing everything as an offering to Him.

27. Doing everything as an offering to Kṛṣṇa	
yat karoṣi yad aśnāsi	Whatever you do, whatever you eat,
yaj juhoṣi dadāsi yat	whatever you offer in sacrifice or give away, and
yat tapasyasi kaunteya	whatever austerities you perform—O son of Kuntī,
tat kuruṣva mad-arpaṇam	do that as an offering to Me.

This is not ananya-bhakti: Kṛṣṇa didn't use the word *bhakti* in this verse. Yet, this is predominately *bhakti* with some mixture of other elements. It is similar to *karma-yoga* because activities are performed, but it superior to *karma-yoga* or *niṣkāma-karma-yoga* because all activities, even beyond the prescribed duties, are offered to the Lord without desire. It is similar to *jñāna-miśra-bhakti* because the person has knowledge of *ātmā* and *Paramātmā*. But it is superior to *jñāna-miśra-bhakti* because it has abundant appreciation of the Lord's personal features as well. But because the consciousness is *not always* fixed on the Lord and one does the activities he wants to do and then offers them to Kṛṣṇa *after* performing them, rather than *before*. Thus it cannot be called as *ananyā bhakti*, in which one knows what actions are pleasing to the Lord, and then performs them, thereby offering those activities to Kṛṣṇa even *before* performing them.

28. Result of offering everything to Kṛṣṇa: You will be freed from bondage to *karma* (an obstacle to *bhakti*) and its auspicious and inauspicious (pious and sinful) results. Then, with your mind fixed on Me in this principle of renunciation (*sannyāsa-yoga-yuktātmā*[1]), you will be liberated and come to Me.

Yukta-vairāgya is to act in Kṛṣṇa consciousness under superior direction and the fruits are given to Kṛṣṇa. Actions performed with such renounced spirit clean one's mind, and one gradually makes progress in spiritual realization and becomes completely surrendered to the Supreme Lord and is liberated.

29. Kṛṣṇa is equal to all, but specially inclined to a devotee	
samo 'haṁ sarva-bhūteṣu	I am equally disposed to all living beings.
na me dveṣyo 'sti na priyaḥ	I envy no one, nor am I partial to anyone.
ye bhajanti tu māṁ bhaktyā	But whoever renders service unto Me in devotion
mayi te teṣu cāpy aham	is a friend, is in Me, and I am also a friend to him.

Kṛṣṇa is reciprocal: Lord Kṛṣṇa is just like a cloud that rains everywhere equally whether on rock or land or water. But for His devotees, He gives specific attention. This is not discrimination; but it is natural. Someone may be charitably disposed to all, yet he has a special interest in his own children. Although every living being is a child of God, only the devotees have the consciousness of acting like God's children. Thus Kṛṣṇa specially reciprocates with them. (See 4.11, *ye yathā māṁ prapadyante...*).

30-31. Kṛṣṇa excuses and purifies an imperfect devotee	
api cet su-durācāro	Even if one commits the most abominable action,
bhajate mām ananya-bhāk	if he is engaged in devotional service to please Me,
sādhur eva sa mantavyaḥ	I consider him My saintly devotee because,
samyag vyavasito hi saḥ	he is properly fixed in his determination on Me.
kṣipraṁ bhavati dharmātmā	He quickly becomes righteous devoid of contamination
śaśvac-chāntiṁ nigacchati	and attains lasting peace.
kaunteya pratijānīhi	O son of Kuntī, declare it boldly
na me bhaktaḥ praṇaśyati	that My devotee never perishes.

[1] *Sannyāsa* means renunciation from matter. *Yoga* means connection with spirit. So, *sannyāsa-yoga* means to be disconnected from matter while connecting with the spirit.

Accidental mistakes: *Bhakti* is like declaration of war against *māyā*. As long as one is not perfect, there may be accidental falldowns from the path of saintly character. However, the circumstantial despicable activities of Kṛṣṇa's devotee, due to the power of material impressions, does not make him abominable, just as the spots on the moon do not become an impediment to the diffusion of moonlight.

Repentance: When a devotee commits sin, he becomes repentant and feels disguist for his actions. By remembering Lord Kṛṣṇa, he will atone for all his mistakes and he quickly becomes righteous.

Kṛṣṇa's attachment to His devotee is His very nature. That attachment does not decrease even if the devotee commits wrong, for Kṛṣṇa makes him come up to the highest standard. But, taking advantage of Kṛṣṇa's kindness, a devotee shouldn't *intentionally* commit mistakes.

Kṛṣṇa asked Arjuna to declare that His devotee never perishes. Because, Kṛṣṇa will uphold the declaration made by His devotee under all circumstances, whereas He can break His own promise if needed and accept criticism for that. For instance, although Kṛṣṇa promised not to take a weapon on the battle of Kurukṣetra, He picked up a chariot wheel to attack Bhīṣma just to protect Bhīṣma's words.

Bhakti unto Kṛṣṇa does not consider not only the *incidental* faults arising by actions of a misbehaving devotee, but *bhakti* does not even consider the *inherent* faults of such a person which arise from his very birth.

32. People of sinful birth also can attain Kṛṣṇa	
māṁ hi pārtha vyapāśritya	O son of Pṛthā, those who take shelter in Me,
ye 'pi syuḥ pāpa-yonayaḥ	though they be of lower or sinful birth,
striyo vaiśyās tathā śūdrās	women, merchants and workers,
te 'pi yānti parāṁ gatim	Everyone can attain the supreme destination.

The process of *bhakti* and the association of Kṛṣṇa's devotees is so powerful that it can purify any impure person coming even from sinful backgrounds.

33. What to speak of qualified people?	
kiṁ punar brāhmaṇāḥ puṇyā	How much more this is so of the pious *brāhmaṇas*,
bhaktā rājarṣayas tathā	the devotees and the saintly kings. Therefore,
anityam asukhaṁ lokam	having come to this temporary, miserable world,
imaṁ prāpya bhajasva mām	engage in loving service unto Me (elaborated in 9.34).

34. Conclusion/ Essence: Worship Kṛṣṇa directly (pure bhakti)	
man-manā bhava mad-bhakto	(*i*) Always think of Me, (*ii*) become My devotee.
mad-yājī māṁ namaskuru	(*iii*) Worship Me and (*iv*) offer obeisances to Me.
mām evaiṣyasi yuktvaivam	You will surely come to Me, having absorbed
ātmānaṁ mat-parāyaṇaḥ	yourself completely in Me and taking My shelter.

Bhakti, like River Gaṅga, does not consider who is suitable or unsuitable. Destroying all sins by its very touch, pure *bhakti* is alone considered to be the king of all secrets.

This verse is the most important instruction of the *Gīta* and is considered the essence of the *Gīta*. While concluding His teachings, Kṛṣṇa will again repeat this verse in 18.65.

10. The Opulence of The Absolute

1-7: Knowing that Kṛṣṇa is unknowable and the source of all

- 1-3: Kṛṣṇa is the mysterious origin of everything and one who knows Kṛṣṇa is free from all sins.
- 4-7: Kṛṣṇa is the origin of all qualities and personalities. Accepting His powers leads to surrender unto Him.

8-11: Pure bhakti, the essence of Bhagavad-gīta

- 8-9: Kṛṣṇa is the source of all material and spiritual worlds. The wise people who worship Him are always absorbed in His discussions.
- 10-11: Kṛṣṇa gives intelligence to His devotees from within and mercifully destroys their ignorance.

12-18: Arjuna accepts Kṛṣṇa's supreme position

- 12-13: Kṛṣṇa is the Supreme Absolute Truth, the purest, unborn and the greatest. His supremacy is confirmed by great authorities like Nārada, Vyāsa and so on.
- 14-15: No one knows Kṛṣṇa expect Himself.
- 16-17: Arjuna requests Kṛṣṇa to tell more about His divine opulences as there is no satiation in hearing about Kṛṣṇa.

19-42: Lord Kṛṣṇa describes His vibhūtīs (opulences)

- 19-20: Kṛṣṇa describes only the most prominent of His opulences, as they are unlimited. He is the all-pervading Supersoul, and the beginning, the middle and the end of all entities.
- 21-39: Various opulences of Kṛṣṇa (See the table)
- 40-42: There is no end to Kṛṣṇa's divine opulences. All that is majestic, beautiful and powerful is a spark of Kṛṣṇa's splendor. He pervades and supports the entire universe with a single fragment of His power.

In the previous chapter, Lord Kṛṣṇa concluded with the instruction to fix the mind upon Him (9.34).

In this chapter, Kṛṣṇa describes His opulences on which a devotee can fix his mind and remember Him whenever he sees anything opulent, powerful and beautiful in this world.

In Chapters 7 and 9, Kṛṣṇa has explained how His different energies are working (7.8-12 and 9.16-19). Now in Chapter 10, He will explain His specific manifestations and opulences (*vibhūtis*), knowing which one understands that the Lord is worthy of worship.

1-7: Knowing That Kṛṣṇa Is Unknowable and the Source of All

1. More wonderful knowledge: O mighty-armed Arjuna (*mahā-bāho*), because you are My dear friend filled with love (*prīyamāṇāya*), for your benefit (*hita-kāmyayā*), I shall give you supreme knowledge (*paramaṁ vacaḥ*) greater than what I spoke earlier. Please listen.

2. No one knows Kṛṣṇa, the mysterious origin of everything	
na me viduḥ sura-gaṇāḥ *prabhavaṁ na maharṣayaḥ*	Neither the hosts of devatās nor the great sages know My extraordinary origin or opulences,
aham ādir hi devānāṁ *maharṣīṇāṁ ca sarvaśaḥ*	for, in every respect, I am the source of the devatās and sages.

One cannot understand Kṛṣṇa by scholarship and speculation. One can understand Kṛṣṇa in His actual situation, only by the unprecedented mercy of Kṛṣṇa and His devotees, and from the bona fide books like the *Gīta* and the *Bhāgavatam*.

3. One who knows Kṛṣṇa is freed from all sins	
yo māṁ ajam anādiṁ ca	He who knows Me as the unborn, as the beginningless,
vetti loka-maheśvaram	and as the Supreme proprietor of all the worlds—
asammūḍhaḥ sa martyeṣu	he only, undeluded among men,
sarva-pāpaiḥ pramucyate	is freed from all sinful reactions in this world.

Refer 7.3 for the rarity of a person who knows Kṛṣṇa in truth. The conditioned souls change bodies, but Kṛṣṇa is unborn and His body is not changeable. All the devatās were created within this world, but Kṛṣṇa existed before the creation of this world.

4-6. Kṛṣṇa is the origin of all qualities and personalities	
buddhir, jñānam, asammohaḥ	Intelligence, knowledge, freedom from illusion,
kṣamā, satyaṁ, damaḥ, śamaḥ	forgiveness, truthfulness, sense control, mind control
sukhaṁ, duḥkhaṁ, bhavo, 'bhāvo	happiness, distress, birth, death,
bhayaṁ, cābhayam eva ca	fear, fearlessness
ahiṁsā, samatā, tuṣṭis	nonviolence, equanimity, satisfaction,
tapo, dānaṁ, yaśo, 'yaśaḥ	austerity, charity, fame and infamy—
bhavanti bhāvā bhūtānāṁ matta eva pṛthag-vidhāḥ	all these various qualities of living beings are created by Me alone.
Genealogical synopsis of the universal population: The 7 great sages, the 4 Kumāras and the Manus (progenitors of mankind) came from Me, born from My mind (they were absorbed in thinking of Me), and all the living beings descend from them.	

7. Accepting Kṛṣṇa's powers leads to surrender: One who is convinced of this opulence and mystic power (*vibhūtis*) of Mine (described in this chapter), engages in unalloyed devotional service (*avikalpena yogena*) undoubtedly.

etāṁ vibhūtiṁ yogaṁ ca mama yo vetti tattvataḥ
so 'vikalpena yogena yujyate nātra saṁśayaḥ

The highest summit of spiritual perfection is knowledge of the Supreme Personality of Godhead. Generally people know that God is great, but they do not know in detail how God is great. The following are the details.

8-11: Pure Bhakti, The Essence of Bhagavad-gīta

Kṛṣṇa summarizes the *Bhagavad-gīta* in these four essential verses (often called as *catuḥ-ślokī* also), describing the *bhakti* of topmost devotees and the real nature of Himself which generates and nourishes that *bhakti*.

8. Kṛṣṇa is the source of everything	
ahaṁ sarvasya prabhavo	I am the source of all spiritual and material worlds.
mattaḥ sarvaṁ pravartate	Everything emanates from Me and operates due to Me.
iti matvā bhajante māṁ	Those who know this engage in My devotional service.
budhā bhāva-samanvitāḥ	Such wise people lovingly worship Me with their hearts.

9. Symptoms of pure devotees of Kṛṣṇa	
mac-cittā *mad-gata-prāṇā*	With their minds absorbed in Me (*smaraṇam*), their lives fully devoted to My service[1],
bodhayantaḥ parasparam	My pure devotees enlighten one another (*śravaṇam*),
kathayantaś ca māṁ nityaṁ	by conversing about Me always (*kīrtanam*),
tuṣyanti ca ramanti ca	and thus experience great satisfaction and bliss.

Bhakti or devotional service unto Lord Kṛṣṇa gives satisfaction in the stages of both practice (*sādhana*) and perfection (*sādhya*).

This great joy that a devotee experiences by glorifying Kṛṣṇa is spiritual bliss beyond the modes. But how does he grasp Kṛṣṇa who is infinite in form, qualities and powers. Who gives them the method of realizing Kṛṣṇa? The previous verse described how devotees worship Kṛṣṇa and the next two verses describe how Kṛṣṇa reciprocates with them.

10. Kṛṣṇa gives intelligence to His devotees	
teṣāṁ satata-yuktānāṁ	To those who are constantly engaged in
bhajatāṁ prīti-pūrvakam	serving Me with love and devotion
dadāmi buddhi-yogaṁ taṁ	I give them the necessary understanding
yena mām upayānti te	by which they can come to Me.

Buddhi-yoga is the process by which one gets out of the entanglement of this material world. The ultimate goal of progress is Kṛṣṇa. To achieve this goal, the path is slowly but progressively traversed.

When a person knows the goal of life but is addicted to the fruits of activities, he is acting in *karma-yoga*. When he knows that the goal is Kṛṣṇa but he takes pleasure in mental speculations to understand Kṛṣṇa, he is acting in *jñāna-yoga*. And when he knows the goal and seeks Kṛṣṇa completely in Kṛṣṇa consciousness and devotional service, he is acting in *bhakti-yoga*, or *buddhi-yoga*, which is the complete *yoga*. This complete *yoga* is the highest perfectional stage of life.

11. Kṛṣṇa mercifully destroys ignorance	
teṣām evānukampārtham	To show them special mercy,
aham ajñāna-jaṁ tamaḥ *nāśayāmy ātma-bhāva-stho*	I, dwelling in their hearts, destroy the darkness born of ignorance,
jñāna-dīpena bhāsvatā	with the shining lamp of knowledge.

[1] They cannot maintain their lives without Me just like a fish out of water.

12-18: Arjuna Accepts Lord Kṛṣṇa's Supreme Position

After hearing the above four essential verses from Kṛṣṇa, Arjuna, in the following verses, glorifies Kṛṣṇa's supremacy and expresses his desire to hear more about His *vibhūtīs*:

12-13. Kṛṣṇa's supremacy confirmed by the authorities	
paraṁ brahma *paraṁ dhāma*	You are the Supreme Personality of Godhead, the ultimate abode,
pavitraṁ, paramaṁ bhavān	the purest, and the Absolute truth.
puruṣaṁ śāśvataṁ, divyam	You are the eternal personality, transcendental,
ādi-devam, ajaṁ, vibhum	the original Lord, unborn and the greatest.
All the great sages such as Nārada, Asita, Devala and Vyāsa confirm this truth about You, and now You Yourself are declaring it to me.	

14. No one knows You, O Kṛṣṇa. I totally accept as truth all that You have told me. Neither the devatās nor the demons can understand You.

15. Only You know Yourself, by Your own internal potency. O Supreme Person (*puruṣottama*), origin of all (*bhūta-bhāvana*), Lord of all beings (*bhūteśa*), God of gods (*deva-deva*), Lord of the universe (*jagat-pate*)!

16-17. Please tell me more of Your divine opulences (*divyā hy ātma-vibhūtayaḥ*) by which You pervade all these worlds. How shall I constantly think of You, know You and remember You? In what all forms do You manifest?

Questions for common people: By Kṛṣṇa's grace, Arjuna has personal experience, intelligence and knowledge by which he has understood Kṛṣṇa to be the Supreme Lord. Yet he asked Kṛṣṇa to describe His *all-pervading nature* on behalf of common people. Because people in general and especially the impersonalists are more concerned with the all-pervading nature of the Supreme in this physical world.

18. No satiation in hearing about You, O Janārdana. Please describe in detail Your mystic power, *vibhūtīs* and *bhakti-yoga*. The more I hear the more I want to taste the nectar of Your words.

19-42: Lord Kṛṣṇa Describes His Vibhūtīs (Opulences)

19. My opulence is limitless, so I will tell you only the prominent (*prādhānyataḥ*) ones of My splendorous manifestations.

Our limited senses do not allow us to understand the totality of Kṛṣṇa's powers. Still the devotees try to understand Kṛṣṇa, because the very topics of Kṛṣṇa are so relishable. "*Vibhūti*," in this verse refers to the opulences by which Kṛṣṇa controls the universe.

20. I am the Supersoul in the hearts of all living entities. I am the beginning, the middle and the end (creation, maintenance and destruction) of all beings.

The mood of understanding Kṛṣṇa's vibhūtis: 10.21-39 describe a few of Kṛṣṇa's infinite opulences or *vibhūtīs*. For easy readability they are presented in a table. The first column gives the verse number. The second column presents a 'broad category' and the last column presents 'the representative of Kṛṣṇa' in that broad category.

For instance when Kṛṣṇa says that He is sun among the luminaries (10.21), it means that sun is the *chief* of all the luminaries and thus *represents* the Supreme Lord Kṛṣṇa. Even the powerful sun gets its power from Lord Kṛṣṇa's potent energy. All the entries in the following table have to be understood in a similar manner.

	Among the –	Kṛṣṇa is –
21	Ādityas	Viṣṇu (Vāmana)
	Luminaries	Sun
	Maruts (winds)	Marīci
	Stars	Moon
22	Vedas	Sāma Veda
	Devatās	Indra
	Senses	Mind
	Living beings	Consciousness
23	Rudras	Śankara
	Yakṣas and Rākṣasas	Kuvera
	Vasus	Agni (fire)
	Mountains	Meru
24	Priests	Bṛhaspati
	Commanders	Kārtikeya
	Water bodies	Ocean
25	Great sages	Bhṛgu
	Vibrations	Oṁ
	Sacrifices	Japa (chanting)
	Immovable things	Himālayas
26	Trees	Banyan tree
	Sages among devatās	Nārada
	Gandharvas	Citraratha
	Perfected beings	Kapila

	Among the –	Kṛṣṇa is –
27	Horses	Uccaiḥśravā
	Lordly elephants	Airāvata
	Men	King
28	Weapons	Thunderbolt
	Cows	Surabhi / Kāmadhenu
	Causes of procreation	Lust for producing progeny (Kandarpa)
	Serpents	Vāsuki
29	Many-hooded snakes	Ananta/ Śeṣa
	Aquatics	Varuṇa
	Ancestors	Aryamā
	Dispensers of law	Yama
30	Demons	Prahlāda
	Subduers	Time
	Beasts	Lion
	Birds	Garuḍa
31	Purifying agents	Wind
	Holders of weapons	Rāma/ Paraśurāma
	Fishes	Makara/ Shark
	Rivers	Gaṅgā

	Among the –	Kṛṣṇa is –
32	Creations	Beginning, middle and end
	Knowledge	Spiritual knowledge
	Arguments of logicians	Conclusive truth (*vāda*)
33	Letters	'A'
	Compound words (*sāmāsika*)	Dual compound (*dvandvaḥ*)
	Destroyers	Time
	Creators	Brahmā
34	Deaths (that take place at every moment)	Death that devours everything including memory
	Future manifestations or transformations	Generating principle (birth)
	Women (feminine opulences)	Fame, fortune, memory, fine speech, patience, intelligence, steadfastness.
35	Sāma veda hymns	Bṛhat-sāma
	Poetry (*chandasa*)	Gāyatrī
	Months	Mārgaśīrṣa (Nov-Dec)
	Seasons	flower-bearing spring

	Among the –	Kṛṣṇa is –
36	Cheaters	Gambling
	Splendid	Splendor
	Victorious	Victory
	Those who endeavor	Effort/ adventure
	Strong	Strength
37	Descendants of Vṛṣni	Vāsudeva
	Pāṇḍavas	Arjuna
	Sages	Vyāsa
	Thinkers	Uśanā (Śukrācārya)
38	Means of suppressing lawlessness	Punishment (*daṇḍa*)
	Victory seekers	Morality (*nīti*)
	Secrets	Silence (*maunam*)
	Wise	Wisdom (*jñāna*)
39	All existences	Seed (*bījam*): No moving or non-moving being exists without Me

40. There is no end to My divine *vibhūtīs* and grandeur. What I have spoken to you is but a mere indication of My infinite opulences.

Having explained His *vibhūtis* individually, Lord Kṛṣṇa will now speak of them as a whole.

41. A spark of Kṛṣṇa's splendor: Know that all majestic (*vibhūtimat*), beautiful (*śrīmat*) and powerful (*ūrjitam*) creations in past, present and future, spring from but a fragment (*aṁśa*) of My splendor (*mama-teja*).

yad yad vibhūtimat sattvaṁ śrīmad ūrjitam eva vā
tat tad evāvagaccha tvaṁ mama tejo-'ṁśa-sambhavam

In this verse Lord Kṛṣṇa gathers together all the *vibhūtis* which He did not mention. One should consider that all glorious objects are non-different from Kṛṣṇa by being under His control and by being pervaded by Him.

42. All-pervasive Supersoul: But what is the need of all this detailed knowledge? With a single fragment of Myself I pervade and support this entire universe.

atha vā bahunaitena kiṁ jñātena tavārjuna
viṣṭabhyāham idaṁ kṛtsnam ekāṁśena sthito jagat

Three Supersouls: Kṛṣṇa is the source and basis of everything in this universe. He is all-pervading (*antaryāmī*) by the expansion of His partial representation, the Supersoul (*paramātmā*), who enters into everything that exists and maintains it. There are three *puruṣa* incarnations, who are the *antaryāmīs* (Supersouls) of *prakṛti* (material nature).

- **Kāraṇodaka-śāyī Viṣṇu** or Mahā-viṣṇu, who lies on the causal ocean (*kāraṇa-samudra*) and from whom innumerable material universes emanate. He is the Supersoul of entire material realm.
- **Garbhodaka-śayī Viṣṇu,** who lies on the Garbhodaka ocean within each material universe. He is the Supersoul of an individual universe.
- **Kṣīrodaka-śayī Viṣṇu,** who lies on the milk ocean, and who expands as the Supersoul in the heart of every single living entity and even an atom.

Since Kṛṣṇa pervades everything, all the wonderful or powerful objects should be understood as His *vibhūtis*. Kṛṣṇa is not an incarnation. He is the source of all incarnations. Therefore Lord Śrī Kṛṣṇa is most worshipable and worthy of service. Understanding this with intelligence and realizing this with devotion, one will be able to taste Kṛṣṇa's sweetness.

11. The Universal Form

1-4: Arjuna requests Kṛṣṇa to show His universal form	"O Kṛṣṇa, my illusion has been dispelled. Please show me Your powerful form by which You enter, pervade and support this universe, if You think I can behold it."
5-8: Lord Kṛṣṇa describes His universal form	"O Arjuna, I will give you divine eyes (divya cakṣu) to behold My mystic opulence (yogam aiśvaram)."
9-14: Sañjaya describes Arjuna's vision of the universal form	9-12: Arjuna sees unlimited faces, arms, eyes, weapons and so on in that wonderful effulgent universal form.
	13-14: Seeing everything in the universe at one place, Arjuna bows down.
15-31: Arjuna's Experience of Seeing the Universal Form	15-19: Arjuna's realizations upon seeing the Viśva-rūpa – difficult to behold, and indicates Kṛṣṇa's supremacy.
	19-25: Arjuna's description of Kāla-rūpa, the form of time – no origin, middle or end, spread everywhere with unlimited strength as the devatās offered prayers. Arjuna becomes fearful.
	26-30: Arjuna sees the future outcomes of the war – Warriors entering the all-devouring Viśva-rūpa's mouth.
	31: Arjuna asks – (i) Who are You? (ii) What is Your mission?
32-34: Kṛṣṇa's reply – "Time I am, become My instrument"	I am time, the ultimate destroyer. I have already killed Droṇa, Bhīṣma, Jayadratha, Karṇa and the other warriors. You just become My instrument.
35-46: Arjuna's prayers	36-38: Glorification – of the pleasing and ferocious forms that are objects of attraction and repulsion.
	39-40: Obeisances – from all sides.
	41-44: Apologies – for offenses committed in friendly relationship.
	45-46: Requests – to show the pleasant, four-armed form.

47-55: Pure bhakti is the prerequisite to see any form of Kṛṣṇa

- 47-49: Rarity of seeing Kṛṣṇa's universal form – no one has seen it before Arjuna.
- 50-51: Kṛṣṇa reveals His four-handed form and then His two-handed form.
- 52-55: Conclusion – Kṛṣṇa is known and seen only by ananya-bhakti, so perform bhakti to attain Kṛṣṇa.

In the previous chapter, Kṛṣṇa said that He pervades and supports the entire universe with a single fragment of His power (10.42).

In this chapter, Arjuna expresses his desire to see that all-pervasive form of Lord Kṛṣṇa, and in response Kṛṣṇa shows His universal form (*viśva-rūpa*).

1-4: Arjuna Requests Kṛṣṇa to Show His Universal Form

1. My illusion has been dispelled by Your great mercy in explaining to me these most confidential spiritual subjects (about *vibhūtis*).

2. I have heard from You, O lotus-eyed Lord (*kamala-patrākṣa*), about the creation and dissolution of all beings arising from You. I have also realized Your inexhaustible glories (*māhātmyam api cāvyayam*) in being unaffected by this (aloof).

In the previous chapters, Arjuna heard various glories of Kṛṣṇa that Kṛṣṇa is the supreme creator, maintainer, controller and all pervading (7.6, 9.4, 10.42 etc.).

3. I desire to see Your universal form: O Supreme Lord (*parameśvara*), greatest of all (*puruṣottama*), You are present before Me as have described Yourself (I have no doubt about Your Supreme position). Yet, I wish to see Your powerful form (*rūpam aiśvaraṁ*) by which You enter and support this universe.

The universal form of Kṛṣṇa (*viśva-rūpa*) is a temporary form in the material realm. It is not eternally situated in the spiritual sky like Kṛṣṇa's other forms. As the material nature is manifested and unmanifested, similarly this universal form is manifested and unmanifested. Devotees of Kṛṣṇa are not very eager to see this form.

Request for others' sake: Arjuna is pesonally convinced that Kṛṣṇa is the Supreme Absolute Truth, the source of everything, and he even acknowledged it (in 10.11). And he is completely satisfied by reciprocations with the personal sweet form of Kṛṣṇa, and has no special desire to see His powerful universal form. Still he asked Kṛṣṇa to show the universal form, because he wanted –

- To substantiate Kṛṣṇa's statements and convince people about His divinity, so that the people could understand that Kṛṣṇa not only theoretically or philosophically presented Himself as the Supreme but actually presented Himself as such.

- To set a criterion for accepting someone as the Supreme Lord. Because in the future, imposters would pose themselves as God's incarnations. One who claims to be God should be prepared to show his universal form.

4. If You think that I can behold Your cosmic form, O master of all mystic power (*yogeśvara*), then kindly show me that unlimited universal Self.

Graceful revelation: Arjuna humbly *requested* Kṛṣṇa to show the universal form, he didn't *demand*. One can understand the unlimited Lord when He reveals Himself gracefully, not by one's own mental speculations.

5-8: Lord Kṛṣṇa Describes His Universal Form

5. Now see My opulences, O Arjuna – My hundreds of thousands of wonderful divine forms of varied types, colors and shapes.

6. Behold the many wonderful things, which no one has ever seen or heard of before. See the Ādityas, Vasus, Rudras, Aśvinī-kumāras and all the other devatās.

7. See within My body, whatever you wish to see – this whole universe with its moving and nonmoving entities is here completely, in one place, at one time.

8. I will give you divine eyes (*divyaṁ cakṣuḥ*), because you cannot see Me with your present eyes. Behold My mystic opulence (*paśya me yogam aiśvaram*)!

Special vision: Arjuna, being an *ananya-bhakta*, had the superior vision of affection with which he is accoustomed to see the sweetness of Kṛṣṇa's human form and pastimes. Now Kṛṣṇa is giving Arjuna a celestial vision to see His majestic form with thousands of heads, eyes and so on, in order to cause astonishment in Arjuna.

9-14: Sañjaya Describes Arjuna's Vision of the Universal Form

Everything visible at one place: These manifestations of the universal form were distributed throughout the universe, but by the grace and inconceivable potency of Lord Kṛṣṇa, Arjuna could see them all while sitting in one place. What Arjuna saw was indescribable, yet Sañjaya tried to give a mental picture of that great revelation to Dhṛtarāṣṭra, in this section.

9. Kṛṣṇa displays the universal form: Having spoken thus, Kṛṣṇa, the Supreme Lord of all mystic power (*mahā-yogeśvaro hariḥ*), displayed His supremely powerful majestic universal form (*rūpam aiśvaram*) to Arjuna.

10-11. Arjuna saw in that form unlimited faces, eyes, wonderful visions, holding many weapons, wearing celestial garlands, garments, ornaments and divine scents. The form was wondrous, brilliant, infinite, all-expanding with faces in all directions (*viśvato mukham*).

12. The effulgence of the universal form is greater than the effulgence of thousands of suns rising at once in the sky.

13. Everything in the universe is seen at that one place (as various parts of the body of the universal form) in various ways divided into many details.

Both Arjuna and Kṛṣṇa were on the chariot when Arjuna saw the universal form. Others on the battlefield could not see it, because Kṛṣṇa gave the vision only to Arjuna.

14. Arjuna bowed down, bewildered and astonished (*vismaya* or *adbhuta rasa*), his hair standing on end. With folded hands, he began to pray to the Supreme Lord:

15-31: Arjuna's Experience of Seeing the Universal Form

15-19: Arjuna's realizations upon seeing the Viśva-rūpa

15. Dear Lord, I see in Your body all the devatās, all living entities, Brahmā sitting on lotus, Śiva, all the sages and divine serpents.

16. O form of the universe (*viśva-rūpa*[1]), O Lord of the universe and the origin of the universal form (*viśveśvara*), I see in Your unlimited form (*ananta-rūpam*), many arms, bellies, mouths and eyes expanded everywhere without limit. I see no end, no middle and no beginning of this form.

aneka-bāhūdara-vaktra-netraṁ
paśyāmi tvāṁ sarvato 'nanta-rūpam
nāntaṁ na madhyaṁ na punas tavādiṁ
paśyāmi viśveśvara viśva-rūpa

17. It is difficult to see (*durnirīkṣyaṁ*) this glowing form (*tejo-rāśim*) adorned with crowns, clubs and discs, because of its glaring effulgence (*dīpti-mantam*), spreading on all sides, with immeasurable radiance (*aprameyam*) like blazing fire or the sun.

18. I am convinced of Your supremacy	
tvam akṣaraṁ paramaṁ veditavyaṁ	You are infallible, the supreme primal objective, knowable by liberation-seekers.
tvam asya viśvasya paraṁ nidhānam	You are the ultimate basis, resting place and shelter of this universe (after destruction).
tvam avyayaḥ śāśvata-dharma-goptā	You are inexhaustible, You are the maintainer of the eternal religion,

[1] This indicates the first Puruṣa incarnation – Mahā Viṣṇu.

sanātanas tvaṁ puruṣo mato me	You are the eternal ancient Personality of Godhead. This is my opinion.

19-25: Arjuna's description of the Kāla-rūpa, the form of time

19a. You have no origin, middle or end (*anādi-madhyāntam*[1]). Your strength is unlimited (*ananta-vīryam*). You have numberless arms (*ananta-bāhuṁ*). The sun and moon are Your eyes (*śaśi-sūrya-netram*).

19b. I see blazing fire emanating from Your mouth, burning this universe.

20. You are spread throughout the sky and the planets and all space between. Seeing this astonishing and ferocious form, all the three worlds are perturbed.

Along with Arjuna, the Lord also gave celestial eyes to the residents of other planetary systems to see the universal form, so that they could witness His powers.

21. Prayers of devatās and sages: Hosts of devatās are surrendering before You, entering into You. Some are praising You out of fear. Hosts of sages and perfected beings, crying "*Svasti* – All peace!" are praying to You by singing the Vedic hymns.

22. All are looking at You in astonishment, including the Rudras, Ādityas, Vasus, Sadhyas, Viśvas, Aśvins, Maruts, Pitṛs, Gandharvas, Yakṣas, Asuras, and Siddhas.

23. All planets and devatās are agitated seeing Your great form, with many faces, eyes, arms, thighs, legs, bellies and terrible teeth; so am I, O mighty-armed one.

Arjuna expresses his pitiful state in the next two verses, so that the Lord will withdraw this ferocious form.

24. I am also fearful and unable to maintain my steadiness and mental equilibrium, seeing You touching the sky, with many radiant colors, gaping mouths and glowing eyes, O all-pervading Viṣṇu.

25. Please be merciful to me (*prasīda*), O Lord of lords (*deveśa*), refuge of the worlds (*jagan-nivāsa*). I cannot keep my balance seeing Your blazing deathlike faces and awful teeth. I cannot recognize the directions.

In 11.7, Kṛṣṇa told Arjuna that he can see whatever he wish to see. That indicates – "See in My body the future victory and defeat in this war." In the next five verses, Kṛṣṇa will show Arjuna the future outcomes of the Kurukṣetra war.

---

[1] Arjuna repeatedly glorifies Kṛṣṇa as beginningless. Out of great joy or astonishment (*mahā-vismaya-rasa*) devotees glorify the Lord repeatedly and it is not a literary flaw.

26-30: Arjuna sees the future outcomes of the war

26-29. Warriors entering Viśva-rūpa's mouth: All the sons of Dhṛtarāṣṭra, their allied kings, Bhīṣma, Droṇa, Karṇa and also our chief warriors—are rushing into Your fearful blazing mouths just like – (*i*) rivers enter the ocean, and (*ii*) moths enter the fire to meet their destruction. Some of them are being trapped with heads smashed between Your teeth.

This is an indication that after the death of nearly all the persons assembled at Kurukṣetra, Arjuna will emerge victorious.

30a. I see You devouring all these people from all sides with Your flaming mouths.

30b. Your effulgence is spread all over the universe by Your terrible, scorching rays, burning it up, O Viṣṇu. (You are spread throughout the universe! It is impossible to flee from You.)

31. Arjuna's two questions: I offer my respects, to You O Lord of lords; please be gracious to me (*prasīda*). You are the primal Lord.

i. Who are You, in this ferocious form (*ugra-rūpa*)?
ii. What is Your mission?

32-34: Kṛṣṇa's Reply – "Time I am, Become My Instrument"

32. I am time, the ultimate destroyer	
kālo 'smi loka-kṣaya-kṛt pravṛddho	Time I am, the great destroyer of the worlds,
lokān samāhartum iha pravṛttaḥ	and I have come here to destroy all people.
ṛte 'pi tvāṁ na bhaviṣyanti sarve	With the exception of you [the Pāṇḍavas], all
ye 'vasthitāḥ pratyanīkeṣu yodhāḥ	the soldiers here on both sides will be slain.

Kṛṣṇa's plan: Arjuna wanted to give up fighting and was indecisive (2.6). But even if Arjuna did not fight, the death of every one in the battlefield couldn't be checked, for that was Kṛṣṇa's plan. Time is destruction, and all manifestations are to be vanquished by the desire of the Supreme Lord. That is the law of nature.

33. Just be an instrument in Kṛṣṇa's plan	
tasmāt tvam uttiṣṭha yaśo labhasva	Therefore get up, fight (dutifully) and win glory.
jitvā śatrūn *bhuṅkṣva rājyaṁ samṛddham*	Conquer your enemies and enjoy a flourishing kingdom.
mayaivaite nihatāḥ pūrvam eva	They all have been killed by My plan already.
nimitta-mātraṁ bhava savya-sācin	O Savyasācī, just become an instrument.

Rare glory: Warriors such as Bhīṣma who cannot be conquered by the devatās, have been defeated by Arjuna with ease! Such will be Arjuna's fame in future. However, they have already been killed by Kṛṣṇa, at the time of their offending Draupadī. They are proceeding like puppets to give Arjuna fame.

Savyasāci means one who is skilful in shooting arrows on the battle (with both hands).

34. I have already killed Droṇa, Bhīṣma, Jayadratha, Karṇa and the other warriors. Therefore, simply fight and kill them and do not be disturbed or fearful (that they have celestial weapons). You will vanquish your enemies easily.

Kṛṣṇa gives credit to devotees: Every plan is made by the Lord, but He is so kind and merciful that He wants to give credit to the devotees who carry out His plan according to His desire.

35-46: Arjuna's Prayers

35. Hearing these words (outcome of the battle) from the Lord, Arjuna, with folded hands, trembling, offered obeisances again and again and fearfully spoke in a faltering voice in the mood of wonder, as follows:

36-38: Glorification

36. Kṛṣṇa's pleasing and ferocious forms are objects of attraction and repulsion: O master of the senses (*hṛṣīkeśa*), the universe rejoices (*prahṛṣyati*) by hearing Your glorification (*prakīrtya*) and becomes attracted to You (*anurajyate*). The perfected devotees offer You homage, but the frightened demons flee in all directions.

Kṛṣṇa is called Hṛṣīkeśa here, because He inspires the senses (*hṛṣīka*) either toward Him (for the devotees) or against Him (for the atheists).

37. Kṛṣṇa is worshipable by all: O great one (*mahātma*), original creator (*ādi-kartre*), greater than even Brahmā. Why should they not offer respects to You? O limitless one (*ananta*), God of gods (*deveśa*), shelter of the universe (*jagannivāsa*)! You are imperishable (*akṣaram*), transcendental to material cause and effect (*sad-asat param*).

38. Kṛṣṇa is the ultimate shelter of everything	
tvam ādi-devaḥ puruṣaḥ purāṇas	You are the original God, primeval person,
tvam asya viśvasya paraṁ nidhānam	ultimate refuge of world (after destruction)
vettāsi vedyaṁ ca paraṁ ca dhāma	knower of all, supreme knowable and shelter,
tvayā tataṁ viśvam ananta-rūpa	all-pervading and unlimited form!

39-40: Obeisances

39. My repeated respects unto You thousands of times! You are the devatās – Vāyu (air), Yama (controller), Agni (fire), Varuṇa (water), Śaṣāṅka (moon), Prajāpati (Brahmā), *prapitāmaha* (great-grandfather).

40. Obeisances unto You from all sides! O unbounded power (*ananta-vīrya*), the master of limitless might (*amita-vikramaḥ*), all-pervading, You are everything!

41-44: Apologies

41-42. Please forgive all my offenses, whatever I did in madness (*pramadā*) or love (*praṇaya*), considering You my friend. Not knowing Your glories, I rashly addressed You, "O Kṛṣṇa, Yādava, O friend (*he kṛṣṇa he yādava he sakheti*)." I dishonored You many times, jesting, laying, sat or ate together, alone and in front of others. O infallible one.

43. Kṛṣṇa's incomparable powers	
pitāsi lokasya carācarasya	You are the father of this world, of all the moving and the nonmoving beings.
tvam asya pūjyaś ca gurur garīyān	You are the most worshipable of all worshipable people, and the supreme spiritual master.
na tvat-samo 'sty abhyadhikaḥ kuto 'nyo	No one is equal to You. Where can there be anyone greater than You within the
loka-traye 'py apratima-prabhāva	three worlds, O Lord of immeasurable power.

44. Please tolerate me just as a father tolerates his son, or a friend tolerates his friend or a husband tolerates wife's familiarity. O most worshipable Lord, I prostrate my body to offer You respects and ask Your mercy.

45-46: Requests

45. I am both gladdened and frightened seeing Your universal form, which was never seen before. Please be merficul and reveal Your pleasing form again, O Lord of lords, O abode of the universe (*prasīda deveśa jagan-nivāsa*).

46. I wish to see Your four-armed form with helmeted head, holding club, disc, conch and lotus. O thousand-armed universal form, please appear in that form.

11.45-46 prove that Kṛṣṇa is the Supreme Lord and the source of all forms including the four-handed form of Lord Viṣṇu. Kṛṣṇa's humanlike form is more pleasing than the majestic universal form which is distasteful to the mind and eye.

In response to Arjuna's requests, Kṛṣṇa will now comfort him by withdrawing His ghastly univeral form and revealing His pleasant four-armed and two-armed forms. He will also describe *bhakti* as the supreme process to see any form of Kṛṣṇa.

47-55: Pure Bhakti Is the Prerequisite to See Any Form of Kṛṣṇa

47-49: Rarity of seeing Kṛṣṇa's universal form

47. Dear Arjuna, I have shown this supreme, effulgent, unlimited universal form, by My internal potency, being pleased with you. No one has ever seen this before you.

Never seen before: Because Kṛṣṇa is merciful to Arjuna, the residents of the higher planets also saw the universal form now. When Kṛṣṇa attempted to persuade Duryodhana from war, Duryodhana tried to capture Kṛṣṇa. At that time also, Kṛṣṇa showed His universal form, but that was different from what Arjuna saw now.

48. No one has seen this form, because neither by Vedic study (*veda-adhyayanaiḥ*), nor by sacrifices (*yajña-adhyayanaiḥ*), charity (*danaiḥ*), pious acts (*kriyābhiḥ*), penances (*tapobhiḥ*) can I be seen in this form (I am seen only by *bhakti*).

Only by divine vision which is a result of pure devotion (*bhakti*) can one actually see Kṛṣṇa's universal form. The pure devotees, however, are not interested to see the universal form, for it does not enable one to reciprocate loving feelings. Therefore, Arjuna desired to see the four-handed form of Kṛṣṇa as Viṣṇu.

49. Let this vision be over: You were afraid and bewildered by seeing this horrible feature (*ghoram*) of Mine. Now be free from fear. With a peaceful mind, again see the form you desire.

50-51. Kṛṣṇa then revealed His four-armed form and His original two-armed form1, thus encouraging the fearful Arjuna. **Arjuna said:** "O Janārdana, seeing this pleasant humanlike form (*mānuṣaṁ rūpaṁ*), so very beautiful, I regained composure, and restored to my original nature."

52-55: Conclusion – Glory of Kṛṣṇa's personal form and bhakti

52-53. Rarity of seeing Kṛṣṇa's humanlike form: This human form of Mine which you are seeing is still very difficult to see (*su-durdarśam*). Even the devatās are

---

[1] Kṛṣṇa knew that Arjuna was more interested in His two-handed form and thus He show it. When Kṛṣṇa appeared as the son of Vāsudeva and Devakī, He first appeared as four-armed Nārāyaṇa, but His parents requested Him to transform like an ordinary child. Then Kṛṣṇa showed His two-handed form.

longing to see this form (*darśana-kāṅkṣiṇaḥ*). This form cannot be understood simply by Vedic study, penances, charity etc. (This can be understood only by *bhakti*).

In 11.48, Kṛṣṇa told Arjuna that the universal form with thousands of heads etc., is difficult to be seen by pious acts, sacrifices, etc. Now Kṛṣṇa says that His two-handed form as Śyāmasundara is still more confidential and rare to see. His two-handed and four-handed forms are eternal. Even when He descends in that form, He is not visible to foolish persons who deride Him (7.25, 9.11).

54. Kṛṣṇa is known and seen only by ananya-bhakti	
bhaktyā tv ananyayā śakya	Only by undivided devotional service
aham evaṁ-vidho 'rjuna	can I be understood as I am, O Arjuna.
jñātuṁ draṣṭuṁ ca tattvena	Only in this way, it is possible to know Me, see Me and
praveṣṭuṁ ca parantapa	enter into mysteries of My understanding, O Arjuna.

For one who does not take guidance from a bona fide spiritual master, it is impossible to even begin to understand Kṛṣṇa.

55. Essence of Bhagavad-gīta: Perform bhakti and attain Kṛṣṇa	
mat-karma-kṛn mat-paramo	He who works for Me, considering Me the Supreme,
mad-bhaktaḥ saṅga-varjitaḥ	who is devoted to Me, without material attachments,
nirvairaḥ sarva-bhūteṣu	without enemity towards any living being,
yaḥ sa mām eti pāṇḍava	will surely attain Me, O Arjuna.

Kṛṣṇa is the source of all forms: Kṛṣṇa's universal form (*viśva-rūpa*), which is a temporary manifestation in this world, and the form of time (*kāla-rūpa*) which devours everything, and even the four-handed form of Viṣṇu, have all been exhibited by Kṛṣṇa. Thus Kṛṣṇa is the origin of all these manifestations. There are hundreds and thousands of Viṣṇus, but for a devotee no form of Kṛṣṇa is important but the original form, two-handed Śyāmasundara. This is confirmed in *Brahma-saṁhitā*.

12. Devotional Service

1: Arjuna's Inquiry – 'Who is better - Personalist or Impersonalist?'	A personalist devotee worships Kṛṣṇa and an impersonalist meditator worships impersonal Brahman. Who is better?
2-7: Personalists Vs. Impersonalists – Supremacy of Kṛṣṇa-bhakti	2. Pure devotees of Kṛṣṇa are most perfect in yoga
	3-5: The path of impersonal Brahman worshipers is troublesome
	6-7: Bhakti is the simple and easy path of personalists (ananya-bhaktas)
8-12: Progressive stages of Bhakti (See the table)	8-9: Bhakti with internal senses (samraṇa-ātmika, manana-ātmikā and abhyāsa-rūpa bhaktis) – fixing mind and intelligence on Kṛṣṇa, and if it is diffucult, endeavour to do so.
	10: Bhakti with external senses – If endeavouring is also difficult, work for Kṛṣṇa.
	11: If working for Kṛṣṇa is difficult, give up the results of work.
	12: Abhyāsa (practice) < Jñāna (knowledge) < Dhyāna (meditation) < Tyāga (renouncing fruits of work)
13-20: Qualities that endear one to Lord Kṛṣṇa	Various qualities of a devotee – of which devotion to Kṛṣṇa is primary and the rest are secondary (See the table)

In the previous chapter, Kṛṣṇa concluded (in 11.55) with the supremacy of *bhakti-yoga* or devotional service unto His personal form as Śyāmasundara. Attachment to Kṛṣṇa's personal form is the highest spiritual realization. It has been emphasized in the earlier chapters as well (6.47, 7.1, 8.5 etc) and Arjuna personally experienced this in the previous chapter. Nevertheless, there are people who prefer to meditate on the impersonal Brahman.

In this chapter, Arjuna inquires about these two classes of people. He thus clarifies his own position of being attached to the personal form of Kṛṣṇa. In response, Kṛṣṇa establishes that pure *bhakti-yoga* is the highest process for realization of the Absolute Truth and the easiest means for attaining His association. Kṛṣṇa also describes how *bhakti* can be practiced at multiple levels and the qualities of a *bhakta* that make one dear to Kṛṣṇa.

1: Arjuna's Inquiry – 'Who Is Better- Personalist or Impersonalist?'

1. Who is the perfect knower of *yoga* or the process of quickly attaining You (*yoga-vittamaḥ*) amongst the following two?

i. A *personalist* devotee who always worships You (*bhaktās tvām paryupāsate*) (as in 11.55)

ii. An *impersonalist* meditator who worships the transcendental (*akṣaram*), unmanifest (*akṣaram*) impersonal Brahman (as in 9.15)

This important question will clarify the distinction between the impersonal and personal conceptions of the Absolute Truth.

2-7: Personalists Vs. Impersonalists – Supremacy of Kṛṣṇa-bhakti

2. Pure devotees of Kṛṣṇa are most perfect in yoga	
mayy āveśya mano ye māṁ	Those who fix their minds on My personal form and
nitya-yuktā upāsate	are always worshiping Me desiring to associate with Me
śraddhayā parayopetās	endowed with great and transcendental faith
te me yuktatamā matāḥ	are considered by Me to be most perfect (Such *ananya-bhaktas* quickly attain Me).

3-4. Process and destination of impersonal Brahman worshipers	
ye tv akṣaram anirdeśyam avyaktaṁ paryupāsate	But those who fully worship the – (*i*) unmanifested, (*ii*) which is beyond sense perception, (*iii*) indefinite,
sarvatra-gam acintyaṁ ca	(*iv*) all-pervading, (*v*) inconceivable,
kūṭa-stham acalaṁ dhruvam	(*vi*) unchanging, (*vii*) fixed and (*viii*) immovable,
sanniyamyendriya-grāmaṁ	by the process of – (*a*) controlling various senses,

sarvatra sama-buddhayaḥ	(*b*) being equally disposed to everyone,
te prāpnuvanti mām eva	such persons, at last achieve Me (impersonal Brahman)
sarva-bhūta-hite ratāḥ	(*c*) being engaged in the welfare of all.

If the impersonalists also attain Kṛṣṇa, what is the foundation for Kṛṣṇa's saying (in 12.2) that the personalist devotees are superior attainers of Him?

5. Troublesome path of the impersonalists	
kleśo 'dhikataras teṣām	Advancement is very troublesome for those
avyaktāsakta-cetasām	whose minds are attached to the unmanifested, impersonal feature of the Supreme.
avyaktā hi gatir duḥkhaṁ	To make progress towards the unmanifest is difficult
dehavadbhir avāpyate	for those who are embodied.

Bhakti-yoga Vs. jñāna-yoga:

- Those who worship the the impersonal feature of the Supreme Lord are called *jñāna-yogīs*, and those who perform devotional service in full Kṛṣṇa consciousness are called *bhakti-yogīs.*
- Like the Supreme Lord, the living entity is also originally *sat-cit-ānanda:* eternal, knowledgeable and blissful. By *jñāna-yoga*, an embodied soul may realize the eternal and knowledgeable aspects of his original nature, but the blissful portion is realized only by *bhakti-yoga,* which is easier and is natural for the soul.
- By the grace of some devotee, a transcendentalist, highly learned in the process of *jñāna-yoga*, may come to the point of *bhakti-yoga.*
- Even that goal of impersonal Brahman which is attained by *jñāna-yogīs* by such suffering is only by having a mixture with *bhakti.* Without *bhakti* to the Lord, the worshippers of the impersonal Brahman obtain only suffering, and not Brahman.
- Though the *bhakti-yogīs* also endure difficulty in controlling senses and engaging in the various *aṅgas* of *bhakti*, because of the appearance of Kṛṣṇa's blissful form, they do not experience the same suffering as impersonalists.

6-7. Bhakti – the simple and easy path of personalists (ananya-bhaktas)	
ye tu sarvāṇi karmāṇi mayi sannyasya mat-parāḥ	But for those who give up all their activities unto Me, being devoted to Me
ananyenaiva yogena	without deviation, engaged in devotional service
māṁ dhyāyanta upāsate	and always meditating upon Me and worshiping Me,
teṣām ahaṁ samuddhartā	for them, I am the swift deliverer
mṛtyu-saṁsāra-sāgarāt	from the ocean of birth and death.

bhavāmi na cirāt pārtha	I deliver them quickly, O son of Pṛthā,
mayy āveśita-cetasām	because they fixed their minds upon Me.

Thus Kṛṣṇa explained the difference between worshiping His personal and impersonal features. While there is no reciprocation from the impersonal feature, there is full protection and swift deliverance from the personality Kṛṣṇa.

Having established the supremacy of *bhakti,* Kṛṣṇa will now explain in the next five verses, multiple levels of *bhakti* beginning with the highest stage (descending ladder).

8-12: Progressive Levels of Bhakti

8-9: Bhakti with internal senses

8a. Fix your mind on Me exclusively (*mayy eva mana ādhatsva*) by remembering Me always. This is *smaraṇa-ātmika bhakti.*

8b. Fix your intelligence in Me (*mayi buddhiṁ niveśaya*) by contemplating on Me (based on scriptural descriptions). This is *manana-ātmika bhakti.*

Result: Thus you will live in Me always, without a doubt.

9. Try to fix your mind on Kṛṣṇa: If you cannot fix your mind upon Me without deviation, then endeavor to fix the mind on Me (*abhyāsa-yoga*) by following the regulative principles of *bhakti* (*sādhana-bhakti*), i.e, withdraw the mind repeatedly from sense objects and fix it on Me. This is *abhyāsa-rūpa bhakti.*

Result: In this way one can develop a desire to attain Me.

Abhyāsa-yoga: Under the guidance of a *guru*, one can follow the prescribed practices of *bhakti-yoga* like chant the holy names of Kṛṣṇa, offering flowers and foodstuffs to the Deity, taking *prasādam*, hearing scriptures from devotees and so on.

The above three types of *bhakti* (*smaraṇa-ātmika, manana-ātmika* and *abhyāsa-rūpa*) are performed internally with mind and intelligence. Intelligent and inoffensive people can perform them easily, while less intelligent people find them difficult. As the mind is fickle like the wind, one may not be able to restrain it. For those who cannot even gradually fix the mind by practice, Kṛṣṇa suggests the following option:

10: Bhakti with external senses

10. Work for Kṛṣṇa: If you cannot practice *sādhana-bhakti*, then just try to perform your activities for My pleasure (*mat-karma-paramo bhava*), though your mind is not on Me. *Result:* Thus you will attain perfection.

Working for Kṛṣṇa includes offering charity to build Kṛṣṇa's temples or publish books. By doing such work even without remembering Kṛṣṇa, one can still attain perfection. Voluntary work done for satisfaction of Kṛṣṇa is spiritual activity.

Those who can do *bhakti* by both internal and external senses are most outstanding. But one may not be able to even work for Kṛṣṇa because of social, familial and religious considerations or other impediments. Kṛṣṇa will now advice such people to sacrifice the results of their activities, if not fully, at least some percentage of the results.

11. Giving up results of work: If you cannot offer all your actions to Me, then try to act giving up all results of your work *(sarva-karma-phala-tyāgam)* and try to be self-situated.

12. Abhyāsa < Jñāna < Dhyāna < Tyāga	
śreyo hi jñānam abhyāsāj	Knowledge (*jñāna*) is better than practice (*abhyāsa*)
jñānād dhyānaṁ viśiṣyate	Meditation (*dhyāna*) is better than knowledge.
dhyānāt karma-phala-tyāgas	Renunciation (*tyāga*) of fruits of work is better than meditation.
tyāgāc chāntir anantaram	*Result of renunciation:* one can attain peace of mind.

This verse has been explained by different *ācāryas* in different ways, and all of them establish the superiority of *bhakti-yoga* over the other processes. They described the four key words highlighted above differently. The following table depicts those explanations along with the stages mentioned in the previous verses of this section.

Kṛṣṇa's statement (Levels of bhakti: highest to lowest)	Śrīla Prabhupāda's explanation	Śrīla Viśvanātha Cakravarti's explanation	Śrīla Baladeva Vidyābhūṣaṇa's explanation
8a. Mayy eva mana ādhatsva	*Bhakti* on the pure stage of love: Offering one's mind and intelligence to Kṛṣṇa entirely and thereby live in Him.	*Smaraṇa-ātmika bhakti* – Remembeing the form of Śyāmasundara in mind	Offering full consciousness to Kṛṣṇa with complete ease and steadiness
8b. Mayi buddhiṁ niveśaya		*Manana-ātmika bhakti* – contemplation on Kṛṣṇa with intelligence	
9. Abhyāsa-yoga	*Sādhana-bhakti* or practice regulative principles of *bhakti-yoga* to develop a desire to attain Kṛṣṇa.	*Abhyāsa-rūpa bhakti* – Endeavoring to attain Kṛṣṇa by withdrawing the wandering mind repeatedly and fixing it on Kṛṣṇa	Withdrawing the wandering mind by repeated practice and gradually fixing it on Kṛṣṇa

10. Mat-karma-paramo bhava	Working for Kṛṣṇa by contributing to His service	Directly serving Kṛṣṇa with external senses even if mind is not on Him	Offering one's activities to Kṛṣṇa.
11. Sarva-karma-phala-tyāgaṁ	Giving up results of work for some good cause	Doing *niṣkāma-karma* offered to Kṛṣṇa (as described in the first six chapters)	Perform all activities devoid of desire for results with controlled mind
12a. Śreyo hi jñānam abhyāsāt	For those who cannot follow the principles of Kṛṣṇa consciousness, it is better to cultivate knowledge (*jñāna*)	*Jñānam* or *manana-ātmika bhakti* (in 12.8b) is better than *abhyāsa-yoga* (in 12.9)	If *abhyāsa* or practicing remembrance of Kṛṣṇa is difficult, then one may cultivate *jñāna* or realization of *ātmā*
12b. Jñānād dhyānaṁ viśiṣyate	*Dhyāna* is better than *jñāna*, because knowledge gradually develops into meditation	*Dhyāna* or *smaraṇa-ātmika bhakti* (in 12.8a) is better than *jñāna* or *manana-ātmika bhakti* (in 12.8b)	*Dhyāna* or practice of meditation on *ātmā* is preferable if *jñāna* or realization of *ātmā* is difficult to accomplish.
12c. Dhyānāt karma-phala-tyāgas	If one cannot do meditation, then one can renounce the results of his prescribed work for some good cause	By *dhyāna* one develops distaste for the fruits of action	Better than unsuccessful practice of meditation is renunciation of results of work
12d. Tyāgāc chāntir anantaram	By renunciation one attains peace	By such distate one attains peace in the form of stopping the senses from dwelling on all objects except Kṛṣṇa's form and qualities.	From giving up results of work, one attains purification of mind (with pure mind one can do meditation).

13-20: Qualities That Endear One to Lord Kṛṣṇa

Bhakti-yoga is the most effective path of spiritual advancement. A *bhakti-yogī* exhibits transcendental qualities which make him dear (*priya*) to Kṛṣṇa. Kṛṣṇa is pleased with such a devotee as He describes in this section by using the word "*priya*" in most verses.

13-20. Qualities that endear one to Kṛṣṇa	
adveṣṭā sarva-bhūtānāṁ	(1) Not envious towards anyone including the envious
maitraḥ *karuṇa eva ca*	(2) Friendly to all (3) Kind / Merciful to all
nirmamo *nirahaṅkāraḥ*	(4) Free from sense of proprietorship (5) Free from false ego or identification with body
sama-duḥkha-sukhaḥ *kṣamī*	(6) Equal in happiness and distress (7) Forgiving and tolerant
santuṣṭaḥ satataṁ yogī	(8) Satisfied always in devotional service
yatātmā *dṛḍha-niścayaḥ*	(9) Self-controlled (10) Determined
mayy arpita-mano-buddhir	(11) Mind and intelligence fixed on Me
yo mad-bhaktaḥ sa me priyaḥ	—such a devotee of Mine is very dear to Me.
yasmān nodvijate loko	(12) No one is agitated by him
lokān nodvijate ca yaḥ	(13) He is not agitated by anyone
harṣāmarṣa-bhayodvegair *mukto yaḥ sa ca me priyaḥ*	(14) Equipoised in joy and distress, fear and anxiety, —such a devotee is very dear to Me.
anapekṣaḥ *śucir* *dakṣa*	(15) Neutral: devoid of all expectations from his work (16) Pure/ clean (17) Expert / skillful in all situations
udāsīno *gata-vyathaḥ*	(18) Without cares/ unattached to material persons (19) Free from all pains (as free from all designations)
sarvārambha-parityāgī	(20) Free from all material endeavors
yo mad-bhaktaḥ sa me priyaḥ	—such a devotee is very dear to Me
yo na hṛṣyati na dveṣṭi	(21) Neither rejoices nor grieves
na śocati na kāṅkṣati	(22) Neither laments nor desires
śubhāśubha-parityāgī	(23) Renounces all auspicious and inauspicious things
bhaktimān yaḥ sa me priyaḥ	—such a devotee is very dear to Me.

samaḥ śatrau ca mitre ca	(24) Equal to friends and enemies,
tathā mānāpamānayoḥ *śītoṣṇa-sukha-duḥkheṣu*	(25) Equipoised in all dualities: honor and dishonor, heat and cold, happiness and distress,
samaḥ saṅga-vivarjitaḥ	(26) Always free from contaminating association.
tulya-nindā-stutir *maunī*	(27) Equal in criticism and praise (28) Silent, i.e., speaks only essential topics
santuṣṭo yena kenacit	(29) Satisfied with whatever comes of its own accord
aniketaḥ *sthira-matir*	(30) Doesn't care for any residence, (31) Steady in mind/ fixed in knowledge
bhaktimān me priyo naraḥ	—such a devotee is very dear to Me.
ye tu dharmāmṛtam idaṁ *yathoktaṁ paryupāsate*	Those who follow this imperishable path of devotional service and completely engage
śraddadhānā mat-paramā	with **faith**, making Me the supreme goal,
bhaktās te 'tīva me priyāḥ	—such devotees are very, very dear to Me.

Lord Kṛṣṇa used the words "*mad-bhakta*" and "*bhaktimān*" in the above verses to indicate a person who has a devotion unto Him. Such *devotion* is the most esential quality (*svarūpa-lakṣaṇa*) in a devotee, while the remaining qualities in the above list are his secondary qualities (*taṭastha-lakṣaṇa*), that depend on his *bhakti*. They automatically result from the devotee's surrender to Kṛṣṇa and fixing his mind and intelligence on Kṛṣṇa.

Part III

Jñāna-yoga

Chapters 13-18

13. Nature, The Enjoyer and Consciousness

1: Arjuna's Six Questions	About - prakṛti (Q1), puruṣa (Q2), kṣetra (Q3), kṣetra-jña (Q4), jñānaṁ (Q5) and jñeyaṁ (Q6)
2-7: Kṛṣṇa Describes Kṣetra, Kṣetrajña and Jñānaṁ (A3, A4 & A5)	2-3: Kṣetra is body; Kṣetra-jña is both soul and Kṛṣṇa; jñānaṁ is perfect knowledge
	4-5: Kṛṣṇa promises to explain six topics about kṣetra and kṣetrajña and quotes authorities
	6-7: The composition, qualities, changes and origin of the body (kṣetra)
8-12: Jñānaṁ – Process of Acquiring Knowledge (A5)	Twenty elements of knowledge: Humility, pridelessness, nonviolence, tolerance and so on.
13-19: Jñeyaṁ – Object of Knowledge (A6)	Soul and Supersoul are the objects of knowledge; The qualities of the Supersoul
20-26: Prakṛti, Puruṣa and Their Union (A1, A2)	20-22: Prakṛti (nature) and puruṣa (jīva) are eternal; Prakṛti causes all material causes and effects. Jīva associates with modes, changes bodies and causes his own happiness and distress.
	23: Supersoul is the real puruṣa
	24: Knowing prakṛti, puruṣa and guṇas, one attains liberation.
	25-26: Different methods of liberation
27-35: Jñāna-cakṣu – The Vision of Knowledge	27: Every entity is a combination of prakṛti and puruṣa
	28-31: A true seer's vision of jīva, prakṛti and Paramātma
	32-35: The non-doership of the soul

In the middle six chapters, Kṛṣṇa described *bhakti-yoga* along with the precise natures of the *jīva*, the Lord and matter and how they are related. The first six chapters showed how *karma* leads to *bhakti* and the last six chapters will show how *jñāna* leads to *bhakti.*

In the final six chapters, Kṛṣṇa describes *jñāna* mixed with *bhakti* while indirectly showing *kevalā bhakti* to be the supreme. In the thirteenth chapter, Kṛṣṇa speaks detailed knowledge of the body, the *jīva,* the *Paramātmā* and *prakṛti.*

1: Arjuna's Six Questions

1. Arjuna's six questions: My dear Kṛṣṇa, I wish to know about –

Q1: *prakṛti* – material nature
Q2: *puruṣa* – the enjoyer
Q3: *kṣetram* – the field
Q4: *kṣetra-jñam* – the knower of the field
Q5: *jñānaṁ* – knowledge
Q6: *jñeyaṁ* – the object of knowledge

2-7: Kṛṣṇa Describes Kṣetra, Kṣetra-jña and Jñānaṁ (A3, A4 & A5)

2a. Kṣetra is body: *Kṣetra* or the field of activity for the conditioned soul is the material body (a product of matter or *prakṛti*).

The conditioned soul is entrapped in material existence. According to his capacity to dominate material nature and enjoy sense gratification, he is given a body made of material senses, which is his field of activity.

2b. Kṣetra-jña is soul: *Kṣetra-jña* or the knower of body is the individual soul (*jīva*) living within that body. He is different from the body and is its proprietor.

The *kṣetra* or the field is a nonpermanent material thing. However, the *kṣetra-jña*, the knower of the field, is eternal. Those who think that the body is the self are not knowers of the field, since they do not know the real nature and function of the body.

3a. Kṣetra-jña is Kṛṣṇa too: I am also the knower of the field in *all* bodies, as the Supersoul (*kṣetra-jñaṁ cāpi māṁ viddhi sarva-kṣetreṣu bhārata*).

The body consists of the senses. Kṛṣṇa is Hṛṣīkeśa, the controller of the senses of all bodies. Out of the two knowers of the bodies, the Supersoul is the *pradhāna-kṣetrajña*, the chief knower of everyone's body. He is infallible and the individual soul is fallible and subordinate.

3b. Jñānaṁ is perfect knowledge of the material body and its knowers – the soul and the Supersoul (*kṣetra-kṣetrajñayor jñānaṁ yat taj jñānaṁ*). This is My opinion (*mataṁ mama*).

Real knowledge means understanding the separate existence of the Lord, *jīva* and *prakṛti*, though they mix together. This will be shown later in 15.16-17 also.

4. Six topics about kṣetra and kṣetra-jña		Kṛṣṇa explains in
i	Composition of the body (*yat ca*)	13.6
ii	Qualities of the body (*yādṛk*)	13.7
iii	Changes that the body undergoes (*yad-vikāri*)	13.7, 20
iv	Origin of the body (*yataḥ*)	13.6, 21, 22, 30
v	Identity (*svarūpa*) of the knower of the body (*yat*)	13.14-18, 23
vi	Powers of the knower of the body (*yat prabhāva*)	13.14-18

In 13.4, Kṛṣṇa said, He will explain these topics in brief. However, if Arjuna wishes to know in detail Kṛṣṇa tells in 13.5 where it can be found.

5. Kṛṣṇa quotes authorities: This knowledge has been described by many sages in various Vedic writings, especially in *Vedānta-sūtra* with all logic and reasoning.

ṛṣibhir bahudhā gītaṁ chandobhir vividhaiḥ pṛthak
brahma-sūtra-padaiś caiva hetumadbhir viniścitaiḥ

Although Kṛṣṇa has established His own position as the Supreme Personality of Godhead, the highest authority in explaining knowledge, and although He has just said in 13.3, "That is My opinion," nonetheless, He gives evidence from two other authorities (the sages and the scriptures) to substantiate His words. Kṛṣṇa, in the role of *guru*, thus presents corresponding references to *sādhu* and *śāstra*.

6. The body is composed of five great elements (*mahā-bhūta*), false ego (*ahaṅkāra*), intelligence (*buddhi*), the unmanifested state of three material modes called *pradhāna* (*avyakta*), ten senses and mind (*indriyāṇi*), and five sense objects (*indriya-gocara*).

24 elements (of material nature – that constitute *kṣetra* or the material body)

- 5 great elements are earth, water, fire, air and ether.
- 5 knowedge acquiring senses are eyes, ears, nose, tongue and skin.
- 5 working senses are voice, legs, hands, anus and genitals.
- 5 sense objects are smell, taste, form, touch and sound.
- Mind (11th sense), intelligence, false ego and *pradhāna*.
- The aggregate of these 24 elements is called the field of activity. By analytical study of these 24 elements, one can understand the field of activity.

7. The qualities or changes of the body include desire (*icchā*), hatred (*dveṣa*), happiness (*sukham*), distress (*duḥkham*), the aggregate body evolving from the 24 elements (*saṅghāta*), the life symptoms (*cetanā*) and convictions (*dhṛti*).

The qualities given here are not exhaustive. Other qualities include determination, uncertainty, faith, faithlessness, perseverance, lack of perseverance, humility, fear and so on. All these are products of the mind.

The body undergoes six changes (*vikāra*) namely – birth and growth, maintenance, maturity, decline and death.

8-12: JÑĀNAṀ – PROCESS OF ACQUIRING KNOWLEDGE (A5)

Now Kṛṣṇa will answer Q5 more elaborately. As described in 13.3 *jñānaṁ* is knowledge of body, soul and Supersoul. However, the real processs of acquiring that knowledge is to cultivate saintly qualities beginning with humility.

So, in the next five verses, Kṛṣṇa describes different aspects of saintly character, by which the soul (*kṣetra-jña*) could disentangle himself from the material body (*kṣetra*) and attain liberation. Thus the following are the aspects of knowledge and liberation.

8-12. Twenty elements of knowledge	
amānitvam *adambhitvam*	(1) Humility – no expectation of respect (2) Pridelessness – not being anxious to be famous
ahiṁsā *kṣāntir* *ārjavam*	(3) Nonviolence – not putting others into distress (4) Tolerance – bearing insults and dishonor (5) Simplicity – straightforward and nondiplomatic
ācāryopāsanaṁ *śaucaṁ*	(6) Serving a bona fide *guru* – without motivation (7) Cleanliness – both internal (mind) & external (body)
sthairyam *ātma-vinigrahaḥ*	(8) Steadiness – determined to progress in spiritual life (9) Self-control – Rejecting unfavorable things
indriyārtheṣu vairāgyam	(10) Renunciation of the objects of sense gratification
anahaṅkāra eva ca	(11) No false ego – No identification with body
janma-mṛtyu-jarā-vyādhi-duḥkha-doṣānudarśanam	(12) Perception of the evil of birth, death, old age and disease (that they give rise to suffering)
asaktir anabhiṣvaṅgaḥ putra-dāra-gṛhādiṣu	(13) Detachment (14) Freedom from entanglement with children, wife, home and the rest
nityaṁ ca sama-cittatvam iṣṭāniṣṭopapattiṣu	(15) Even-mindedness amid pleasant and unpleasant events;
mayi cānanya-yogena bhaktir avyabhicāriṇī	(16) Constant and unalloyed **devotion to Me** with undeviating attention
vivikta-deśa-sevitvam	(17) Secluded living – Living in devotee association
aratir jana-saṁsadi	(18) Detachment from the general mass of people;
adhyātma-jñāna-nityatvaṁ	(19) Accepting the importance of self-realization;
tattva-jñānārtha-darśanam	(20) Philosophical search for the Absolute Truth

etaj jñānam iti proktam	—all these I declare to be knowledge,
ajñānaṁ yad ato 'nyathā	and besides this whatever there may be is ignorance.

Of these 20 factors, 18 are common to both devotees and *jñānīs*. However the 16th item, i.e., exclusive devotion to Kṛṣṇa is the special qualification of devotees. The other qualities wil automatically manifest for those who have devotion without effort. The last two items are especially for the *jñānīs*.

13-19: JÑEYAṀ – OBJECT OF KNOWLEDGE (A6)

Having taught the process for attaining knowledge, Kṛṣṇa now teaches what is to be known (*jñeyaṁ*) by those means. The real objects of knowledge (*jñeyaṁ*) are *jīvātma,* the individual soul, and *Paramātma*, the Supersoul, who is an expansion and representation of the Supreme Personality of Godhead Kṛṣṇa.

13a. By knowing the knowable (*jñeyaṁ*), you will attain liberation (*amṛtam aśnute*).

13b. Brahman[1], the spirit soul (*jīva*) is beginningless, subordinate to Me (*anādi mat-paraṁ brahma*), and lies beyond the cause and effect[2] of this material world.

14-18: The qualities of Supersoul (Paramātma)	
sarvataḥ pāṇi-pādaṁ tat	Everywhere are His hands and legs.
sarvato 'kṣi-śiro-mukham	Everywhere are His eyes, heads and faces.
sarvataḥ śrutimal loke	Everywhere are His ears.
sarvam āvṛtya tiṣṭhati	He is **all-pervading**.
sarvendriya-guṇābhāsaṁ	He is the source of all senses.
sarvendriya-vivarjitam	Yet He is devoid of material senses.[3]
asaktaṁ sarva-bhṛc caiva	He is unattached, though He is the maintainer of all.
nirguṇaṁ guṇa-bhoktṛ ca	He is the master of modes, yet **transcendental** to them.

---

[1] The word 'Brahman' could refer to both soul and Supersoul depending on the context. *Jīva* is Brahman and the Lord is Supreme Brahman. Brahman is worshiped by the devotees as personal, with qualities, and by the *jñānīs* as impersonal, with no qualities.

[2] Brahman in its essential nature is beyond cause and effect, yet the Supreme Brahman (Paramātmā) is also *the* cause and effect because energy is non-different from the energetic, the source of energy.

[3] The Lord has no material eyes, but He has eyes. He sits in the hearts of all living beings and sees their activities in their past, present and future. He knows everything, but no one knows Him. He has no material legs, but He can travel throughout space with His spiritual legs.

bahir antaś ca bhūtānām acaraṁ caram eva ca	He is outside and inside of all moving and nonmoving beings. He moves and He doesn't move.
sūkṣmatvāt tad avijñeyaṁ	He is subtle and thus not knowable by material senses.
dūra-sthaṁ cāntike ca tat	Although far, far away, He is also near to all.
avibhaktaṁ ca bhūteṣu vibhaktam iva ca sthitam	He is **never divided** although He appears to be divided among all beings. He is situated as one.
bhūta-bhartṛ ca taj jñeyaṁ grasiṣṇu prabhaviṣṇu ca	He is the maintainer of all beings and also their destroyer (by His *kāla-śakti* or time energy) and creator.
jyotiṣām api taj jyotis	He is the source of light in all the luminous objects.
tamasaḥ param ucyate	He is beyond the darkness of matter.
jñānaṁ jñeyaṁ jñāna-gamyaṁ	He is **knowledge,** He is the object of knowledge, and He is the goal of knowledge.
hṛdi sarvasya viṣṭhitam	He is situated in everyone's heart.

19. Qualification to understand: Thus I have described briefly the body (*kṣetra*), knowledge (*jñāna*), and the knowable (*jñeya*). Only My **devotees** understand this, and thus attain to My nature. (Combined, these are called *vijñāna*, or the science of knowledge.)

20-26: Prakṛti, Puruṣa and Their Union (A1, A2)

Kṛṣṇa has described about *Paramātmā* as the knower of the field. Now He will desribe how the *jīva,* who is also the knower of the field, comes in contact with *māyā.*

20. Prakṛti and puruṣa are eternal: Material nature (*prakṛti*) and the *jīvas* or the living entities (*puruṣam*) are beginningless (*anādi*), being the energies of the Supreme Lord (See 7.4-5). Their transformations (*vikārān*) and the material modes (*guṇān*) are products of material nature.

Mystery of material creation: Before the creation, the material nature and the living entities were absorbed in the Supreme Lord, Mahā-viṣṇu. At the time of creation, they was manifested and the living entities were again given a chance to act in the material world and prepare themselves to enter into the spiritual world.

Puruṣa: The Supreme Lord is the supreme *puruṣa,* the master, controller, enjoyer, proprietor and maintainer of this entire cosmos. The *jīva* or the living entity is the energy of the Supreme Lord (See 7.5) and is not the master or the controller, but still the *jīva* is sometimes called *puruṣa* due to his 'mentality of being the master.' Thus the word "*puruṣa*" is used to refer to both the Supreme Lord and the living entity.

21. Roles of prakṛti and jīva	
kārya-kāraṇa-kartṛtve hetuḥ prakṛtir ucyate	**Prakṛti** or the material nature is said to be the cause of all material causes and effects.
puruṣaḥ sukha-duḥkhānāṁ bhoktṛtve hetur ucyate	**Puruṣa** or the living entity (*jīva*) is the cause of his own happiness and distress (due to his enjoying propensity).

Relationship between jīva and prakṛti: *Prakṛti* is the cause of the *jīva's* unfortunate condition in this world, by offering the body (*kārya*), the senses which produce happiness and distress (*kāraṇa*) and the presiding deities of the senses (*kartṛ*). *Jīva* suffers or enjoys due to his (mis)identification with the body produced by the *prakṛti.*

22. Jīva's association with modes and his transmigration	
puruṣaḥ prakṛti-stho hi	The living entity situated in the material nature (body)
bhuṅkte prakṛti-jān guṇān	thinks he is enjoying in the three modes born of *prakṛti.*
kāraṇaṁ guṇa-saṅgo 'sya	This is due to his association with three material modes.
sad-asad-yoni-janmasu	Thus he meets with good and evil in various species.

Soul changing bodies: Under the influence of material desires, the living entity is born sometimes as a devatā, a man, a beast, a bird, a worm, an aquatic, and so on. And in all cases the living entity thinks himself to be the master of his circumstances, yet he is under the influence of material nature and modes. This is due to the *jīva's* misidentification with *prakṛti* and misuse of his minute independence.

23. Supersoul, the real puruṣa: In this body, there is another *puruṣa*, who is called Paramātmā. He is overseer (*upadraṣṭa*), permitter of *jīva's* actions (*anumantā*), the supreme master (*bhartā*), enjoyer (*bhoktā*) and proprietor (*maheśvara*).

upadraṣṭānumantā ca bhartā bhoktā maheśvaraḥ
paramātmeti cāpy ukto dehe 'smin puruṣaḥ paraḥ

24. Result of this knowledge: He who knows about *prakṛti*, *puruṣas*, and modes (*guṇas*) will surely attain liberation from repeated birth.

25. Other methods: Some see Paramātmā through meditation (*dhyāna* or *aṣṭāṅga-yoga*), others by cultivation of knowledge (*sāṅkhya* or *jñāna-yoga*), and still others by working without fruitive desires (*niṣkāma-karma-yoga*).

26. Bhakti by hearing: Others, although not having knowledge (*ajānantaḥ*), worship the Supreme Lord upon hearing about Him. They surpass the path of birth and death due to their faithful hearing (*śruti-parāyaṇāḥ*) from authoritative persons.

27-35: JÑĀNA-CAKṢU – THE VISION OF KNOWLEDGE

Kṛṣṇa has answered all the six questions of Arjuna (in 13.1) about *kṣetra, kṣetrajña, jñāna, jñeya, puruṣa* and *prakṛti*. In the rest of the chapter, He will intigrate and expand on all the topics and explain the vision of one who can understand them from proper perspective.

27. Combination of prakṛti and puruṣa: Every entity, moving and nonmoving, in the material existence, is only a combination of the field of activity and the knower of the field (*kṣetra-kṣetrajña-saṁyogāt*).

All manifestations in this world arise from the combination of the two knowers of the field (*kṣetrajñas* or *puruṣas*) with *prakṛti* (i.e, the material bodies or *kṣetras*). The Lord, controlling the *jīva* and *prakṛti*, puts them in motion. *Jīva* and *prakṛti* then mutually bind themselves up.

28. The true seer's vision of Paramātma	
samaṁ sarveṣu bhūteṣu	The Supersoul is **equally disposed** to all living entities.
tiṣṭhantaṁ parameśvaram	He is residing **in the hearts** of all embodied beings.
vinaśyatsv avinaśyantaṁ	He is **indestructible** situated in the destructible bodies. (Neither the soul nor the Supersoul are ever destroyed.)
yaḥ paśyati sa paśyati	One who sees like this actually sees.

One who has mature vision due to his real knowledge, sees the Supreme Lord, distinct from the *jīvas*, but situated in the bodies (made of with *prakṛti*) of the *jīvas*.

29. Result of such mature vision: No degradation	
samaṁ paśyan hi sarvatra samavasthitam īśvaram	One who sees the Supersoul equally present everywhere, in every living being,
na hinasty ātmanātmānaṁ	does not degrade himself by his deviating mind.
tato yāti parāṁ gatim	Thus he attains the spiritual world.

30. The true seer's vision about the jīva and prakṛti	
prakṛtyaiva ca karmāṇi kriyamāṇāni sarvaśaḥ	**Prakṛti is the doer:** All material activities are performed by the body, which is created of *prakṛti*.
yaḥ paśyati tathātmānam akartāraṁ sa paśyati	**Jīva is non-doer:** The self does nothing[1]. One who sees like this actually sees. (*3.27 is also similar*)

[1] Yet the *jīva* suffers or enjoys due to his misidentification with *prakṛti*, as mentioned before.

31. Brahman vision: Material vision is to see separate identities (*pṛthak-bhāvam*) due to different material bodies. Mature vision is to see how beings of same spiritual nature (souls) are expanded everywhere. By such vision one attains to the Brahman platform (*brahma saṁpadyate*).

At the time of universal destruction, all living entities, who have assumed various forms such as devatās and men, lose such distinctions and become one by entering *prakṛti* (*eka-stham*). At the time of universal creation, they disperse again from *prakṛti* in many forms. In other words, the *jīva* is distinct from *prakṛti* and in conditioned state the *jīva* assumes various temporary forms.

32. The soul is non-doer and is not entangled[1]	
anāditvān nirguṇatvāt paramātmāyam avyayaḥ	The soul is transcendental, beginningless, endless or imperishable and beyond the modes of nature.
śarīra-stho 'pi kaunteya	Despite being situated in the material body, O Arjuna,
na karoti na lipyate	the soul doesn't do anything and is not entangled.

The soul is eternal and changeless, but nevertheless because of being in the material body, does the soul combine with it and gets contaminated by its qualities? To answer such a quation, in the next two verses, Kṛṣṇa gives two analogies.

33. Soul doesn't mix with matter: The soul situated in Brahman vision stays aloof, though situated in the material body, just as the sky although all-pervading (*sarva-gatam*), doesn't mix with anything (*nopalipyate*) due to its subtle nature.

34. The soul illuminates the entire body by consciousness, just as the sun alone illuminates the whole universe.

Consciousness is not a product of the combinations of matter. It is the symptom of the soul. The consciousness of one particular body does not share with that of another body. But the Supersoul, who is situated in all bodies as the friend of the soul, is conscious of all bodies. That is the difference between supreme consciousness and individual consciousness.

35. Summary – Phala-śruti	
kṣetra-kṣetrajñayor evam antaraṁ jñāna-cakṣuṣā	Those who see with eyes of knowledge the difference between the body and the knowers of the body, and
bhūta-prakṛti-mokṣaṁ ca ye vidur yānti te param	also understand the process of liberation from bondage in material nature, attain the supreme goal.

[1] The same description can be applied to the Supersoul as well.

14. The Three Modes of Material Nature

- **1-13:** The conditioning of the soul by the material modes
  - 1-2: Kṛṣṇa glorifies the pure knowledge
  - 3-4: The jīva's contact with prakṛti (matter)
  - 5–9: How the material modes bind the pure jīva
  - 10-13: Recognizing the prominence of a mode
- **14-18:** Effect of conditioning by the modes
  - 14-15: Destination after death in different modes
  - 16-18: Result of action in different modes
- **19–27:** Transcending the modes (becoming guṇātīta)
  - 19. Seeing the modes as doers and the Lord as transcendental
  - 20: Result of transcending the modes
  - 21: Arjuna's three questions about guṇātīta (Q1-Q3)
  - 22: A1 – Symptoms of guṇātīta
  - 23-25: A2 – Behaviour of guṇātīta
  - 26: A3 – By pure bhakti one transcends the modes and comes to the level of Brahman
  - 27: Kṛṣṇa is the source of that Brahman

In the previous chapter, Lord Kṛṣṇa said (in 13.22) that the living entity takes up repeated birth and death due to association with the modes of material nature (*guṇas*).

In this chapter, Kṛṣṇa explains what those modes of material nature are, how they work, how they bind the living entity and how they are destroyed by *kṛṣṇa-bhakti*.

1-13: The Conditioning of the Soul by the Material Modes

1-2: Kṛṣṇa glorifies pure knowledge

In the first two verses, Kṛṣṇa glorifies the knowledge that He is going to reveal in this chapter (similar to the way He has done in Chapters 7, 9 and 10).

1. Kṛṣṇa speaks the highest knowledge	
paraṁ bhūyaḥ pravakṣyāmi jñānānāṁ jñānam uttamam	Again I shall declare to you this supreme wisdom, the best of all knowledge,
yaj jñātvā munayaḥ sarve	knowing which all the sages
parāṁ siddhim ito gatāḥ	have attained the supreme perfection.

2. Result of attaining that knowledge	
idaṁ jñānam upāśritya	By taking shelter of this knowledge,
mama sādharmyam āgatāḥ	(*i*) one can attain same nature or form as Mine,
sarge 'pi nopajāyante pralaye na vyathanti ca	(*ii*) one is freed from repeated birth and death → doesn't take birth again (in universal creation) or experience the pain of death (at universal dissolution).

Having glorified the knowledge, Kṛṣṇa will now begin to explain the relationship between the *jīvas*, the *prakṛti* and Himself.

3-4: The jīva's contact with prakṛti (matter)

3. The Lord impregnates prakṛti: The material nature or *prakṛti* (*mahad-brahma* or *mahat-tattva*) is the womb that I impregnate, making possible the births of all *jīvas*.

Prakṛti is called *mahat*, because it extends through all place and time continuously. It is called *brahma* because it is the cause of expansion.

4. Kṛṣṇa is the father and Prakṛti is the mother of all jīvas	
sarva-yoniṣu kaunteya	All species of life, O son of Kuntī,
mūrtayaḥ sambhavanti yāḥ	are made possible by birth
tāsāṁ brahma mahad yonir	in this material nature (the mother).
ahaṁ bīja-pradaḥ pitā	I (as Mahā Viṣṇu) am the seed-giving father.

5-9: How the material modes bind the pure jīva

5. The jīva's bondage under the spell of modes	
sattvaṁ rajas tama iti	Goodness, passion and ignorance –
guṇāḥ prakṛti-sambhavāḥ	these three *guṇas* are produced of material nature.
nibadhnanti mahā-bāho	O mighty-armed one, they bind the
dehe dehinam avyayam	the changeless living entity in the material body.

6. Bondage by sattva-guṇa	
tatra sattvaṁ nirmalatvāt	The mode of goodness is the purest of the three modes.
prakāśakam anāmayam	It is illuminating, and frees one from sins and distress.
sukha-saṅgena badhnāti jñāna-saṅgena cānagha	Those situated in this mode become conditioned by a sense of happiness and knowledge, O sinless Arjuna.

7. Bondage by rajo-guṇa	
rajo rāgātmakaṁ viddhi tṛṣṇā-saṅga-samudbhavam	The mode of passion is born of desire – attachment for the attained and longing for the unattained.
tan nibadhnāti kaunteya karma-saṅgena dehinam	O son of Kuntī, and because of this the embodied living entity is bound to material fruitive actions.

The mode of passion is characterized by the attraction between man and woman. And when the passion is increased, one develops hankering for material enjoyment and works very hard and becomes bound to his activities.

8. Bondage by tamo-guṇa	
tamas tv ajñāna-jaṁ viddhi mohanaṁ sarva-dehinām	Know that the mode of darkness, born of ignorance, is the delusion of all embodied living entities.
pramādālasya-nidrābhis tan nibadhnāti bhārata	This mode binds the *jīva* with madness, laziness and sleep, O son of Bharata.

9. Summary: Goodness conditions one to happiness; passion conditions one to fruitive action; and ignorance, covering one's knowledge, binds one to madness.

10-13: Recognizing the prominence of a mode

10. Competition amongst modes: Sometimes the mode of goodness becomes prominent, defeating the modes of passion and ignorance. Sometimes passion defeats goodness and ignorance, and at other times ignorance defeats goodness and passion.

The modes appear and disappear according to operation or exhaustion of old *karmas*. The prominence of certain mode is manifested in one's dealings, activities, etc. One who is actually intent on advancing in *bhakti* has to transcend these three modes.

11. When goodness increases, all the nine gates of the body (two eyes, two ears, two nostrils, mouth, genitals and anus) are illuminated by knowledge and happiness (one can see, hear and taste things in the right position).

12. When passion increases, the symptoms of greed, fruitive activity, intense endeavor, and uncontrollable desire and hankering develop. (Passionate person is never satisfied with the position he has already acquired).

13. When ignorance increases, darkness (*aprakāśaḥ*), inertia (*apravṛttiḥ*), madness (*pramādaḥ*) and illusion (*mohaḥ*) are manifested (discrimination is absent).

14-18: Effect of Conditioning by the Modes

14.14-15 describe the long-term effect, i.e., destination after death. 14.16 describes medium-term effect, 14.17 describes immideate effect and 14.18 describes *jīva's* direction in the universe after death. These are summarized and given below.

14-15. Destination after death for a person in –

- **Goodness** → higher planets of great sages, like Brahmaloka or Janaloka.
- **Passion** → birth among those engaged in fruitive activities on the earthly planet.
- **Ignorance** → birth in lower species, the animal kingdom.

16-18. Result of action in –

- **Goodness** → purity without distress (*nirmalaṁ*), knowledge (*jñānaṁ*), higher or heavenly planets, upto Brahmaloka (*ūrdhvaṁ*).
- **Passion** → misery (*duḥkham*), greed (*lobha*), middle or earthly planets (*madhye*).
- **Ignorance** → foolishness (*ajñānaṁ*), madness (*pramāda*), illusion (*moha*), lower or hellish planets (*adho*).

sattvāt sañjāyate jñānaṁ rajaso lobha eva ca
pramāda-mohau tamaso bhavato 'jñānam eva ca
ūrdhvaṁ gacchanti sattva-sthā madhye tiṣṭhanti rājasāḥ
jaghanya-guṇa-vṛtti-sthā adho gacchanti tāmasāḥ

Having described the all-pervasive control of modes, Kṛṣṇa will now describe how to transcend the modes and explains His own position in relation to them.

19-27: Transcending the Modes (Becoming Guṇātīta)

Gist of the section: *Jñāna* stresses discrimination. Discrimination ultimately leads one to appreciate that he is not the body, Kṛṣṇa is Supreme, and that he should take shelter of Kṛṣṇa to become free. Thus *jñāna* is a path that culminates in *bhakti*.

19. Seeing the modes as doers and the Lord as transcendental	
nānyaṁ guṇebhyaḥ kartāraṁ yadā draṣṭānupaśyati	When one sees that there is no other performer of actions than the material modes and
guṇebhyaś ca paraṁ vetti mad-bhāvaṁ so 'dhigacchati	knows that the Supreme Lord (and even the *jīva*) is transcendental to the modes, he attains My spiritual nature crossing beyond this material existence.

20. When one can surpass the modes associated with the body (which give rise to the body), he can become free from birth, death, old age and their distresses and enjoy nectar even in present life (and attains eternal life).

Hearing the result of surpassing the modes, Arjuna will ask Kṛṣṇa about the process of transcending the modes and the symptoms and behaviour of such a person who has transcended the modes (*guṇātīta*).

21. Arjuna's questions about guṇātīta		**Kṛṣṇa's answers**
Q1	By what **symptoms** is he known?	**A1** 14.22
Q2	What is his **behaviour**?	**A2** 14.23-25
Q3	What is the **process** of transcending the modes?	**A3** 14.26

Arjuna asked a similar question in 2.54 about the qualities and activities of a *sthita-prajña*. But at that time he didn't ask how one could transcend the material modes. Here he inquires about that.

22-26: Kṛṣṇa's answers to Arjuna's questions about guṇātīta

22. [A1] Symptoms of a guṇātīta: Doesn't hate illumination, attachment and delusion when they are present or long for them when they disappear.

23-25. [A2] Behaviour of a guṇātīta (external conduct)

- Neutral (*udāsīna*) and undisturbed by the reactions of modes (*guṇair yo na vicālyate*), knowing that the modes alone are active.
- Equal to happiness and distress (*sama-duḥkha-sukhaḥ*)

- Firmly situated in the self (*sva-sthaḥ*)
- Sees a lump of earth, a stone and gold as the same (*sama-loṣṭāśma-kāñcanaḥ*)
- Equal toward the dear and not dear (*tulya-priyāpriyo*)
- Steady (*dhīra*)
- Equal towards praise and blame (*tulya-nindātma-saṁstutiḥ*)
- Equal in honor and dishonor (*mānāpamānayos tulyas*)
- Treats friend and enemy alike (*tulyo mitrāri-pakṣayoḥ*)
- Renounces all material activities (*sarvārambha-parityāgī*)

26. [A3] Pure bhakti is the process of transcending modes	
māṁ ca yo 'vyabhicāreṇa bhakti-yogena sevate	One who engages in full devotional service, unfailing in all circumstances,
sa guṇān samatītyaitān brahma-bhūyāya kalpate	at once transcends the modes of material nature and thus comes to the level of Brahman.

Kṛṣṇa said that by *bhakti* one will attain Brahman. But a devotee doesn't desire Brahman realization but wants to serve Kṛṣṇa. Therefore, Kṛṣṇa describes His own relationship with Brahman and thus stresses *bhakti* again.

27. Kṛṣṇa is the source of Brahman	
brahmaṇo hi pratiṣṭhāham	I am the basis or shelter of the impersonal Brahman,
amṛtasyāvyayasya ca	which is immortal, imperishable and
śāśvatasya ca dharmasya	eternal and is the constitutional position
sukhasyaikāntikasya ca	or platform of ultimate bliss.

When one has attained the level of Brahman (i.e., freedom from the contamination of the modes of nature), he becomes qualified to engage in the *bhakti* devotional service of Para-brahman (the Supreme Brahman), Kṛṣṇa. Kṛṣṇa is the basis of the eternal process of *bhakti* that gives the realization of the Personality of Kṛṣṇa. Both Brahman and Paramātmā are within the Supreme Person Kṛṣṇa. Thus the realization of Brahman, or eternity is included in *bhakti* unto Kṛṣṇa and is already possessed by a devotee. And Kṛṣṇa is also the basis of the bliss of the unalloyed devotee.

15. The Yoga of The Supreme Person

1-6: From material world to spiritual world – by detachment and surrender

- 1-2: Material world is an upside down banyan tree – branches are planets, the three modes are watering process, twigs are sense objects and secondary roots are fruitive activities.
- 3-6: Cut the tree of material world with the axe of detachment and surrender unto the Supreme Lord (process explained) and thus attain the spiritual world (qualities described).

7-11: Transmigration of the living entities

- 7-9: The jīva is part and parcel of Kṛṣṇa, but struggling in this world due to the five senses and the mind and thus changing material bodies.
- 10-11: Soul's transmigration – Who can and who can't see?

12-15: Appreciating Kṛṣṇa's position as our maintainer in this world

- 12-13: Kṛṣṇa is our maintainer at cosmic level – as source of light, sustenence and juice of life
- 14-15: Kṛṣṇa is our maintainer at personal level – as digestion fire and Paramātma in the heart

16-18: Summary of the Vedas and the Vedānta

- 16: Two kinds of living entities – kṣara and akṣara
- 17: The Supersoul, beyond kṣara and akṣara
- 18: Lord Kṛṣṇa, the Supreme Lord

19-20: Knowing Kṛṣṇa means knowing everything

- Knowing Kṛṣṇa one engages in His bahkti. Whoever understands this will attain knowledge, realization and perfection

In the previous chapter, Kṛṣṇa said that He is the basis and supreme shelter of Brahman (in 14.27). Kṛṣṇa also said that by performing *bhakti*, one can transcend the material modes and attain the status of Brahman (in 14.26). But to attain devotion and attachment to Kṛṣṇa, one needs to also develop detachment from this material world.

In this chapter, Kṛṣṇa describes the process of breaking attachment to this material world. He compares this world (*saṁsāra*) to a banyan tree (*aśvattha vṛkṣa*) and 'detachment' to an 'axe' to cut it. He then describes *Puruṣottama-yoga*.

After knowing the importance of *bhakti-yoga*, one may question, "What about the Vedas?" This chapter explains that the purpose of Vedic study is to understand Kṛṣṇa.

1-6: From Material World to Spiritual World – by Detachment and Surrender

1. Material world is an upside-down banyan tree	
ūrdhva-mūlam adhaḥ-śākham *aśvatthaṁ prāhur avyayam*	It is said that there is an imperishable banyan tree that has its roots upward and its branches down
chandāṁsi yasya parṇāni	and whose leaves are the Vedas.
yas taṁ veda sa veda-vit	One who knows this tree is the knower of the Vedas.

Reflection tree: A tree with its branches down and roots upward, is the reflection of a real tree in the water. The tree of this material world is only a reflection of the real tree of the spiritual world.

Desire: Just as a tree's reflection is situated on water, the reflection of the spiritual world is situated on desire. One can be free from entanglement within material world by cultivating a transcendental desire to enter into spiritual world.

Knowing the Vedas: One who is attracted by rituals of Vedas, is just attracted by the beautiful green leaves of the banyan tree and does not know the purpose of Vedas. Knowing the Vedas means to cut off one's attchment to the tree of material world.

2a. Its branches spreading up and down, represent planets with different species.

On the lower parts of the branches there are planets with living entities like human beings, animals, horses, cows, dogs, cats, etc. On the upper parts are higher forms of living entities: the devatās, Gandharvas etc. Brahma-loka lies at the root.

2b. It is nourished (watering process) by the three modes (*guṇa pravṛddhāḥ*)

2c. Its twigs are the sense objects (*viṣaya pravālāḥ*); The tips of the branches are the senses attached to the sense objects.

2d. Its secondary roots extending everywhere, bind the human society to fruitive actions (*karma anubandhīni*).

The subsidiary roots are attachments and aversions, which are by-products of different varieties of suffering and sense enjoyment. The tendencies toward piety and impiety develop from these secondary roots.

The fruits of this tree are *dharma, artha, kāma* and *mokṣa.*

This tree is eternal (*avyayam*) in the sense of being continuous, because it does not disappear except through the discriminating knowledge given in the *Gīta*.

3-4. Cut the tree with the axe of detachment: The real form of this tree, its beginning, end and foundation, cannot be perceived in this world. But one must cut this strongly rooted tree with the axe of detachment (*asaṅga-śastreṇa*), sharpened by determination (*dṛḍhena*). Then one should search for that place from which, having gone, one never returns, by **surrendering** unto that original Person (*ādyaṁ puruṣaṁ prapadye*) from whom everything originated.

5. The surrendering process	
nirmāna-mohā *jita-saṅga-doṣā*	Those who are free from false prestige and illusion, who have conquered over false association,
adhyātma-nityā *vinivṛtta-kāmāḥ*	who understand the eternal, who are done with material lust,
dvandvair vimuktāḥ *sukha-duḥkha-saṁjñair*	who are freed from the dualities of happiness and distress, and
gacchanty amūḍhāḥ *padam avyayaṁ tat*	who, unbewildered, know how to surrender unto the Supreme Person, attain that eternal spiritual world.

Now Kṛṣṇa will describe the nature of the spiritual world, which is the goal of the surrendering process described above.

6. Qualities of the spiritual world (Kṛṣṇaloka or Goloka Vṛndāvana)	
na tad bhāsayate sūryo	It is not illumined by the sun
na śaśāṅko na pāvakaḥ	or moon, nor by fire or electricity.
yad gatvā na nivartante	Those who reach it never return to this material world.
tad dhāma paramaṁ mama	That is the supreme abode of Mine.

A living entity will not be satisfied until he reaches that Supreme abode. Because it is his constitutional position to be related with Kṛṣṇa as explained in 15.7.

7-11: Transmigration of the Living Entities

7-9: Mind's power to determine the jīva's future

7. Identity of the living entity	
mamaivāṁśo jīva-loke jīva-bhūtaḥ sanātanaḥ	The living entities in this world are My eternal fragmental parts.
manaḥ-ṣaṣṭhānīndriyāṇi prakṛti-sthāni karṣati	Due to conditioned life, they are struggling hard in the material nature with the six senses, including the mind.

Kṛṣṇa will elaborate on how the *jīva* carrying the senses is struggling (*karṣati*) in this world.

8. Change of the bodies: The living entity carries his different conceptions of life (in the mind) from one material body to another, just as the air carries aromas.

9. Thus taking another gross body, the *jīva* obtains new ears, eyes, tongue, nose and sense of touch, all grouped about the mind and thus he enjoys sense objects.

Consciousness is originally pure, like water. But just as we mix water with a certain color, it changes, consciousness changes according to the association of the material modes. Real consciousness is Kṛṣṇa consciousness.

10-11. Soul's transmigration – Who can and who can't see?	
utkrāmantaṁ sthitaṁ vāpi	This quitting of the body and staying in a body
bhuñjānaṁ vā guṇānvitam	and enjoying under the spell of material modes
vimūḍhā nānupaśyanti	is not perceived by foolish people,
paśyanti jñāna-cakṣuṣaḥ	but those who have eyes of knowledge can see this.
yatanto yoginaś cainaṁ paśyanty ātmany avasthitam	The endeavoring transcendentalists who are situated in self-realization can see all this clearly.
yatanto 'py akṛtātmāno nainaṁ paśyanty acetasaḥ	But those with impure consciousness cannot see this, though they may try.

Even sense enjoyment is impossible without the help of the Lord. One can develop his Kṛṣṇa consciousness, even while living in this world, by appreciating Kṛṣṇa as the maintainer of the phenomenal world. The folowing verses help us to know how things are taking place in this material world and thus be established in knowledge.

12-15: Appreciating Kṛṣṇa's Position as Our Maintainer in This World

12-13: Kṛṣṇa is our maintainer at cosmic level

12. I am the source of light of the sun, moon and fire that dissipate the darkness of this world.

13a. I enter into each planet, and by My energy I sustain all living beings.

13b. I become the moon and supply the juice of life to all plants and vegetables.

14-15: Kṛṣṇa is our maintainer at personal level

14. Kṛṣṇa is the digestion fire	
ahaṁ vaiśvānaro bhūtvā	I am the fire of digestion
prāṇināṁ deham āśritaḥ	in the bodies of all living entities.
prāṇāpāna-samāyuktaḥ	I join with the air of life, outgoing and incoming,
pacāmy annaṁ catur-vidham	to digest the four kinds of foodstuff.

Four kinds of foodstuff: (*i*) *Bhakṣya* – Chewed; (*ii*) *Bhojya* – sipped; (*iii*) *Lehya* – licked; (*iv*) *Coṣya* – sucked.

15. As Paramātmā, Kṛṣṇa initiates all activities	
sarvasya cāhaṁ hṛdi sanniviṣṭo	I am seated in everyone's heart.
mattaḥ smṛtir *jñānam apohanaṁ ca*	From Me come remembrance, knowledge and forgetfulness.
vedaiś ca sarvair aham eva vedyo	By all the Vedas, I am to be known.
vedānta-kṛd *veda-vid eva cāham*	I am the compiler of Vedānta (as Vyāsadeva) I am the knower of the Vedas.

The living entity forgets everything of his past life, but the Supersoul, the witness of all his work, gives him remembrance and required knowledge to start his deeds. Thus, the Lord is not only all-pervading; He is also localized in everyone's heart.

Having concluded that He is the goal of Vedas, Kṛṣṇa will speak the essence of Vedānta in the three verses, that conclusively establishes His position as the Supreme.

16-18: Summary of the Vedas and the Vedānta

16. Two kinds of living entities – kṣara and akṣara	
dvāv imau puruṣau loke	There are two classes of beings,
kṣaraś cākṣara eva ca	(*i*) *kṣara:* the fallible, who deviates from his true nature (*ii*) *akṣara:* the infallible, who doesn't deviate
kṣaraḥ sarvāṇi bhūtāni	In the material world every living entity is fallible.
kūṭa-stho 'kṣara ucyate	In the spiritual world every living entity is infallible.

17. The Supersoul, beyond kṣara and akṣara	
uttamaḥ puruṣas tv anyaḥ	Superior to these two, there is the greatest personality,
paramātmety udāhṛtaḥ	called the Paramātma, the Supreme Soul.
yo loka-trayam āviśya	He has entered the three worlds.
bibharty avyaya īśvaraḥ	That inexhaustible Lord is thus maintaining the worlds.

The two classes of beings mentioned in 15.16 are the conditioned (*kṣara*) and liberated (*akṣara*) *jīvas*. The position of supporting and protecting the universe (mentioned in 15.17) cannot refer to the conditioned *jīva* because he cannot perform such actions. It cannot refer to the liberated *jīva* because he is devoid of interaction with the world. It can refer only to the Supreme Lord. No one can surpass the Supreme Lord—neither the conditioned soul nor the liberated soul.

Having spoken about the object of worship of the *yogīs*, Paramātmā, Kṛṣṇa now speaks about the object of worship of the devotees, *Bhagavān*.

18. Lord Kṛṣṇa, the Supreme Lord	
yasmāt kṣaram atīto 'ham *akṣarād api cottamaḥ*	Because I am transcendental, superior to both the fallible and the infallible, and because I am the greatest,
ato 'smi loke vede ca *prathitaḥ puruṣottamaḥ*	I am celebrated both in the world and in the Vedas as that Supreme Person.

Kṛṣṇa will now speak about the position and disposition of a person who has assimilated the essence of the last three verses, especially that Kṛṣṇa is the Supreme Perosnality of Godhead.

19-20: Knowing Kṛṣṇa Means Knowing Everything

19. Knower of Kṛṣṇa knows everything	
yo māṁ evam asammūḍho jānāti puruṣottamam	Whoever knows Me as the Supreme Personality of Godhead, without doubting,
sa sarva-vid bhajati māṁ	is the knower of everything. He engages in devotional service unto Me
sarva-bhāvena bhārata	in all respects, O son of Bharata.

20. Summary and phala-śruti: Thus I have spoken this most confidential part of the Vedic scriptures. Whoever understands this will have knowledge and realization and perfection in all his endeavors.

iti guhyatamaṁ śāstram idam uktaṁ mayānagha
etad buddhvā buddhimān syāt kṛta-kṛtyaś ca bhārata

We learn from this chapter that the person who is different from the conditioned and liberated souls, and who supports and is superior to both of them, is the Supreme Lord Kṛṣṇa.

16. The Divine and Demoniac Natures

16. The Divine and Demoniac Natures

- 1-3: Daivī sampada – Divine qualities (see the table)
- 4-8: Asura sampada – Demoniac qualities
- 10-20: Activities of the demoniac people and the consequences – their tendencies, conduct, attitude, engagements, thoughts and destination.
- 20-24: Giving up demoniac tendencies (lust, anger and greed which are three gates to hell) and following scriptures.

In the previous chapter, Kṛṣṇa described the Banyan tree of the material world, but its fruits have not been described.

In this chapter, Kṛṣṇa describes the fruits of the tree which are of two varieties: good fruits (divine qualities) that cause liberation and bad fruits (demoniac qualities) that cause bondage. First, he describes the good fruits.

1-3: Daivī sampada – Divine Qualities

1. Daiva or divine qualities (in goodness)	
abhayaṁ *sattva-saṁśuddhir*	(1) Fearlessness – dependence on God (2) Purity of consciousness – by prescribed rules
jñāna-yoga-vyavasthitiḥ	(3) Cultivation of spiritual knowledge
dānaṁ *damaś ca* *yajñaś ca*	(4) Charity – for *gṛhasthas* (5) Self-control – especially in sex life (6) Sacrifice – especially for *gṛhasthas*
svādhyāyas *tapa* *ārjavam*	(7) Vedic study – for *brahmacāris* (8) Austerity – can be of body, mind and tongue (9) Simplicity – being straightforward

ahiṁsā *satyam* *akrodhas*	(10) Nonviolence – not checking one's progressive life (11) Truthfulness – not lying for personal interest (12) Freedom from anger – even in provocation
tyāgaḥ *śāntir* *apaiśunam*	(13) Renunciation – using things in Kṛṣṇa's service (14) Tranquility – unagitated, peaceful, equipoised (15) Aversion to faultfinding unnecessarily
dayā bhūteṣv *aloluptvaṁ*	(16) Compassion for all living entities (17) Freedom from covetousness
mārdavaṁ *hrīr* *acāpalam*	(18) Gentleness – towards all living entities (19) Modesty – no abominable activities (20) Steady determination – not agitated even in failure
tejaḥ *kṣamā* *dhṛtiḥ* *śaucam*	(21) Vigor – protecting the needy (for *kṣatriyas*) (22) Forgiveness – of others' minor offenses (23) Fortitude – mental and emotional strength (24) Cleanliness – internal (mind) and external (body)
adroho *nāti-mānitā*	(25) Freedom from envy – not resentful (26) From the passion for honor – respecting others
bhavanti sampadaṁ daivīm *abhijātasya bhārata*	—these transcendental qualities, O son of Bharata, belong to godly men endowed with divine nature.

The divine qualities are cultivated according to one's *varṇa* and *āśrama*. The demoniac qualities described below cause bondage and lay a royal road to hell.

4-8: ASURA SAMPADA – DEMONIAC QUALITIES

4. Āsuric or demoniac qualities (in passion and ignorance)	
dambho *darpo* *abhimānaś ca*	(1) Pride – want to make a show of religion even if sinful (2) Arrogance – pride in one's wealth and education (3) Conceit – desire to be worshiped by others
krodhaḥ *pāruṣyam eva ca*	(4) Anger – over trifles (5) Harshness – rough language in front of others
ajñānaṁ, *cābhijātasya* *pārtha sampadam āsurīm*	(6) Ignorance – lack of discrimination, whimsical action —these qualities belong to those of demoniac nature, O son of Pṛthā.

Hearing about the divine and demoniac qualities, Arjuna might doubt whether his own participation in the battle as a warrior – and therefore as a killer – will be due to possessing a demoniac temperament. So, Kṛṣṇa clarifies this now.

5. Destiny of divine and demoniac: The divine qualities are conducive to liberation (*daivī sampad vimokṣāya*), and the demoniac qualities cause bondage (*nibandhāya āsurī matā*). Do not worry, O son of Pāṇḍu, you are born with the divine qualities.

Seeing that Arjuna's lamentation didn't go away, Kṛṣṇa begins to describe the qualities of demoniac people.

6. In this world there are two kinds of beings – divine (daiva) and demoniac (asura). I have already explained the divine qualities. Now hear about the demoniac.

7a. They do not know what is to be done (*pravṛttim*) and not to be done (*nivṛttim*).

7b. They don't have cleanliness (*śaucam*), good behavior (*ācāraḥ*) or truthfulness (*satyam*).

8. Their conclusions about this world – (*i*) false (*asatyam*), (*ii*) without foundation (*apratiṣṭham*), (*iii*) with no God in control (*anīśvaram*), (*iv*) has arisen without cause (*aparaspara sambhūtam*), (*v*) produced of sex desire or lust (*kāma-haitukam*).

9a. Thus they are lost to themselves (*naṣṭātmānaḥ*) and have no intelligence (*alpa-buddhayaḥ*).

9b. They engage in unbeneficial, horrible works (*ugra-karmāṇaḥ*) meant to destroy the world.

10-20: Activities of the Demoniac People and the Consequences

10. Demoniac tendencies and conduct	
kāmam āśritya duṣpūraṁ	Taking shelter of insatiable thirst for enjoyment, and
dambha-māna-madānvitāḥ	absorbed in the conceit of pride and false prestige,
mohād gṛhītvāsad-grāhān	they are illusioned, attracted by the impermanent,
pravartante 'śuci-vratāḥ	and are always sworn to unclean vows.

11. Attitude: Believing in the ultimate goal of gratifying senses (*kāmopabhoga*), they take unlimited anxieties until the end of life.

12. Engagement: Bound by a network of thousands of desires (*āśā-pāśā*) and absorbed in lust and anger, they secure money by illegal means for sense gratification.

The laws of nature do not allow a second beyond what one is destined to enjoy. Not knowing that there is a witness (Supersoul) within his heart, such fools feel free to do anything for sense enjoyment, regardless of the consequences.

13-15. Thoughts upon gaining wealth: "I gained this wealth today, I will gain more as per my desires. I killed this enemy, and will also kill my other enemies. I am the lord and enjoyer. I am perfect, powerful and happy. I am the richest and high born.

No one is so powerful and happy as I am. I shall perform sacrifices, give some charity, and thus rejoice." In this way, such persons are deluded by ignorance.

16. Destination of demoniac people – Hell	
aneka-citta-vibhrāntā	Thus perplexed by various anxieties,
moha-jāla-samāvṛtāḥ	bound by a network of illusions,
prasaktāḥ kāma-bhogeṣu	they become strongly attached to sense enjoyment,
patanti narake 'śucau	and fall down into an unclean hell (like Vaitaraṇī, filled with blood and pus).

17. Demoniac hypocritical nature	
ātma-sambhāvitāḥ stabdhā	Self-complacent and always impudent
dhana-māna-madānvitāḥ	deluded by wealth and false prestige
yajante nāma-yajñais te	they sometimes proudly do sacrifices in name only,
dambhenāvidhi-pūrvakam	without following any scriptural rules or regulations.

18. Further results of demoniac activities	
ahaṅkāraṁ balaṁ darpaṁ *kāmaṁ krodhaṁ ca saṁśritāḥ*	They take shelter of false ego, strength, pride, lust and anger and are thus **bewildered**.
māṁ ātma-para-deheṣu *pradviṣanto 'bhyasūyakāḥ*	They become **envious** of Me, who is situated in their own bodies and in the bodies of others. They **blaspheme** against the real religion.

19-20. Kṛṣṇa's treatment of the demoniac	
tān ahaṁ dviṣataḥ krūrān *saṁsāreṣu narādhamān* *kṣipāmy ajasram aśubhān* *āsurīṣv eva yoniṣu*	I perpetually cast the envious, cruel, and the lowest among men, into the ocean of material existence, into various demoniac species of life.
āsurīṁ yonim āpannā *mūḍhā janmani janmani*	Attaining repeated birth amongst the demoniac species, such fools
māṁ aprāpyaiva kaunteya	can never approach Me, O son of Kuntī.
tato yānty adhamāṁ gatim	Gradually they sink down to the lowest status of life.

The placing of a particular individual soul in a particular body is the prerogative of the supreme will. Those who have *asura* mentality will not get liberation.

21-24: Giving up Demoniac Tendencies and Following Scriptures

21. Three gates to hell	
tri-vidhaṁ narakasyedaṁ dvāraṁ nāśanam ātmanaḥ	There are three gates leading to this hell, that cause the degradation of the soul.
kāmaḥ krodhas tathā lobhas	They are lust, anger and greed.
tasmād etat trayaṁ tyajet	Every sane man should give them up.

22. One who has escaped these three gates performs acts conducive to self-realization and gradually attains the supreme destination (*parām gatim*) or liberation.

One cannot escape form the three gates to hell without practice of ones own *dharma* as prescribed by the scriptures. Kṛṣṇa will now describe the importance of acting according to the scriptural injunctions.

23. Result of disregarding scriptures	
yaḥ śāstra-vidhim utsṛjya	He who discards scriptural injunctions
vartate kāma-kārataḥ	and acts according to his own whims
na sa siddhim avāpnoti	attains neither perfection,
na sukhaṁ na parāṁ gatim	nor happiness, nor liberation (supreme goal).

24. Following the scriptures	
tasmāc chāstraṁ pramāṇaṁ te	Therefore, from the evidence of scriptures,
kāryākārya-vyavasthitau	one should understand what is duty and what is not.
jñātvā śāstra-vidhānoktaṁ	Knowing these regulations of the scriptures,
karma kartum ihārhasi	one should act so that he may gradually be elevated.

Conclusion: This chapter has described how those who follow the scripture attain liberation and those who do not follow scripture go to hell.

17. The Divisions of Faith

17. The Divisions of Faith

- 1: Arjuna's inquiry about the unauthorized worship of those who have some faith which is not based on scriptures
- 2-7: The three modes determine one's faith (śraddhā) and worship
- 8-10: Foods in three modes
- 11-13: Sacrifices in three modes
- 14-16: Three types of austerity
- 17-19: Austerity in three modes
- 20-22: Charity in three modes
- 23-28: Conclusion – Oṁ tat Sat indicate the Supreme Absolute Truth, Viṣṇu. Any sacrifice, charity or austerity done without faith in the Supreme is impermanent and is *asat*

In the previous chapter, Kṛṣṇa has established that 'faithful followers of the scriptures are divine' and that the 'faithless are demoniac.' In 16.23, He has concluded that those who disregard scriptures and behave whimsically do not attain happiness in this life or the next.

In this Chapter, Arjuna asks Kṛṣṇa about the fate of those who have some other faith which is not based on the scriptures. In response, Kṛṣṇa describes about faith and various other items in the three modes.

In short, Kṛṣṇa described in Chapter 16 people of two extremes – those who have scriptual faith (divine) and the faithless (demoniac). In Chapter 17, He describes those who are in the middle, i.e, with non-scriptural faith.

1: Arjuna's Inquiry About Unauthorized Worship

1. Arjuna asked, "O Kṛṣṇa, what is the situation of those who do not follow the scripture but worship according to their own faith? Are they in goodness, in passion or in ignorance?"

Kṛṣṇa will first explain the situation of those who worship without giving up the rules of scripture. After that He will speak about the condition of those who give up the rules of scripture.

2-7: The Modes Determine One's Faith (Śraddhā) and Worship

2. People have three types of faith (*śraddhā*) that arise from their acquired nature (*svabhāva*) due to previous impressions by the influence of the modes. Thus one's faith can be in goodness, in passion or in ignorance. Now hear about this.

But one's nature can be changed if one abides by the teachings of a bona fide spiritual master and the scriptures. Gradually, one can change his position from ignorance or passion to goodness.

3. One's particular faith is evolved according to one's existence under the various modes. He becomes similar to whatever form he worships with such faith.

Everyone has a particular type of faith, regardless of what he is. According to his faith, one associates with certain persons. The real fact is that every *jīva* is originally a fragmental part of the Supreme Lord (15.7) and is therefore transcendental to the three modes. But when one forgets his relationship with the Lord in contact with the material nature, he generates his own position by association with the modes. The resultant artificial faith and existence are only material.

4. Worship in different modes –

- **In goodness,** one worships *devatās* for a purpose.
- **In passion,** one worships demons.
- **In ignorance,** one worships ghosts and spirits.

17.2-4 describe those who have given up scripture out of laziness or because the required worship was troublesome, yet faithfully worship the devatās. 17.5-6, in contrast, describe the demoniac way of worship, which is against the Vedic practices.

5-6. Demoniac austerity –

- Not recommended in the scriptures, but done out of pride and ego (with ulterior motives; for instance, to promote a political or social end)
- Impelled by lust, attachment and strength
- Foolishly torture the body as well as the Supersoul within

7. Even the food, sacrifices, austerities and charity of people are of three kinds, according to the three modes of material nature. Now hear about them.

One can make out a person's mode of *faith* by seeing his activities of eating (*āhāra*), sacrifice (*yajña*), austerity (*tapa*) and charity (*dāna*). Kṛṣṇa will describe the three types of each of these four items.

8-10: Foods in Three Modes

8. Foods in mode of goodness	
āyuḥ-sattva-balārogya-	One's lifespan, purity, strength, health,
sukha-prīti-vivardhanāḥ	happiness and satisfaction will increase by such foods.
rasyāḥ snigdhāḥ sthirā hṛdyā	They are juicy, fatty, wholesome, and pleasing to heart.
āhārāḥ sāttvika-priyāḥ	Such are the foods dear to people in goodness.

9. Foods in mode of passion	
kaṭv-amla-lavaṇāty-uṣṇa-	Foods that are excessively bitter, sour, salty, hot,
tīkṣṇa-rūkṣa-vidāhinaḥ	pungent, dry and burning
āhārā rājasasyeṣṭā	are dear to those in the mode of passion.
duḥkha-śokāmaya-pradāḥ	They cause distress, lamentation and disease.

10. Foods in mode of ignorance	
yāta-yāmaṁ gata-rasaṁ	Foods which are stale, tasteless,
pūti paryuṣitaṁ ca yat	bad-smelling, decomposed, and
ucchiṣṭam api cāmedhyaṁ	consisting of remnants and untouchable things
bhojanaṁ tāmasa-priyam	is dear to those in the mode of darkness.

Remnants of food may be eaten only when they are first offered to the Supreme Lord or eaten by saintly persons, especially the spiritual master. The Vaiṣṇavas or devotees do not eat any food not offered to the Supreme Lord, even if it is food in goodness.

11-13: Sacrifices in Three Modes

11. Sacrifices in goodness

- Performed according to the scripture
- As a matter of duty
- Without desire for material results.

12. Sacrifices in passion

- Performed for some material benefits in this world (or elevation to heaven)
- For the sake of pride

13. Sacrifices in ignorance

- Performed without regard for the directions of scripture
- Without distribution of *prasādam* [spiritual food]
- Without chanting of Vedic hymns
- Without remunerations to the priests
- Without faith

14-19: Austerity in Three Modes

14-16: Three types of austerity

14. Austerity of body	
deva-dvija-guru-prājña-pūjanaṁ śaucam ārjavam	Worship of the Supreme Lord, *brāhmaṇas*, *guru* and superiors like the parents and cleanliness, simplicity
brahmacaryam ahiṁsā ca	celibacy and nonviolence –
śārīraṁ tapa ucyate	all these constitute the austerity of body.

15. Austerity of speech	
anudvega-karaṁ vākyaṁ	Speaking words that do not agitate others
satyaṁ priya-hitaṁ ca yat	that are truthful, pleasing, beneficial,
svādhyāyābhyasanaṁ caiva	and regular recition of Vedic literature –
vāṅ-mayaṁ tapa ucyate	all these constitute the austerity of speech.

Unagitating words: A teacher may speak the truth for the instruction of his students, but he should not speak to those who are not his students if he will agitate their minds. Besides that, one should not talk nonsense. Speaking in spiritual circles is to say something upheld by the scriptures, in a pleasing manner to elevate people.

16. Austerity of mind	
manaḥ-prasādaḥ saumyatvaṁ	Satisfaction, simplicity (no duplicity),
maunam ātma-vinigrahaḥ	gravity (silence), self-control
bhāva-saṁśuddhir ity etat	and purity of heart
tapo mānasam ucyate	are the austerities of the mind.

Mind's austerity is to detach it from unnecessary sense gratification. It should be so trained that it can be always thinking of doing good for others.

The above three types of austerity can be perfomed in three modes as described in the following three verses.

17-19: Austerity in three modes

17. Austerity in goodness is performed – (*i*) with transcendental faith, (*ii*) not expecting material benefits, and (*iii*) only for the sake of the Supreme.

18. Austerity in passion is performed – (*i*) out of pride, (*ii*) for respect, honor and worship from others; (*iii*) It is neither stable nor permanent.

19. Austerity in ignorance is performed – (*i*) out of foolishness, (*ii*) with self-torture or (*iii*) to destroy or injure others.

20-22: Charity in Three Modes

20. Charity in goodness is given – (*i*) out of duty, (*ii*) without expectation of return (*anupakāriṇe*), (*iii*) at the proper time and place, and (*iv*) to a worthy person.

21. Charity in passion is given – (*i*) with the expectation of reciprocation, (*ii*) with a desire for fruitive results, (*iii*) in a grudging mood, unwillingly.

22. Charity in ignorance is given – (*i*) at an impure place, (*ii*) at an improper time, (*iii*) to undeserving persons, or (*iv*) with disregard and discourtesy.

Contributions for indulgence in intoxication and gambling are not encouraged. Such charity is not beneficial; rather, sinful persons are encouraged.

So far, Kṛṣṇa has described the existence of a person under the three modes by his worship, food, austerity, sacrifice and charity, that determines one's quality of faith. All three modes and their combinations are defective and bind one to the material world. Now Kṛṣṇa will explain that all defects can be removed by chanting *Oṁ tat sat* (the names of Lord Viṣṇu) and that the activity itself will become transcendental. Thus the person who has non-scriptural faith can be gradually elevated.

23-28: Conclusion – Oṁ tat Sat

This section describes the right spirit of performing sacrifice (*yajña*), charity (*dāna*) and austerity (*tapa*), which is dedication to the Supreme Lord.

23. 'Oṁ tat sat' – these three words indicate the Supreme Absolute Truth (Viṣṇu) and are chanted by *brāhmaṇas* during sacrifices for the satisfaction of the Supreme.

24. 'Oṁ' – is always chanted in the beginning by those who perform sacrifice, charity and austerity in accordance with scriptural regulations, to attain the Supreme.

25. 'Tat' – is uttered by persons aspiring for liberation from material entanglement, perform sacrifice, austerity and charity without desiring fruitive results.

26-27. 'Sat' – is used to indicate the Absolute Truth (*sad-bhāve*) and also the knower or seeker of Absolute Truth and the performer of sacrifice (*sādhu-bhāve*). All auspicious works of sacrifice, austerity and charity are performed to please the Supreme Person. Any work dedicated to the Lord is permanent and is called *sat.*

28. Asat: Any sacrifice, charity or austerity done without faith in the Supreme is impermanent. It is called *asat* and is useless both in this life and the next.

aśraddhayā hutaṁ dattaṁ tapas taptaṁ kṛtaṁ ca yat
asad ity ucyate pārtha na ca tat pretya no iha

18. Conclusion: The Perfection of Renunciation

- **1-12:** Freedom from bondage through Karma-yoga
  - 1: Arjuna's inquiry on sannyāsa and tyāga
  - 2-6: Kṛṣṇa defines sannyāsa and tyāga. He gives two opinions on tyāga and then His own opinion.
  - 7-9: Renunciation (tyāga) in three modes
  - 10-12: The wise and true renunciant; The result of not renouncing
- **13-17:** The five factors of action
  - 13-15: Causes of all right and wrong actions – adhiṣṭhānaṁ (body), kartā (doer), karaṇam (senses), cestā (effort) and daivam (Supersoul)
  - 16-17: Doership and non-doership mentalities
- **18-40:** The modes control all activities and all beings
  - 18-19: Three motivators and three constituents of action
  - 20-22: Knowledge (jñāna) in three modes
  - 23-25: Work (karma) in three modes
  - 26-28: Worker (karta) in three modes
  - 29-32: Intelligence or understanding (buddhi) in three modes
  - 33-35: Determination (dhṛti) in three modes
  - 36-40: Happiness (sukhaṁ) in three modes
- **41-48:** Purification through prescribed duties of Varṇāśrama
  - 41-44: The four social orders (varṇas) and their qualities
  - 45-48: Importance of sticking to one's prescribed duty
- **49-55:** Brahman platform (Confidential knowledge)
  - 49-53: The perfect stage of sannyāsa and the process of attaiining Brahman
  - 54-55: From Brahma-bhūta stage to bhakti by which one can know Kṛṣṇa and attain His abode

- **56-66:** Pure Bhakti – Acting in Kṛṣṇa Consciousness
  - 56-60: Working and not working in Kṛṣṇa consciousness
  - 61-63: Surrendering to the Supersoul (More confidential knowledge)
  - 64-66: Surrendering to Lord Kṛṣṇa (Most confidential knowledge)
- **67-78:** The conclusion
  - 67-71: Glory of studying and teaching Bhagavad-gīta
  - 72-73: Realizations of Arjuna
  - 74-78: Realizations of Sañjaya

In the previous chapters, a description of various systems of *yoga* has been presented and the supremacy of *bhakti-yoga* has been emphasized.

In this final chapter, Lord Kṛṣṇa gives an overview of *Bhagavad-gīta*, and stresses that *bhakti*, devotional service in loving surrender to Kṛṣṇa, is the ultimate goal of life. Kṛṣṇa begins by reiterating His prescription that Arjuna should renounce the fruit of work, not work itself. Thus Kṛṣṇa reviews that "dutiful, detached work is true renunciation which brings no reaction."

1-12: Freedom From Bondage Through Karma-yoga

Gist of the section: Performing prescribed actions in the mood of renunciation is better than renouncing the action itself. This is a summary of the first six chapters.

1. Arjuna's inquiry on sannyāsa and tyāga: "O Keśi-niṣūdana, O Hṛṣīkeśa (master of the senses), O Mahā-bāho (mighty armed one), I wish to understand the purpose of renunciation (*tyāga*) and of the renounced order of life (*sannyāsa*)."

Doubts are compared to demons. Arjuna addresses Kṛṣṇa as Keśi-niṣūdana, the killer of Keśī demon, expecting Him to kill the demon of his doubt. Arjuna wanted to know if two words *sannyāsa* and *tyāga* that Kṛṣṇa spoke earlier have different or similar meanings? Now Kṛṣṇa will explain this subject as follows:

2. Kṛṣṇa defines sannyāsa and tyāga	
kāmyānāṁ karmaṇāṁ nyāsaṁ sannyāsaṁ kavayo viduḥ	**Sannyāsa** or renounced order of life is giving up of *kāmya-karmas* or activities based on material desire. The learned say so.
sarva-karma-phala-tyāgaṁ prāhus tyāgaṁ vicakṣaṇāḥ	**Tyāga** or renunciation is giving up the *results* of all activities. The wise say so.

Two type of activities:

i. *Nitya-karmas* – daily obligatory activities prescribed by the scriptures (like *sandhyā-vandana* etc)

ii. *Kāmya-karmas* – activities for fulfilling particular personal desires (like elevation to heavens, getting a good son etc).

Sannyāsa Vs. tyāga: In *sannyāsa* one gives up *kāmya-karmas*, and performs *nitya-karmas*. In *tyāga* one performs all *kāmya-karmas* and *nitya-karmas*, but without seeking results. Acting for results has to be given up. But activities leading to advanced spiritual knowledge, purification and liberation are not to be given up.

3. Two opinions about tyāga

i. **Give up all** fruitive activities as faulty, because there is a possibility of violence in the acts of sacrifice (the followers of Kapila's *sāṅkhya* say so).

ii. **Never give up** the acts of sacrifice (*yajña*), charity (*dāna*) and austerity (*tapa*), because one incurs no sin from performing what is prescribed in the Vedas, even if it involves violence (the followers of Jaimini say so).

After describing different opinions about *tyāga*, Kṛṣṇa states His own opinion in the next few verses.

4-6: Kṛṣṇa's opinion about tyāga

4. Renunciation is of three kinds (see 18.7-9), in terms of the modes of nature in which it is performed, O *puruṣa-vyāghra* (tiger amongst men[1]).

5. Never give up acts of sacrifice, charity and austerity	
yajña-dāna-tapaḥ-karma	Acts of sacrifice, charity and austerity
na tyājyaṁ kāryam eva tat	are not to be given up; they must be performed.
yajño dānaṁ tapaś caiva	Indeed, sacrifice, charity and austerity
pāvanāni manīṣiṇām	purify even the great souls.

6. Mood of performing actions –

i. without attachment or doership mentality (*saṅgaṁ tyaktvā*)

ii. without expectation of result (*phalāni ca*).

iii. as a matter of duty (*kartavyāni*)

---

[1] Kṛṣṇa calls Arjuna tiger amongst men, because just as a tiger cannot be overcome by small animals in the forest, a devotee like Arjuna cannot be overcome by misconceptions or varied opinions of philospohers.

In Kṛṣṇa's opinion, *tyāga* and *sannyāsa* are essentially the same, i.e., there is no difference between renounced order of life and renunciation of the fruits of work. Thus both these words are equated as "renunciation."

7-9: Renunciation (tyāga) in three modes

7. Tyāga in ignorance: Giving up prescribed, obligatory duties (*nitya-karma* or *niyataṁ karma*) due to illusion (*mohāt*) or lack of scriptural knowledge.

A *sannyāsī* may give up *kāmya-karmas* since they are not obligatory, but not the *nitya-karmas*, because they give liberation through the knowledge inherent in them.

8. Tyāga in passion: Giving up prescribed duties as troublesome or out of fear of bodily discomfort (*kāya kleśa bhāyāt*). It never leads to elevation.

9. Tyāga in goodness: To perform prescribed duty only because it is ought to be done, without material association (*saṅgam tyaktvā*) and desire for results (*phalam caiva*), i.e., without a sense of doership.

10. The wise renunciant (*medhāvī*) fixed in goodness (*sattvic tyāga*) is neither hateful of inauspicious work (uncomfortable for the body) nor attached to auspicious work (pleasurable for the body); he has no doubts about work.

na dveṣṭy akuśalaṁ karma kuśale nānuṣajjate
tyāgī sattva-samāviṣṭo medhāvī chinna-saṁśayaḥ

Is it better to completely give up actions rather than simply giving up the results? – Actually completely giving up action is impossible (see 3.5 also)!

11. A true renunciant (*tyāgī*) is he who renounces the results of action (*karma-phala-tyāgī*), for it is impossible for an embodied being to completely give up all actions.

12. If one is not renounced (*atyāginām*), his actions will lead to three kinds of results after death – (*i*) *iṣṭam:* desirable, heavenly enjoyment, (*ii*) *aniṣṭam:* undesirable, hellish suffering, and (*iii*) *miśram:* mixed, human birth. One who is renounced has no such result to suffer or enjoy. He is free from bondage.

Since any action must have some reaction, how is it that a *karma-yogī* with the spirit of renunciation avoids bondage to *kārmic* reactions? – "There is no *kārmic* reaction when one works without the false identification as the doer and with conviction that the Supreme Lord is the main doer. Such a person has the knowledge (*jñāna*) of the various causes of action." – In order to establish this principle, Lord Kṛṣṇa speaks the next five verses.

13-17: The Five Factors of Action

13-14. The five causes of an action according to the Vedānta are –

i. **adhiṣṭhānaṁ:** the place of action or the body of the *jīva*
ii. **kartā:** the doer of action, or the consciousness reflected in the false ego
iii. **karaṇaṁ:** the instruments of action, the various senses
iv. **ceṣṭā:** the effort exerted by the life airs with various functions
v. **daivam:** the Supersoul who sets everything into motion by His supreme will

adhiṣṭhānaṁ tathā kartā karaṇaṁ ca pṛthag-vidham
vividhāś ca pṛthak ceṣṭā daivaṁ caivātra pañcamam [14]

15. These five factors cause all the right actions prescribed in the scriptures (*nyāyyaṁ*) and the wrong actions opposed to the scriptures (*viparītam*), that a man performs by body, words and mind (physical, vocal and mental actions).

The *jīva's* acting as a doer takes place only with the Lord's permission, and depends upon the body and senses given by the Lord. But one who sees only the *jīva* as the doer of action is foolish.

16. Doership mentality: One who thinks himself the *only* doer of actions, not considering these five factors, is certainly foolish (*durmati*) due to impure intelligence (*akṛta-buddhitvāt*) and cannot see things as they are, like a blind man.

17. Non-doership mentality: One who is not motivated by false ego (*nāhaṅkṛto*), whose intelligence is not entangled, does not actually kill people even though he kills them and thus he is not contaminated or bound by his actions.

18-40: The Modes Control All Activities and All Beings

18a. Three motivators of action

i. *jñānaṁ* – knowledge
ii. *jñeyaṁ* – object of knowledge
iii. *parijñātā* – knower

18b. Three constituents of action

i. *karma* – work
ii. *karaṇaṁ* – instruments of work (senses)
iii. *karta* – worker / doer

An action is motivated by the knower (*parijñātā*) who has the knowledge (*jñānaṁ*) of the knowable (*jñeyaṁ*). In other words, an activity is motivated by a person (knower) perceiving a desirable object or goal. With such inspiration or impetus, the doer (*karta*) carries out the work (*karma*) with the senses (*karaṇaṁ*).

Even the motivators of action and the constituents of action are under the dictates of the material modes of nature. Kṛṣṇa will now describe the effects of the three modes of nature (as He did in Chapters 14 and 17) in the next section. He begins with how the three modes will affect three of the six factors He mentioned in 18.18.

19. According to the three modes, there are three kinds of knowledge (*jñāna*), work (*karma*) and worker (*karta*). Now hear of them from Me.

20-22: Knowledge (jñāna) in three modes

20. Jñāna in goodness is that by which one undivided spiritual nature (spirit soul) is seen in all living beings, though they exist in innumerable forms like a devatā, human being, animal, bird, beast, aquatic or plant and so on.

21. Jñāna in passion is that by which one sees that there is a different type of living entity in different types of bodies (various opinions about the soul).

Different opinions about soul: The body is the soul; the soul is different from the body but the same size as the body; the soul is just momentary knowledge; the soul is God, consisting of eternal knowledge; the soul, different from the body, is a conscious, all pervasive entity giving shelter to different qualities and so on.

22. Jñāna in ignorance is that by which one is attached to one kind of work as all in all, without knowing the truth, and which is very meager.

Summary: Knowledge about the spirit soul beyond this body is in *sattva-guṇa*, knowledge producing many theories by dint of mundane logic and speculation is the product of *rajo-guṇa*, and knowledge concerned only with keeping the body comfortable is said to be in *tamo-guṇa*.

23-25: Work (karma) in three modes

23. Karma in goodness	24. Karma in passion	25. Karma in ignorance
• Regulated (*niyatam*) • Done with detachment (*saṅga-rahitam*) • Without like or dislike (*arāga-dveṣa*) • With no desire for fruitive results (*aphala-prepsunā*)	• Done with great labor (*bahula-āyāsam*) • Done seeking to gratify one's desires (*kāma-īpsunā*), • Done with false ego (*sa-ahaṅkāreṇa*)	• Leads to bondage by Yamadūtas (*anubandhaṁ*), • Destructive (*kṣayaṁ*) • Harmful to self and others (*hiṁsām*) • Without considering consequences (*anapekṣya*) • Disregarding scriptures, • In illusion (*mohāt*)

26-28: Worker (karta) in three modes

26. Karta in goodness	27. Karta in passion	28. Karta in ignorance
• Detached (*mukta-saṅga*)	• Attached to work (*ragī*) • Desires to enjoy results	• Acts against the scriptures (*ayuktaḥ*)

• Devoid of false ego (*anahaṁ*) • Determined (*dhṛti*) • Enthusiastic (*utsāha*) • Unwavering in success or failure (*nirvikāraḥ*)	• Greedy (*lubdha*) • Envious (*hiṁsā-ātmakaḥ*) • Impure (*aśuciḥ*) • Subject to joy and sorrow (*harṣa-śoka-anvitaḥ*)	• Materialistic and whimsical (*prākṛtaḥ*) • Obstinate (*stabdhaḥ*) • Cheating (*śaṭhaḥ*) • Expert in insulting others (*naiṣkṛtikaḥ*) • Lazy (*alasaḥ*) • Morose (*viṣādī*) • Procrastinating (*dīrgha-sūtrī*)

29. O conqueror of wealth, now hear about the three types of intelligence (*buddhi*) and determination (*dhṛti*), according to the three modes of material nature.

30-32: Intelligence or understanding (buddhi) in three modes

30. Buddhi in goodness	27. Buddhi in passion	28. Buddhi in ignorance
One knows what is – • to be done and not to be done • to be feared and not to be feared • binding and liberating	One cannot distinguish between – • religion and irreligion, • action to be done and not to be done	• Considers irreligion to be religion and religion to be irreligion • Takes everything in the opposite direction of the truth

33-35: Determination (dhṛti) in three modes

33. Dhṛti in goodness	34. Dhṛti in passion	35. Dhṛti in ignorance
• unbreakable • sustained by *yoga* practice • controls the activities of the mind, life and senses	Desiring fruitive results (*phalākāṅkṣī*) in religion, economic development and sense gratification, in the association of similar people (*prasaṅgena*).	Cannot go beyond dreaming[1] (*svapnam*), fearfulness (*bhayam*), lamentation (*śokam*), moroseness (*viṣādam*) and illusion (*madam*)

[1] It should not be concluded that a person in the mode of goodness does not dream. Here "dream" means too much sleep. Dreaming is a natural occurrence and is present in any mode.

36-39: Happiness (sukhaṁ) in three modes

36-37. Sukhaṁ in goodness	38. Sukhaṁ in passion	39. Sukhaṁ in ignorance
• Brings joy and destroys sorrow by practice • Like poison in the beginning • Becomes nectar at the end • Arises from purity of intellect, awakens one to self-realization	• Arises from contact of the senses with sense objects • Appears like nectar in the beginning • Becomes poison at the end	• Blind to self-realization • Delusion from beginning to end • Arises from sleep, laziness and illusion or intoxication

40. Summary of the influence of modes: There is no being existing on earth or heavens, which is freed from these three modes born of material nature.

na tad asti pṛthivyāṁ vā divi deveṣu vā punaḥ
sattvaṁ prakṛti-jair muktaṁ yad ebhiḥ syāt tribhir guṇaiḥ

Here Kṛṣṇa includes all other things that He did not mention so far. Among all things made of the three *guṇas*, those in the mode of goodness should be accepted because they alone are useful, and those things in the lower modes should be rejected.

The living body filled with the three modes becomes successful by worshipping the Supreme Lord by prescribed activities according to one's acquired nature. This is described in the next six verses.

41-48: Purification Through Prescribed Duties of Varṇāśrama

41-44: The four social orders (varṇas) and their qualities

41. The four varṇas – *brāhmaṇas, kṣatriyas, vaiśyas* and *śūdras* are distinguished by the activities and qualities born of their own natures in accordance with the modes.

42. Qualities of brāhmaṇas	
śamo damas tapaḥ śaucaṁ	Peacefulness, self-control, austerity, cleanliness,
kṣāntir ārjavam eva ca	tolerance, honesty,
jñānaṁ vijñānaṁ āstikyaṁ	knowledge, wisdom and religiousness—these are the
brahma-karma svabhāva-jam	natural qualities by which the *brāhmaṇas* work.

43. Qualities of kṣatriyas	
śauryaṁ tejo dhṛtir dākṣyaṁ	Heroism, power, determination, resourcefulness,
yuddhe cāpy apalāyanam	courage in battle (not fleeing),
dānam īśvara-bhāvaś ca	generosity and leadership (controlling others)
kṣātraṁ karma svabhāva-jam	are the natural qualities of work for the *kṣatriyas*.

44. Qualities of vaiśyas and śūdras	
kṛṣi-go-rakṣya-vāṇijyaṁ	Farming, cow protection and business
vaiśya-karma svabhāva-jam	are the natural duties for the *vaiśyas*.
paricaryātmakaṁ karma	Labor and service to other *varṇas*
śūdrasyāpi svabhāva-jam	are the natural duties of *śūdras*.

Modes of varṇas –

- *Brāhmaṇa* are predominantly in *sattva-guṇa*.
- *Kṣatiryas* are predominantly in *rajo-guṇa* with *sattva* as a secondary mode
- *Vaiśya* are predominantly in *raja-guṇa* with *tamas* as secondary mode
- *Śūdra* are predominantly in *tamo-guṇa* with *rajas* as a secondary mode

45-48: Importance of sticking to one's prescribed duty

45-46. Everyone can become perfect by performing his particular duties and **worshiping the Supreme Lord**, who is all-pervading and the source of all beings.

yataḥ pravṛttir bhūtānāṁ yena sarvam idaṁ tatam
sva-karmaṇā tam abhyarcya siddhiṁ vindati mānavaḥ

The worship consists of offering the work in the mind, thinking, "By this work may the Lord be satisfied."

Because the duties of the *kṣatiryas* and others are composed of the lower *guṇas*, should one perform the duties of the *brāhmaṇas* in *sattva guṇa*?

47. It is better to do one's own duties (as a *brāhmaṇa, kṣatriya, vaiśya* and *śūdra*) even imperfectly, than to do another's duties perfectly. Duties prescribed according to one's own nature are not affected by sinful reactions.

śreyān sva-dharmo viguṇaḥ para-dharmāt sv-anuṣṭhitāt
svabhāva-niyataṁ karma kurvan nāpnoti kilbiṣam

48. All endeavors are covered by some fault, just as fire is covered by smoke. So, one should not give up the work born of his nature, even if it has some fault.

A *brāhmaṇa* has to perform sacrifices in which animal killing is necessary. A *kṣatriya*, however pious he may be, has to fight enemies. Similarly, a merchant must sometimes hide his profit to stay in business and a *śūdra* may sometimes have to serve a bad master. Despite these flaws, one should continue to carry out his prescribed duties, for they are born out of his own nature. Just as by removing the smoke, the fire is useful for removing darkness and cold, so by removing the faulty portion of one's work, the good portion is useful for purification of one's existence.

49-55: BRAHMAN PLATFORM (CONFIDENTIAL KNOWLEDGE)

Gist of the section: In this section Kṛṣṇa describes the transition from reaction-free work through *jñāna-yoga* to the Brahman platform to pure devotioanl service. The perfection of *jñāna-yoga* is to understand the nature of the self and it's relationship with Kṛṣṇa; thus *bhakti* is the culmination of *jñāna*.

Reaction-free work through Jñāna-yoga → Brahman Platform → Pure Bhakti

The first type of *sannyāsī* gives up the doership mentality in work and attachment to the results of work. When that *sannyāsī* perfects his *sādhana* over time, then he gives up the work completely. That is called *yogārūḍha* stage. That is the second type of *sannyāsa* that Kṛṣṇa mentions now:

49. Perfect stage of sannyāsa: One – (*i*) whose intelligence is detached from all material objects (*asakta-buddhiḥ sarvatra*), (*ii*) whose mind is controlled (*jitātmā*) and (*iii*) who is without material desires (*vigata-spṛhaḥ*) – by complete renunciation of all activities (*sannyāsena*), attains the highest perfection of no action and reaction (*naiṣkarmya-siddhiṁ*).

50. Know how to attain Brahman: Having attained such perfection by cessation of all work, one realizes Brahman, the stage of highest knowledge, *jñāna*. Now hear the process of realizing that Brahman.

51-53. The process of attaining Brahman (Brahma-bhūta stage)	
buddhyā viśuddhayā yukto	(1) Being purified by *sattvic* intelligence
dhṛtyātmānaṁ niyamya ca	(2) controlling the mind with determination
śabdādīn viṣayāṁs tyaktvā	(3) giving up all sense objects like sound
rāga-dveṣau vyudasya ca	(4) being freed from attachment and repulsion
vivikta-sevī *laghv-āśī*	(5) living in a secluded place (6) eating little

yata-vāk-kāya-mānasaḥ	(7) controlling one's speech, body and mind
dhyāna-yoga-paro nityaṁ	(8) absorption in meditating on the Lord
vairāgyaṁ samupāśritaḥ	(9) taking shelter of detachment
ahaṅkāraṁ balaṁ darpaṁ kāmaṁ krodhaṁ parigraham	(10) freed from false ego, false strength, false pride, lust, anger, and material possessions
vimucya nirmamaḥ śānto	(11) freed from false proprietorship and (12) peaceful (like an ocean without waves)
brahma-bhūyāya kalpate	—such a person can attain Brahman (self-realization).

In the stage of *brahma-bhūta,* one is completely devoid of all contamination of the material modes, and becomes fully joyful or peaceful, a pure soul (*prasanna-ātmā*). After realizing one's self in this way, one can attain pure *bhakti* unto Lord Kṛṣṇa.

54. Brahma-bhuta stage to Bhakti (Brahman realization to Bhagavān realization)	
brahma-bhūtaḥ prasannātmā	One who is thus situated (18.51-53) at once realizes the Supreme Brahman and becomes fully joyful.
na śocati na kāṅkṣati	He never laments or desires anything.
samaḥ sarveṣu bhūteṣu	He is equally disposed toward every living entity.
mad-bhaktiṁ labhate parām	In that state (beyond the modes) he attains pure devotional service unto Me (*prema-bhakti*).

The *brahma-bhūta* stage of self-realization or liberation is the final aspiration of an impersonalist. But *bhakti* is beyond Brahman realization. A personalist, or pure devotee, aspires to do *bhakti* or pure devotional service unto Lord Kṛṣṇa. A devotee is already in a state of liberation or oneness with the Absolute. Without being one with the Lord on a spiritual platform, one cannot render service unto Him.

55. By bhakti one can know Kṛṣṇa and attain His abode	
bhaktyā mām abhijānāti yāvān yaś cāsmi tattvataḥ	One can understand Me as I am, as the Supreme Personality of Godhead, only by devotional service.
tato māṁ tattvato jñātvā	And when one thus knows Me fully in truth, and is in full consciousness of Me,
viśate tad-anantaram	he can enter the spiritual world, the kingdom of God.

Supreme Lord Kṛṣṇa is not revealed to everyone (See 7.25). He and His expansions or incarnations cannot be understood by scholarship or speculation. He is known only by performing *bhakti* under the guidance of a pure *bhakta.*

Having described how a *jñānī* progresses step by step by giving up the results of work, then the work itself and then attains liberation (*sāyujya*), Kṛṣṇa will now explain how His devotee (*bhakta*) attains Him.

56-66: Pure Bhakti – Acting in Kṛṣṇa Consciousness

56-60: Working and not working in Kṛṣṇa consciousness

56. Activities in bhakti lead to Kṛṣṇa's abode	
sarva-karmāṇy api sadā kurvāṇo mad-vyapāśrayaḥ	My pure devotee, although doing all kinds of activities always, is under My protection,
mat-prasādād avāpnoti	By My mercy, he reaches
śāśvataṁ padam avyayam	the eternal and imperishable abode of Mine.

57. So, work in Kṛṣṇa consciousness	
cetasā sarva-karmāṇi mayi sannyasya mat-paraḥ	Offer all your activities unto Me and just depend on My protection, making Me the goal of your life.
buddhi-yogam upāśritya	Taking shelter of *bhakti-yoga* with fixed intelligence,
mac-cittaḥ satataṁ bhava	be always conscious of Me (while doing your actions).

Acting in Kṛṣṇa consciousness means to act under the direction of the Supreme Lord just like a faithful servant, not independently. Acting according to the direction of Kṛṣṇa in the *Bhagavad-gīta*, and acting under the guidance of a bona fide *guru*, Kṛṣṇa's representative, are the same. While working according to Kṛṣṇa's orders, one naturally has to think of Kṛṣṇa. This is perfect Kṛṣṇa consciousness.

58a. Result of working in Kṛṣṇa consciousness	
mac-cittaḥ sarva-durgāṇi mat-prasādāt tariṣyasi	If you become conscious of Me, you will cross over all the obstacles in life by My grace.

For one who acts in Kṛṣṇa consciousness, Kṛṣṇa becomes the most intimate friend and always looks after His friend's comfort. Kṛṣṇa gives Himself to His friend and removes all of his sufferings.

58b-60. Result of not following Kṛṣṇa	
atha cet tvam ahaṅkārān na śroṣyasi vinaṅkṣyasi	But if do not hear Me, and act out of pride and false ego, you will perish.

59-60. One works as per his nature anyway: Out of false identity (*ahaṅkāra*), and illusion (*mohāt*), if you think of not fighting, such resolve is only misdirection. You will fight anyway, even against your own will (*avaśaḥ*), as you are bound by actions arising from your *kṣatriya* nature (*svabhāvajena karmaṇā*) and the modes, O Arjuna.

Voluntarily acting according to the Lord's directions keeps one safe in all situations, because no one can ascertain one's destiny as the Supreme Lord can. Otherwise, he is compelled to act by the modes in which he is situated.

Seeing that Arjuna still seemed to have the false concept of thinking he knew everything, and because of Arjuna's inability to give that up, Lord Kṛṣṇa teaches him in a different way in the next two verses.

61-63: Surrendering to the Supersoul (More confidential knowledge)

61. Supersoul is the master and director	
īśvaraḥ sarva-bhūtānāṁ hṛd-deśe 'rjuna tiṣṭhati	The Supreme Lord is situated in the heart of all living entities (See 15.15 also), O Arjuna.
bhrāmayan sarva-bhūtāni	He is directing the wanderings of all of them,
yantrārūḍhāni māyayā	who are seated as on a machine (body), under the spell of material energy (like dolls moving by strings).

After changing bodies, the living entity forgets his past deeds. Kṛṣṇa, as the Supersoul in heart, the knower of the past, present and future, remains as the witness of all his activities. By His order, the material nature fashions a particular type of body to a particular type of *jīva* so that he may work according to his past desires.

62. Surrender unto Supersoul	
tam eva śaraṇaṁ gaccha	Take shelter of the Supersoul
sarva-bhāvena bhārata	with full devotion (all of heart's emotions), O Arjuna.
tat-prasādāt parāṁ śāntiṁ	By His mercy you will attain transcendental peace
sthānaṁ prāpsyasi śāśvatam	and you will attain the supreme eternal abode.

The purpose of the knowledge just revealed is to take shelter of the Lord. This surrender to the Supersoul is for worshippers of Kṛṣṇa's expansion as the Supersoul (Paramātmā), whereas the worshippers of Bhagavān surrender directly to the personality of Kṛṣṇa, which will be explained in 18.65-66.

63. Now do as you wish: Thus I have explained to you this greatly confidential knowledge of the scripture *Gīta* (the means of understanding *karma*, *bhakti* and *jñāna*). Deliberate on this fully, and then do what you wish to do.

iti te jñānam ākhyātaṁ guhyād guhyataraṁ mayā
vimṛśyaitad aśeṣeṇa yathecchasi tathā kuru

The concluding words *yathecchasi tathā kuru*—"As you like, you may act"—indicate that God does not interfere with our little independence. He doesn't force anyone to act according to his instructions, but gives knowledge and then allows people to act as per their choice.

Arjuna stood silently reviewing the very deep meaning of the *Gīta* scripture. Glancing at His dear friend, Kṛṣṇa's merciful heart melted like butter and He spoke. "O My dear friend Arjuna, I will now speak the essence of the whole scripture in few verses. Forget about the difficulties in having to review everything to understand it." Thus the following verses reveal the essence of *Bhagavad-gīta*, to be applied in everyone's life.

64-66: Surrendering to Lord Kṛṣṇa (Most confidential knowledge)

Kṛṣṇa has given Arjuna the confidential knowledge of Brahman (18.51-54) and still more confidential knowledge of the Supersoul (18.61-63), and now He will give the most confidential knowledge of surrendering unto the Supreme Personality of Godhead (18.64-66).

64. Again hear My supreme instruction (*paramaṁ vacaḥ*), the **most confidential knowledge** of all (*sarva-guhyatamaṁ*). I speak this for your benefit, because you are My very dear (*iṣṭa*) friend, having faith in My authority.

sarva-guhyatamaṁ bhūyaḥ śṛṇu me paramaṁ vacaḥ
iṣṭo 'si me dṛḍham iti tato vakṣyāmi te hitam

Kṛṣṇa tells Arjuna to *again* (*bhūyaḥ*) hear the supreme and most secret knowledge (greater than what He said in 18.62), because He has already revealed it at the end of Chapter Nine (9.34). Kṛṣṇa will now repeat it to stress the essence of the teachings of *Bhagavad-gīta*; in fact it is the essence of all scriptures. There is no secret greater than this, in any place, from any cause, by any means.

65. Essence of Bhagavad-gīta – Devotion to Kṛṣṇa	
man-manā bhava mad-bhakto	(*i*) Always think of Me, (*ii*) become My devotee,
mad-yājī māṁ namaskuru	(*iii*) worship Me and (*iv*) offer your respects to Me.
mām evaiṣyasi satyaṁ te	Thus you will come to Me without fail.
pratijāne priyo 'si me	I promise you this because you are My dear friend.

Man-manā or concentration of the mind on Kṛṣṇa constitutes the most confidential part of knowledge. That original form of Godhead, Kṛṣṇa, is with two hands carrying a flute, the bluish boy with a beautiful face and peacock feathers in His hair.

Bhava mad-bhakto is to be Kṛṣṇa's devotee. Kṛṣṇa excludes the other possibilities of thinking of Him by being a *jñānī* or a *yogī* etc. One should serve Kṛṣṇa by all one's senses by hearing, chanting, seeing His deity, cleaning temple, picking flowers etc.

Mad-yājī means worshiping Kṛṣṇa by offering Him flowers, garlands, ornaments, incense, lamp, *gandha*, *naivedya*, umbrella and *cāmara*.

Māṁ namaskuru means to fall on the ground with the whole body, offer respects to Kṛṣṇa, by touching the body to the ground with eight limbs.

Mām eva eṣyasi means by doing any one or all of the abive four activities—one can attain Kṛṣṇa. **Satyam te**: Kṛṣṇa makes an oath, "I will give Myself to you."

"How is it possible for men whose hearts are contaminated with unlimited sins to perform pure *bhakti* to Kṛṣṇa like this, unless those sins are first destroyed (Kṛṣṇa also says this in 7.28) by following prescribed *dharma* with atonements?" – Kṛṣṇa will now answer that even if one is not freed from sins, one can surrender to Him and He will deliver them from those sins.

66. Conclusion of Bhagavad-gīta – Surrender unto Kṛṣṇa	
sarva-dharmān parityajya	Give up all varieties of religion.
mām ekaṁ śaraṇaṁ vraja	Just surrender unto Me alone (not devatās or others).
ahaṁ tvāṁ sarva-pāpebhyo *mokṣayiṣyāmi mā śucaḥ*	I shall deliver you from all sinful reactions. Do not fear or worry.

The final conclusion: Kṛṣṇa described in the *Gīta* various kinds of knowledge—about Brahman, Supersoul, *varṇāśrama*, *sannyāsa*, *tyāga*, sense and mind control, meditation, etc. He has described in so many ways different types of *dharmas*. Now, in concluding the *Gīta*, He says that Arjuna should give up all such processes and simply surrender to Kṛṣṇa.

Kṛṣṇa is instructing the whole world taking Arjuna as the means. One should give up anxiety for one's own welfare or that of others, and surrender unto Kṛṣṇa by one's thoughts and actions in contentment. One should confidently accept Kṛṣṇa as the supreme savior of all living entities, with faith and love. Kṛṣṇa has accepted the burden of protecting such surrendered souls and freeing them from all sin, and this *saṁsāra* (See 9.22 also).

Having completed His teachings, Kṛṣṇa will now speak of the glory of the *Gīta* and the result of hearing it (*phala-śruti*). Having given the instructions of the scripture of the *Gītā*, the Lord now indicates the process for passing on this knowledge.

67-78: Glory of Studying and Teaching Bhagavad-gīta

67-78: Glory of studying and teaching Bhagavad-gīta

67. These teachings of the Gīta are not to be given to those who are –

i. *atapaskāya* – not austere and sense controlled
ii. *abhaktāya* – without true devotion
iii. *aśuśrūṣave* – unwilling to hear or not engaged in obedient service
iv. *abhyasūyati* – envious of Me

68-69. Benefits of teaching Bhagavad-gīta	
ya idaṁ paramaṁ guhyaṁ mad-bhakteṣv abhidhāsyati	One who explains this supreme secret of *Bhagavad-gīta* to My devotees, will –
bhaktiṁ mayi parāṁ kṛtvā	(*i*) attain pure devotional service unto Me
mām evaiṣyaty asaṁśayaḥ	(*ii*) come back to Me without doubt
na ca tasmān manuṣyeṣu kaścin me priya-kṛttamaḥ bhavitā na ca me tasmād anyaḥ priyataro bhuvi	(*iii*) become most dear to Me: There is no servant in this world more dear to Me than he, nor will there ever be one more dear in future.

70. Benefits of studying Bhagavad-gīta: One who studies (*adhyeṣyate*) this sacred conversation (*dharmyam saṁvādam*) of ours worships Me by his intelligence or sacrifice of knowledge (*jñāna yajña*).

In 4.28, Kṛṣṇa stated the sacrifice of knowledge (*jñāna yajña*) is superior to the sacrifice of materials (*dravya-yajñāḥ*).

71. Benefits of hearing Bhagavad-gīta: One who listens with faith (*śraddhāvān*) and without envy (*anasūyaḥ*) – (*i*) becomes free from sinful reactions (*muktaḥ*) and (*ii*) attains to the auspicious planets where the pious dwell.

In 18.67, Kṛṣṇa said that the *Gīta* cannot be taught to non-devotees. But although not everyone is a devotee, still there are many men who are not envious of Kṛṣṇa. They have faith in Him as the Supreme Lord. If such persons hear from a bona fide devotee about the Lord, they attain the results mentioned in 18.71. So, the devotees sometimes hold public classes and give opportunity to common people to become devotees.

Thus either by teaching the *Gīta*, or by studying the *Gīta* or atleast hearing the *Gīta*, one will attain great transcendental results.

72-73: Realizations of Arjuna

72. Lord Kṛṣṇa asked Arjuna, "O Pārthā, have you heard this with an attentive mind (*ekāgreṇa cetasā*)? Are your ignorance (*ajñāna*) and bewilderment (*sammohaḥ*) now dispelled?

As per the request of Arjuna in 2.7, Kṛṣṇa acted as his *guru* and taught him the *Gīta*. Now Kṛṣṇa is dutifully asking His student whether he understood the *Bhagavad-gītā* in its proper perspective. If not, Kṛṣṇa was ready to re-explain it.

73. Arjuna informs Kṛṣṇa of his realizations	
naṣṭo mohaḥ *smṛtir labdhā*	(*i*) My illusion is now dispelled. (*ii*) I have regained my memory.
tvat-prasādān mayācyuta	All this happened by Your mercy, O infallible Lord.
sthito 'smi gata-sandehaḥ	(*iii*) I am now firm and free from all doubts.
kariṣye vacanaṁ tava	(*iv*) I am ready to follow Your instructions.

Kṛṣṇa consciousness is acting according to Kṛṣṇa's order. The constitutional position of a living entity, represented by Arjuna, is to act in such Kṛṣṇa consciousness. Here Arjuna says, "What else can I ask? Having given up all duties, surrendering to You completely, without worries, I now completely trust You and follow Your orders."

In the beginning of *Bhagavad-gītā*, Dhṛtarāṣṭra inquired from his secretary Sañjaya, about the scene on the Battlefield of Kurukṣetra. By the grace of Vyāsadeva, his *guru*, Sañjaya could see that scene within his heart and describe it to Dhṛtarāṣṭra. Now Sañjaya is sharing his realizations:

74-78: Realizations of Sañjaya

74. The conversation of Kṛṣṇa and Arjuna that I have heard is so wonderful (*adbhutaṁ*) that my hair is standing on end (*roma-harṣaṇam*).

75. By the mercy of Vyāsa, I have heard the most confidential talks (on *bhakti-yogaṁ*) directly from the master of all mysticism Kṛṣṇa, (*yogeśvarāt kṛṣṇāt*), who was speaking personally to Arjuna.

As Arjuna was fortunate enough to understand Kṛṣṇa directly, so, by the grace of his *guru* Vyāsa, Sañjaya was also able to hear Kṛṣṇa directly. One can understand Kṛṣṇa through the medium of the *guru*.

76. I repeatedly recall this wonderful, sacred conversation between Kṛṣṇa and Arjuna, and I take pleasure, being thrilled at every moment.

77. As I remember Kṛṣṇa's wonderful form (*rūpam aty-adbhutaṁ hareḥ*), I am struck with wonder (*vismaya*) more and more, and I rejoice (*hṛṣyāmi*) repeatedly and my hairs stand on end again and again.

78. The amazing combination of Kṛṣṇa and Arjuna	
yatra yogeśvaraḥ kṛṣṇo	Wherever there is Kṛṣṇa, the master of all mystics, and
yatra pārtho dhanur-dharaḥ	wherever there is Arjuna, the supreme archer,
tatra śrīr vijayo bhūtir dhruvā nītir matir mama	there will certainly be – (*i*) opulence or prosperity, (*ii*) victory, (*iii*) extraordinary power and (*iv*) morality. That is my opinion.

Victory: Dhṛtarāṣṭra was hopeful of the victory of his sons, assisted by great warriors like Bhīṣma, Droṇa and Karṇa. But after describing the scene on the battlefield, Sañjaya directly confirmed to him that victory will be on the side of Pāṇḍavas due to the presence of Kṛṣṇa and Arjuna.

Thematic Compilations

1. KṚṢṆA, THE SUPREME PERSONALITY OF GODHEAD

Lord Kṛṣṇa, the divine speaker of the *Bhagavad-gīta*, is referred to as *Bhagavān,* the Supreme Personality of Godhead. *Bhagavān* is a person who is full in six opulences, namely strength, fame, wealth, knowledge, beauty and renunciation. While Kṛṣṇa was present on this earth, He displayed all six opulences in full. Kṛṣṇa's greatness and sweetness are unparalleled. Kṛṣṇa's majestic opulence is awe-inspiring and His loving reciprocation is heart touching. The following compilation of *Gīta* verses give a glimpse of Lord Kṛṣṇa's unparalleled glories and prove that Kṛṣṇa is the Supreme Godhead, and not just one amongst many gods.

1. Kṛṣṇa is the source and basis of everything

- There is no truth superior to Kṛṣṇa. Everything rests upon Him, as pearls are strung on a thread. (*7.7 mattaḥ parataraṁ nānyat…*)
- Kṛṣṇa is the eternal divine person, the Supreme Absolute Brahman. (*10.12 paraṁ brahma paraṁ dhāma…*)
- Kṛṣṇa is the Supreme Person, overseer, permitter and proprietor (*13.23 upadraṣṭā anumantā ca…*)
- Kṛṣṇa is the basis of impersonal Brahman (*14.27 brahmaṇo hi pratiṣṭhāham…*)
- Ultimately everyone pursues Kṛṣṇa only, but in their own way (*4.11 ye yathā māṁ prapadyante…*)
- The entire universe and all the gods are within Kṛṣṇa's cosmic body. (11.5, 7)
- Kṛṣṇa is the origin of everything in all the material and spiritual realms. (*10.8 ahaṁ sarvasya prabhavo…*)
- The gods do not know Kṛṣṇa's origin, for He is their origin. (*10.2 na me viduḥ sura-gaṇāḥ…*)
- All opulent, beautiful and glorious creations are but a spark of Kṛṣṇa's splendor. (*10.41 yad yad vibhūtimat sattva…*)
- Kṛṣṇa pervades everything, all beings are in Him, yet He is not in everyone. (*9.4 mayā tatam idaṁ sarvaṁ…*)

- Although He is everywhere, He is not part of this cosmic manifestation. (*9.5 na ca mat-sthāni bhūtāni...*)
- Kṛṣṇa is the source of our memory and knowledge. (*15.15 sarvasya cāhaṁ hṛdi...*)
- Kṛṣṇa is the knower of everyone's body (*13.3 kṣetra-jñaṁ cāpi māṁ viddhi...*)

2. Kṛṣṇa, the seed-giving father of all

- The seven great sages, four Kumaras and the Manus come from Kṛṣṇa through His mind. (*10.6 maharṣayaḥ sapta pūrve...*)
- Kṛṣṇa is the seed-giving father of all species as He impregnates the mother material nature. (*14.3-4 sarva-yoniṣu kaunteya...*)
- Kṛṣṇa is generating seed of all existences, no being – moving or nonmoving – can exist without Him. (*10.39 yac cāpi sarva-bhūtānāṁ...*)
- Kṛṣṇa is our supreme father and mother (*9.17 pitāham asya jagato...*)
- Living entities are Kṛṣṇa's fragmental parts. (*15.7 mamaivāṁśo jīva-loke...*)
- Kṛṣṇa is greater than the Supersoul and the fallible and infallible living entities (*15.17 uttamaḥ puruṣas tv anyaḥ...*)

3. Kṛṣṇa is the creator, maintainer and destroyer

- Kṛṣṇa is both the origin and the dissolution of everything in this world. (*7.6 etad-yonīni bhūtāni...*)
- The whole cosmic order is manifested and annihilated by Kṛṣṇa's will. (*9.8 prakṛtiṁ svām avaṣṭabhya...*)
- Kṛṣṇa is the maintainer of all living entities (*9.5 na ca mat-sthāni bhūtāni...*)
- Kṛṣṇa is time, the ultimate destroyer. (*11.32 kālo 'smi loka-kṣaya-kṛt...*)

4. Kṛṣṇa's compassionate descents

- Kṛṣṇa descends when there is a decline in religious practice and a predominant rise of irreligion. (*4.7 yadā yadā hi dharmasya...*)
- Kṛṣṇa delivers the pious and annihilates the miscreants, and reestablishes religious principles millennium after millennium. (*4.8 paritrāṇāya sādhūnāṁ...*)

5. Kṛṣṇa's Supremacy confirmed by authorities

- Arjuna accepted Kṛṣṇa's supremacy as the purest, the Absolute Truth, eternal, original person etc. All the great sages such as Nārada, Asita, Devala and Vyāsa also confirm this truth. (*10.12-13 paraṁ brahma paraṁ dhāma..., 11.8*)
- Sañjaya's opinion: Wherever there is Kṛṣṇa and Arjuna there will be opulence, victory, extraordinary power, and morality. (*18.78 yatra yogeśvaraḥ kṛṣṇo...*)

6. Kṛṣṇa's Supreme form

- Kṛṣṇa's transcendental body never deteriorates. (*4.6 ajo 'pi sann avyayātmā…*)
- Kṛṣṇa's form is inconceivable, luminous like the sun and transcendental, beyond this material nature. (*8.9 kaviṁ purāṇam anuśāsitāram…*)
- Seeing Kṛṣṇa's beautiful humanlike form, Arjuna was composed in mind. Even the devatās are ever seeking the opportunity to see Kṛṣṇa's form. (11.51-52)
- Sañjaya rejoices, whenever he remembers Kṛṣṇa's form. (18.77)

7. Kṛṣṇa, the bestower of supreme knowledge

- Kṛṣṇa is the source of all transcendental knowledge. (*4.1 imaṁ vivasvate…*)
- Just by hearing the knowledge given by Kṛṣṇa, nothing further remains for us to know. (*7.2 jñānaṁ te 'haṁ sa-vijñānam…*)
- Kṛṣṇa knows past, present and future and all living entities; but Him no one knows. (*7.26 vedāhaṁ samatītāni…*)
- Knowledge given by Kṛṣṇa purifies, gives direct perception of the self, and is the perfection of religion. (*9.2 rāja-vidyā rāja-guhyaṁ…*)
- Kṛṣṇa is the knower in all bodies whereas we can know only our body. (*13.3 kṣetra-jñaṁ cāpi māṁ viddhi…*)
- Kṛṣṇa can remember all births of Himself and all the living entities, but the living entities cannot. (*4.5 bahūni me vyatītāni…*)

8. Result of knowing Kṛṣṇa's transcendental nature

- His birth and activities are transcendental and knowing which one attains His eternal abode. (*4.9 janma karma ca me divyam…*)
- One who knows Kṛṣṇa attains peace from the pangs of material miseries. (5.29 *bhoktāraṁ yajña-tapasāṁ…*)

9. Kṛṣṇa's supreme abode

- One who attains to Kṛṣṇa's abode, never takes birth again in this miserable material world. (*8.16 ā-brahma-bhuvanāl lokāḥ…*)
- Having attained the unmanifest, infallible supreme destination, one never returns to this world. (*8.21 avyakto 'kṣara ity uktas…*)

10. Kṛṣṇa's work doesn't affect Him

- Kṛṣṇa's work doesn't affect Him; nor does He aspire for the fruits of action. (*4.14 na māṁ karmāṇi limpanti…*)

- Work cannot bind Kṛṣṇa. He is ever detached from all these material activities, seated as though neutral. (*9.9 na ca māṁ tāni karmāṇi…*)
- Lord Kṛṣṇa created the four *varṇas*, yet He is nondoer, being unchangeable. (*4.13 cātur-varṇyaṁ mayā sṛṣṭaṁ…*)

11. Kṛṣṇa reciprocates with everyone

- Kṛṣṇa envies no one; He is impartial and equal to all. But a devotee who renders service unto Him is His friend. (*9.29 samo 'haṁ sarva-bhūteṣu…*)
- As all surrender unto Kṛṣṇa, He rewards them accordingly. (*4.11 ye yathā māṁ prapadyante…*)
- Kṛṣṇa does not resent those who ignore Him, but simply gives them what they want and deserve. (*7.21 yo yo yāṁ yāṁ tanuṁ bhaktaḥ…*)

12. Kṛṣṇa's shelter, the ultimate benediction

- People of even sinful birth can attain Kṛṣṇa's abode by taking His shelter. (9.32 *māṁ hi pārtha vyapāśritya…*)
- Just by knowing Kṛṣṇa one is free from all sins. (*10.3 yo mām ajam anādiṁ…*)
- For one who takes shelter of Kṛṣṇa is delivered from all sinful reactions. (*18.66 sarva-dharmān parityajya…*)
- One can easily cross over this material ocean by surrendering to Kṛṣṇa. (*7.14 daivī hy eṣā guṇa-mayī…*)
- Kṛṣṇa personally uplifts those who turn to Him for shelter (*12.7 teṣām ahaṁ samuddhartā…*)
- Kṛṣṇa destroys ignorance of devotees by revealing knowledge from heart. (*10.11 teṣām evānukampārtham…*)
- For His devotees Kṛṣṇa supplies what they lack and preserve what they have. (*9.22 ananyāś cintayanto māṁ…*)

The above glories of Lord Kṛṣṇa are just a small glimpse of His unlimited qualities and powers. All the Vedic literatires praise Him extensively and a drop of those descriptions can enlighten and satisfy the hearts of sincere listeners.

2. Bhakti, The Topmost Yoga

Bhakti-yoga means devotional service unto the Supreme Personality of Godhead Śrī Kṛṣṇa. The ultimate teaching of the *Bhagavad-gīta* is to perfrom *bhakti*. *Yoga* ultimately means *bhakti-yoga*. All the other *yogas*, namely *karma-yoga*, *jñāna-yoga*, *aṣṭāṅga yoga* etc., are different rungs of the *yoga* ladder, and are the means to reach the highest rung of *bhakti*.

1. Lord Kṛṣṇa's opinion

- Bhakti-yogī is the best of all yogīs. (*6.47 yoginām api sarveṣāṁ...*)
- Fight with full surrender, knowledge, detachment and non-doership. (*3.30 mayi sarvāṇi karmāṇi...*)
- Engage your mind always in thinking of Me, become My devotee (*9.34 man-manā bhava mad-bhakto...*)
- Those who perfectly know Me as the source of everything, engage in bhakti with all their hearts. (*10.8 ahaṁ sarvasya prabhavo...*)
- Abandon all varieties of religion and just surrender unto Me. I shall deliver you from all sinful reactions. Do not fear. (*18.66 sarva-dharmān parityajya...*)

2. Bhakti is rare

- Out of many thousands, one may be interested in transcendental realization to try to know the self, the body, and Absolute Truth. (*7.3 manuṣyāṇāṁ sahasreṣu...*)
- After many, many births, one may actually understand that Kṛṣṇa is the ultimate goal of spiritual realization. (*7.19 bahūnāṁ janmanām ante...*)
- After many, many births of pious activities, when one is freed from sins and dualities, and can engage in *bhakti*. (*7.28 yeṣāṁ tv anta-gataṁ pāpaṁ...*)
- The faithless cannot do *bhakti*, even after hearing all Vedic evidence. Being unfixed they return to the path of birth and death. (*9.3 aśraddadhānāḥ puruṣā...*)

3. Bhakti is all-encompassing

- A person who accepts the path of *bhakti* attains the results derived from Vedic study, sacrifices, austerities, charity etc, and at the end reaches the spiritual world. (*8.28 vedeṣu yajñeṣu tapaḥsu caiva…*)
- Even the lowborn people can attain the supreme destination by taking to *bhakti.* (*9.32 māṁ hi pārtha vyapāśritya…*)
- One can perceive results directly (*pratyakṣāvagamaṁ*) by executing *bhakti.* (*9.2 rāja-vidyā rāja-guhyaṁ…*)

4. Bhakti is very easy

- By experiencing a higher taste, one can easily control one's mind and senses from sense objects. (*2.59 viṣayā vinivartante…*)
- Those who fix their minds on the personal form of Kṛṣṇa are most perfect. For the impersonalists, advancement is troublesome. (*12.2-5 mayy āveśya mano ye…*)
- Compared to *aṣṭānga-yoga*, *bhakti* does not demand strict vows like absolute celibacy and so on. (*6.13-14 samaṁ kāya-śiro-grīvaṁ…*)
- *Bhakti* process is blissfully performed (*su-sukhaṁ*). One can simply hear and chanting the Lord's glories, eat *prasāda* and so on. (*9.2 rāja-vidyā rāja-guhyaṁ…*)
- Kṛṣṇa is pleased to accept even a leaf, a flower, little water or fruit offered in genuine love and devotion. (*9.26 patraṁ puṣpaṁ phalaṁ toyaṁ…*)
- Whatever one does, eats, donates and whatever austerities one performs—one may simply do that as an offering to Kṛṣṇa. (*9.27 yat karoṣi yad aśnāsi…*)

5. Bhakti benedictions

- Those who have surrendered unto Kṛṣṇa easily cross beyond the insurmountable material energy. (*7.14 daivī hy eṣā guṇa-mayī…*)
- One who engages in unalloyed *bhakti* transcends the material modes and is elevated to the spiritual platform. (*14.26 māṁ ca yo 'vyabhicāreṇa…*)
- Under the protection of Kṛṣṇa's divine nature, the great souls are not deluded and fully engaged in *bhakti.* (*9.13 mahātmānas tu māṁ pārtha…*)
- Kṛṣṇa personally supplies what a devotee lacks and preserves what he has. (*9.22 ananyāś cintayanto māṁ…*)
- Understanding Kṛṣṇa to be the only enjoyer, proprietor and the real friend of all, one attains real peace. (*5.29 bhoktāraṁ yajña-tapasāṁ…*)

6. Bhakti is the only way to understand and attain Kṛṣṇa

- Whoever quits his body remembering Kṛṣṇa alone at once attains His abode. (*8.5 anta-kāle ca mām eva…*)
- Only by undivided *bhakti* can one understand Kṛṣṇa as He is, and can thus see Him directly. (*11.54 bhaktyā tv ananyayā śakya…*)
- When one is in fully conscious of Kṛṣṇa by devotion, he can enter into the kingdom of God. (*18.55 bhaktyā mām abhijānāti…*)

7. Kṛṣṇa's personal reciprocation with a bhakti-yogī

- Kṛṣṇa gives a devotee sufficient intelligence to attain Him in the spiritual world. (*10.10 teṣāṁ satata-yuktānāṁ…*)
- Kṛṣṇa, dwelling in the heart, shows special mercy by removing the darkness of ignorance by the shining lamp of knowledge. (*10.11 teṣām evānukampārtham…*)
- Even if by accident if a devotee does some mistake, if he is engaged in *bhakti*, Kṛṣṇa considers him a *sadhu*. (*9.30 api cet su-durācāro…*)
- Kṛṣṇa promises to protect His devotees from all accidental falldowns because of his continuous thinking of the Lord. (*9.31 kṣipraṁ bhavati dharmātmā…*)
- Kṛṣṇa is the swift deliverer of His devotees from the material ocean of birth and death due to their undeviated *bhakti*. (*12.7 teṣām ahaṁ samuddhartā…*)

3. Bhakti Throughout the Gīta

Bhakti or devotional service in loving surrender unto Lord Kṛṣṇa is the essential and conclusive message of the *Gīta*. The middle six chapters describe *bhakti* vividly and directly. Yet the first and last six chapters also are meant to teach us *bhakti,* through *karma* and *jñāna*. These chapters also directly describe *bhakti* at several places. The first six chapters explain us why and how to work for Kṛṣṇa. The middle six chapters explain the nature and activities of pure devotional service. The last six chapters explain us how to think and discriminate for advancing in *bhakti*. The following are selected references from each chapter of the *Gīta* that mention about *bhakti*.

Chapter 1

- Kṛṣṇa always protects His surrendered devotees, the Pāṇḍavas, and thus they are ensured of victory regardless of all material odds (1.14-19).
- Kṛṣṇa is called *Acyuta,* as He never fails in affection for His devotees (1.21).
- Kṛṣṇa becomes a servant of His devotees, Arjuna's charioteer (1.21-25).

Chapter 2

- Effects of *bhakti* are never lost (*2.40 nehābhikrama-nāśo 'sti…*)
- Bhaktas are resoulte in their purpose (*2.41 vyavasāyātmikā buddhi…*)
- *Bhakti* is beyond the material modes (*2.45 traiguṇya viṣayā vedā…*)
- Sense control is possible only by dedicated *bhakti* unto Kṛṣṇa – *mat-paraḥ* (*2.61 tāni sarvāṇi saṁyamya…*)

Chapter 3

- Work, which is not done for satisfaction of Viṣṇu, causes bondage in this material world (*3.9 yajñārthāt karmaṇo 'nyatra…*)
- One has to devote all works in Kṛṣṇa's service (*3.30 mayi sarvāṇi karmāṇi…*)

Chapter 4

- Kṛṣṇa's divine appearance and activities are understood only by *bhakti* (4.1-10)

Chapter 5

- Kṛṣṇa is the only enjoyer of all sacrifices, proprietor of all and true friend of all living entities (*5.29 bhoktāraṁ yajña-tapasāṁ….*)

Chapter 6

- *Bhakti-yogī* is the topmost of all *yogīs*. (*6.47 yoginām api sarveṣāṁ…*)

Chapter 7

- Surrender unto Kṛṣṇa is the only way to transcend *māyā*, His material energy (*7.14 daivī hy eṣā guṇa-mayī...*)
- Surrender to Kṛṣṇa is the ultimate goal of *jñāna* (*7.19 bahūnāṁ janmanām...*)
- Devotees of Kṛṣṇa go to Kṛṣṇa's planet (*7.23 mad-bhakā yānti mām api*)
- Pious and sinless souls can engage in *bhakti* with determination (*7.28 yeṣāṁ tv anta-gataṁ pāpaṁ...*)

Chapter 8

- One should always remember Kṛṣṇa in devotion (*8.7 tasmāt sarveṣu kāleṣu...*)
- Constant remembrance of Kṛṣṇa in *bhakti*, Kṛṣṇa is easy to obtain (*8.14 ananya-cetāḥ satataṁ...*)
- By *ananya-bhakti*, Kṛṣṇa is easy to obtain (*8.22 bhaktyā labhyas tv ananyayā*)
- A *bhakta* automatically and effortlessly achieves all the results of *jñāna, yoga, karma* and all the Vedic forms of purification (*8.28 vedeṣu yajñeṣu tapaḥsu caiva...*)

Chapter 9

- *Bhakti-yoga* is the king of all knowledge, most confidential, purest, topmost and is joyfully performed. (*9.2 rāja-vidyā rāja-guhyaṁ...*)
- Pure devotees under the shelter of Kṛṣṇa's divine energy worship Kṛṣṇa and know Him (*9.13 mahātmānas tu māṁ pārtha...*)
- Great devotees perpetualy chant the glories of Kṛṣṇa, worship and remember Him (*9.14 satataṁ kīrtayanto māṁ...*)
- Kṛṣṇa protects and supplies the necessities of His pure devotees (*9.22 ananyāś cintayanto māṁ...*)
- Kṛṣṇa is never lost for His pure devotees. (*9.29 samo 'haṁ sarva-bhūteṣu...*)
- Kṛṣṇa excuses accidental mistakes of devotees (*9.30-31 api cet su-durācāro...*)
- Kṛṣṇa advises full absorption in Him (*9.34 man-manā bhava mad-bhakto...*)

Chapter 10

- One in full knowledge engages in unalloyed devotional service (*10.7 etāṁ vibhūtiṁ yogaṁ ca...*)
- A truly intelligent person takes to the practice of pure *bhakti* (*10.8 ahaṁ sarvasya prabhavo...*)
- The four essential verses of the *Gītā* (*Catuḥ-ślokī*) describe the reciprocation between Kṛṣṇa and His devotees (10.8-11)

Chapter 11

- Only by *ananya-bhakti* can one know or see Kṛṣṇa (*11.54 bhaktyā tv ananyayā śakya...*)
- By working for Kṛṣṇa with devotion, detachment and non-envy, one attains Kṛṣṇa (11.55 *mat-karma-kṛn mat-paramo...*)

Chapter 12

- *Bhakti* is superior to impersonalism and Kṛṣṇa directly takes charge of His devotees (12.1-7 *evaṁ satata-yuktā ye...*)
- Kṛṣṇa recommends pure *bhakti*, yet He presents simpler forms of *bhakti* to accommodate everyone. (12.8-12 *mayy eva mana ādhatsva...*)
- Pure devotees have divine qualities that make them extremely dear to Kṛṣṇa (12.13-20 *adveṣṭā sarva-bhūtānāṁ...*)

Chapter 13

- All good qualities are meant to develop unalloyed *bhakti*, which is the ultimate goal (13.8-12 *amānitvam adambhitvam…*)
- Only a devotee of Kṛṣṇa can properly understand the subjects of *kṣetra, kṣetrajña* and *jñānaṁ*. (13.19 *iti kṣetraṁ tathā jñānaṁ…*)

Chapter 14

- Uninterrupted *bhakti* is the method to transcend three material modes (14.26 *māṁ ca yo 'vyabhicāreṇa…*)

Chapter 15

- The process of surrendering unto Kṛṣṇa includes pridelessness etc. (15.6 *nirmāna-mohā jita-saṅga-doṣā…*)
- Lord Kṛṣṇa is the goal of all Vedas (15.15 *sarvasya cāhaṁ hṛdi sanniviṣṭo…*)
- One who knows Kṛṣṇa engages in His *bhakti* (15.19 *yo mām evam asammūḍho…*)

Chapter 16

- Aversion to the principles of understanding the Supreme Lord is the cause of all degradation, which leads to demoniac life (16.23-24 *yaḥ śāstra-vidhim utsṛjya…*)

Chapter 17

- One's activities can be free from the influence of material modes by dedicating them for pleasure of the Supreme (17.23-28 *oṁ tat sad iti nirdeśo…*)

Chapter 18

- The supreme instruction on morality: 'Give up all other processes and just surrender unto Kṛṣṇa' (18.65 *man-manā bhava mad-bhakto…*, 18.66 *sarva-dharmān parityajya…*)

Ananya-bhakti or *kevala-bhakti* is pure devotional service unto Lord Kṛṣṇa, which is unmixed with any selfish material motivations or intellectual persuits. Such ananya-*bhakti* has been directly discussed in 8.14; 9.13, 9.22, 9.26, 9.30 and 9.34; 10.8-11; 11.54-55; 15.19-20; 18.65-66.

4. Soul and Transmigration

Lord Kṛṣṇa begins His teachings to Arjuna in the *Bhagavad-gīta* by describing the *ātma-jñāna* or the knowledge about the soul. The spirit soul is qualitatively equal to the Superme Spirit Kṛṣṇa and is a part and parcel of Kṛṣṇa. But due to material desires and material deeds under the influence of material modes, the soul is entrapped in the cycle of repeated birth and death and transmigrates from one material body to another in different species. The following is a short compilation on the soul and its transmigration in this world based on the contents of the *Gīta*.

1. Identity and characteristics of the soul

- The soul is a fragmental part of Lord Kṛṣṇa (*15.7 mamaivāṁśo jīva-loke…*)
- The soul is eternally an individual. (*2.12 na tv evāhaṁ jātu nāsaṁ…*)
- For more characteristics of the soul see 2.16-25 in the overview section.

2. Soul changing bodies – examples

- Soul's changing the bodies is compared to a person's changing different dresses. (*2.22 vāsāṁsi jīrṇāni yathā vihāya…*)
- Just as embodied soul passes through different stages of life (boyhood → youth → old age), after death the soul passes into another body. (*2.13 dehino 'smin yathā dehe…*)
- The soul in the material world carries one's different conceptions of life from one body to another as the air carries aromas. (*15.8-9 śarīraṁ yad avāpnoti…*)

3. Role of three modes in the transmigration of soul

- Association with the modes of material nature leads to different good and evil among various species. (*13.22 puruṣaḥ prakṛti-stho hi…*)
- The three modes facilitate the filfillment of soul's desires through providing different bodies, under the supreme direction of Supreme Lord (5.14-15 *na kartṛtvaṁ na karmāṇi…*)

- The material modes govern one's destinations after death. (*14.18 ūrdhvaṁ gacchanti sattva-sthā…*)

4. Role of Supersoul in transmigration

- The Supersoul acts as the supreme proprietor, overseer and permitter for the soul's activities (*13.23 upadraṣṭānumantā ca…*)
- The Supersoul always accompanies the soul in all material bodies (*18.61 īśvaraḥ sarva-bhūtānāṁ…*)

5. Factors that determine the next body

- Thoughts at the time of death determine the future birth (*8.5 anta-kāle ca mām eva… 8.6 yaṁ yaṁ vāpi smaran bhāvaṁ…*)
- State of consciousness throughout the life is carried to the next body (*15.8 śarīraṁ yad avāpnoti…*)
- The bewildered soul, under the influence of modes, thinks himself the doer. (*3.27 prakṛteḥ kriyamāṇāni…*)
- Demons are condemned life after life. (*16.19 tān ahaṁ dviṣataḥ krūrān… 16.20 āsurīṁ yonim āpannā…*)
- By devatā worship one is transferred to devatā planets. (*9.25 yānti deva-vratā devān… 7.23 antavat tu phalaṁ teṣāṁ…*)
- By pure *bhakti* one is transferred to Lord Kṛṣṇa's abode. (*18.55 bhaktyā mām abhijānāti…*)

By performing *bhakti-yoga,* one can rise above the three modes and thus transcend the cycle of repeted birth and death.

5. Self-control

Self-control is a necessity for achieving desired goals and success in any path. Especially one who seeks progress on a spiritual path of *yoga* needs to control the mind and the senses. The following is a short compilation on this theme from various chapters of the *Bhagavad-gīta*.

1. Introduction to mind and senses

- Mind is one of the components of subtle body (*7.4 bhūmir āpo 'nalo vāyuḥ..., 13.6-7 mahā-bhūtāny ahaṅkāro...*)
- Senses are the instruments for any action through which the mind functions (*18.13-14 pañcaitāni mahā-bāho...*)
- Lord Kṛṣṇa says that He is the mind amongst all senses. (*10.22 indriyāṇāṁ manaś cāsmi*)
- Mind is the center of all sense activities and reservoir of all ideas for sense gratification (*15.8-9 śarīraṁ yad avāpnoti...*)
- Hierarchy: Intelligence is higher than the mind, which is higher than the senses (*3.42 indriyāṇi parāṇy āhur...*)

2. Nature of mind and senses

- Mind is very powerful, restless, turbulent, obstinate and strong (*6.34 cañcalaṁ hi manaḥ kṛṣṇa...*)
- Senses are very strong and impetuous. They forcibly carry away the mind even of a man of discrimination who is endeavoring to control them (*2.60 yatato hy api kaunteya...*)
- Contemplating on sense objects within the mind can begin the process of fall down (*2.62 dhyāyato viṣayān puṁsaḥ...*)

3. Analogies on mind and senses

- One who is able to withdraw his senses from sense objects, as the tortoise draws its limbs within the shell, is firmly fixed in perfect consciousness (*2.58 yadā saṁharate cāyaṁ...*)

- As a strong wind sweeps away a boat on the water, even one of the roaming senses on which the mind focuses can carry away a man's intelligence (*2.67 indriyāṇāṁ hi caratāṁ...*)
- Steady mind is like a lamp in a windless place (*6.19 yathā dīpo nivāta-stho...*)
- Mind as the reins of the chariot of body with five senses as the horses (6.34 P)

4. Why control mind and senses?

- Controlled mind is the best friend and uncontrolled mind is the worst enemy (*6.5-6 uddhared ātmanātmānaṁ...*)
- Without mind control, there is no chance of self-realization (*6.36 asaṁyatātmanā yogo...*)
- Whatever one thinks at time of death one will attain that state in the next life (*8.5 anta-kāle ca mām eva...*)
- Uncontrolled senses cause fall down (*2.62-63 dhyāyato viṣayān puṁsaḥ...*). Even in regulated sense enjoyment there is a chance of fall down (3.34P)
- Contact of senses with sense objects is a source of misery and temporary (*5.22 ye hi saṁsparśa-jā bhogā...*)

5. How to control mind and senses?

- One has to tolerate the urges of material senses and desires untill death (*5.23 śaknotīhaiva yaḥ soḍhuṁ...*)
- Senses cannot be artificially controlled by other yogic processes because the slightest agitation can cause fall down (*2.60 yatato hy api kaunteya...*)
- Therefore only by engaging senses in Kṛṣṇa consciousness can one actually control them (*2.61 tāni sarvāṇi saṁyamya...*)
- By engaging the mind in Kṛṣṇa's service and experiencing higher taste, one gets rid of lower engagement (*2.59 viṣayā vinivartante...*)
- By deliberate spiritual intelligence one can control mind and senses (*3.42 indriyāṇi parāṇy āhur..., 3.43 evaṁ buddheḥ paraṁ buddhvā...*)
- Withdraw the mind from wherever it wanders (*6.26 yato yato niścalati...*)
- Mind can be controlled by practice and detachment (*6.35 asaṁśayaṁ mahā-bāho...*)
- By doing one's prescribed duty to engage the mind according to one's proclivities (*8.7 tasmāt sarveṣu kāleṣu...*)
- Try to control the active senses by the mind and begin *karma-yoga* without attachment (*3.7 yas tv indriyāṇi manasā...*)
- Always think of Kṛṣṇa (*9.34 man-manā bhava mad-bhakto...*)
- Self-control is one of the austerities of mind (*17.16 manaḥ-prasādaḥ saumyatvaṁ...*)
- Don't let the senses to come in contact with sense objects, like a tortoise that withdraws the senses when not in use (*2.58 yadā saṁharate cāyaṁ...*)

6. Results of mind and sense control

- The *yogī* whose mind is fixed on *Kṛṣṇa* verily attains the highest perfection of transcendental happiness and rises above the modes and is freed from all reactions to past deeds (*6.27 praśānta-manasaṁ hy enaṁ…*)
- Kṛṣṇa promises that if one always thinks of Him and becomes His devotee, one can attain Him. (*18.65 man-manā bhava mad-bhakto…*)
- One can obtain complete mercy of the Lord (*2.64 rāga-dveṣa-vimuktais tu…*)
- One attains happiness within and becomes completely peaceful (*2.65 prasāde sarva-duḥkhānāṁ…*)
- One is liberated and ultimately attains the Supreme (*2.72 eṣā brāhmī sthitiḥ pārtha…*)

7. Processes for self control and the best of all

- **Role of dharma:** Engaging the senses in one's prescribed duties leads to purification (*3.4-7 na karmaṇām anārambhān…*)
- **Role of buddhi:** Self-control can be achieved by deliberate spiritual intelligence trained in Kṛṣṇa consciousness (*3.43 evaṁ buddheḥ paraṁ buddhvā….*)
- **Role of jñāna:** Using one's discrimination to control the mind and senses (Chapters 13-14, *5.22-23 ye hi saṁsparśa-jā…, 15.1-4 ūrdhva-mūlam adhaḥ…*)
- **Role of aṣṭāṅga yoga:** This process employs meditation as a means to control mind and senses. However, Arjuna rejects this process as very difficult. (*6.33-34 yo 'yaṁ yogas tvayā proktaḥ…*)
- **Role of bhakti:** This process is simple, easy, practical and most recommended –
    - 'Higher taste in service of Lord' is the most effective means for mind and sense control (*2.59 viṣayā vinivartante…*)
    - Performing one's prescribed duty with remembrance of Lord Kṛṣṇa (*8.7 tasmāt sarveṣu kāleṣu…*)
    - Constant remembrance of Kṛṣṇa without deviation (*8.14 ananya-cetāḥ satataṁ…*)
    - Engage the mind and senses filly in the service of Lord Kṛṣṇa (*9.34, 18.65 man-manā bhava mad-bhakto…*)
    - Direct service to Kṛṣṇa is better than impersonal meditation (*12.2 mayy āveśya mano ye māṁ…, 12.6-8 ye tu sarvāṇi karmāṇi…*)
    - *Bhakti* is not only the topmost process but includes the essential elements and results of all other processes (*8.28 vedeṣu yajñeṣu tapaḥsu caiva…*)
    - Devotees regulate their senses and mind, and they use various material things in the spiritual service of the Lord. (*9.27 yat karoṣi yad aśnāsi…*)

6. How to Receive Knowledge

Lord Kṛṣṇa presents the knowledge of *Bhagavad-gīta* to Arjuna because Arjuna is non-envious (*anasūya*), a devotee (*bhakta*) and a friend of Kṛṣṇa. One may think that such privilege of receiving knowledge directly from God is not there now. But if one has favourable qualities, one can receive the same spiritual knowledge from a bona fide representative of Kṛṣṇa. The following is a compilation of few verses of the *Gīta* that throw light on this theme.

1. Method

- Spiritual knowledge is attained thorugh *paramparā* or bona fide disciplic succession (*4.1-4.2 imaṁ vivasvate yogam…*)
- Hearing from Lord Kṛṣṇa or His bona fide representative (*7.1 mayy āsakta-manāḥ pārtha…*)

2. Qualifications

- Arjuna's qualification as a friend and devotee (*4.3 sa evāyaṁ mayā te 'dya…*)
- Submissiveness, service and relevant inquiries from a bina fide *guru* (*4.34 tad viddhi praṇipātena…*)
- Faith and sense control (*4.39 śraddhāvāl labhate jñānaṁ…*)
- Non-enviousness or *anasūya* (*9.1 idaṁ tu te guhyatamaṁ…, 18.67 idaṁ te nātapaskāya…*)
- Knowledge is revealed in the heart by sincerity (*10.10-11 teṣāṁ satata-yuktānāṁ…*)
- 20 qualities form the process of knowledge (*13.8-12 amānitvam adambhitvam…*)
- Especially humility and accepting shelter of a bona fide *guru* are two most important qualities (*13.8 amānitvam adambhitvam…*)
- Pure devotional service is the ultimate goal (*13.11 mayi cānanya-yogena…*)

3. Disqualifications

- Faithlessness in devotional service (*9.3 aśraddadhānāḥ puruṣā…*)
- Doubting mentality (*4.40 ajñaś cāśraddadhānaś ca…*)

7. Death

For a person who is born in this world, death is inevitable. Death doesn't mean the end of person (soul), but the end of a person's tenure within one material body. The soul receives a particular material body in certain species according to one's previous desires and deeds (*karma*). Such an embodied soul passes through different stages of life such as boyhood and youthhood in a body, and when the body becomes old, he leaves it to enter another body as per his activities. That is called as death.

One who performs *bhakti-yoga* throughout life enters the spiritual world after leaving his current material body. The following are some verses from the *Gīta* duly categorized under this topic.

1. What is Death?

- **Who are we?** – We are not this body but eternal individual spirit souls (*2.12 na tv evāhaṁ jātu nāsaṁ…*)
- **What is death?** – It is simply change of bodies (*2.13 dehino 'smin yathā dehe…*)
    - Change of body is like change of dress (*2.22 vāsāṁsi jīrṇāni yathā…*)
- Soul is immutable and never dies – Only the body undergoes six changes namely, birth, growth, existence, reproduction, dwindling and death (2.20 P)
- **Death is inevitable**
    - A sober person is not bewildered by such a change (*2.13 dehino 'smin yathā dehe…*)
    - One who takes birth is sure to die (*2.27 jātasya hi dhruvo mṛtyur…*)
    - Death pervades everywhere in the universe, from the highest planet to the lowest planet (*8.16 ā-brahma-bhuvanāl lokāḥ…*)
- **Kṛṣṇa is death personified –**
    - I am all-devouring death (*10.34 mṛtyuḥ sarva-haraś cāham…*)
    - I am Yama, the lord of death. (*10.29 yamaḥ saṁyamatām aham*)
    - I am immortality, and I am also death personified (*9.19 amṛtaṁ caiva mṛtyuś ca*)

2. Different Times of Departure and Destinations

- **Yogic process**
  - Path of light – One attains the Supreme and does not come back to this world (*8.24 agnir jyotir ahaḥ śuklaḥ…*)
  - Path of darkness – One reaches the moon planet but again comes back (*8.25 dhūmo rātris tathā kṛṣṇaḥ…*)
- **Devotional process:** Since a devotee of Kṛṣṇa is completely dependent on the Lord, he is beyond the considerations of auspicious and inauspicious times. Lord Kṛṣṇa personally takes charge of him (*8.27 naite sṛtī pārtha jānan…, 12.7 ye tu sarvāṇi karmāṇi…*)

3. Death in different modes

- Death in mode of goodness: One goes to the higher planets (14.14)
- Death in mode of passion: One attains earthly planets (14.15)
- Death in mode of ignorance: One attains birth in lower species or hellish planets (14.15)
- Summary (*14.18 ūrdhvaṁ gacchanti sattva-sthā…*)

4. Consciousness at the time of death

- Consciousness while dying determines the future birth (*8.6 yaṁ yaṁ vāpi smaran bhāvaṁ…*)
- Remembrance of Kṛṣṇa takes one to Kṛṣṇa (*8.5 anta-kāle ca mām eva…*)
- Remembrance of Kṛṣṇa in full devotion is possible only by proper training (*8.10 prayāṇa-kāle manasācalena…*)

5. How to transcend death / Death for a devotee

- Buddhi-yoga – *Buddhi-yoga* provides complete freedom from fruitive bondage and cycle of birth and death (*2.51 karma-jaṁ buddhi-yuktā hi…*)
- Equanimity – By attaining equanimity of mind one can conquer birth and death (*5.19 ihaiva tair jitaḥ sargo…*)
- Kṛṣṇa's personal care – Kṛṣṇa personally delivers those engaged in pure devotional service (*12.7 ye tu sarvāṇi karmāṇi…*)
- Submissive hearing – By the process of sincere hearing from the bona fide authorities, one can transcend birth and death (*13.26 anye tv evam ajānantaḥ…*)

8. Devatā Worship

Devatās are empowered administrators who manage various affairs of the material universe, on behalf of the Supreme Lord Kṛṣṇa. They are the representatives of the Supreme Lord and are dependent on Him. They are very respectable for holding such great responsibilities; however, some people consider them to be independent of Kṛṣṇa and worship them to fulfil their material desires. Ultimately it is Lord Kṛṣṇa who bestows the benedictions upon those devatā worshipers, as He says in the *Gīta*. The following are some references from the *Gīta* about devatā worship.

1. **Introduction:** Kṛṣṇa establishes the process of sacrifice and the dutiful worship of the devatās, for the fulfilment of the basic necessities of the human society. One who enjoys the results of one's work without offering them in a sacrifice, is a thief. (3.10-14)
2. **Motivation:** Devatā worshipers look for quick fulfillment of material desires, without knowledge of their ultimate welfare (*4.12 kāṅkṣantaḥ karmaṇāṁ siddhiṁ…*)
3. **Knowledge:** Kṛṣṇa calls devatā worshipers as less intelligent. (*7.20 kāmais tais tair hṛta-jñānāḥ…*)
4. **Temporary results:** Devatā worshipers go to devatā planets, which are also temporary. Thus, they undergo repeated cycle of birth and death (*9.21 te taṁ bhuktvā svarga-lokaṁ viśālaṁ…, 9.25 yānti deva-vratā devān…*)
5. **Faith:** It is Kṛṣṇa who makes the faith of devatā worshipers steady (*7.21 yo yo yāṁ yāṁ tanuṁ bhaktaḥ…*)
6. **Results:** It is Kṛṣṇa who bestows benefits to the living entities through the devatās (*7.22 sa tayā śraddhayā yuktas…*)
7. **Improper:** Devatā worship without knowledge of Kṛṣṇa's supremacy is called "*avidhi-pūrvakam*" – improper method of worship (*9.23 ye 'py anya-devatā-bhaktā…*)

9. Equanimity and Satisfaction

Equanimity (*samatvam*) and satisfaction (*tuṣṭi*) are emphasized in the *Gīta* as most essential qualities for a spiritual seeker. One needs to be tolerant and equipoised towards dualities[1] with detachment and be satisfied with whatever comes of its own accord in life. The following is a list of verses from the *Gīta* that highlight these qualities. Only the gist of verses is given below. The readers are requested to refer to the respective verses for more details.

Tolerance and Equanimity

1. Duty needs to be performed with equanimity abandoning all attachment to success or failure. Such equanimity is called *yoga*. (*2.48 samatvaṁ yoga ucyate*)
2. An equipoised devotee is eligible for liberation (*2.15 yaṁ hi na vyathayanty..., 5.25*)
3. By being equipoised in dualities, one shall never incur sin (*2.38 sukha-duḥkhe same kṛtvā...*)
4. A devotee sees a learned *brāhmaṇa*, a cow, an elephant, a dog and a dog-eater with equal vision. (*5.18 vidyā-vinaya-sampanne...*)
5. One attains the Supreme Lord by controlling senses and being equally disposed to everyone. (*12.4 sanniyamyendriya-grāmaṁ...*)
6. An equipoised person regards alike all kinds of dualities (*14.22-26, 6.7-9, 2.56-57*)
7. People with equal vision conquer birth and death (*5.19-20*)
8. The Lord considers an equipoised devotee as the topmost. (*6.32 ātmaupamyena sarvatra...*)

---

[1] **Dualities described in the Gīta:** Cold and heat, joy and sorrow (2.14, 6.7, 12.18, 18.27, 15.5); gain and loss, victory and defeat (2.38); success and failure (2.48, 4.22, 18.26); love and hate (2.64, 3.34, 18.23, 18.51); honor and dishonor (6.7, 12.19, 14.25); earth, stone and gold (6.8, 14.24); friend and enemy (6.9, 12.18, 14.25); chastisement and praise (12.19, 14.24); pleasing and displeasing (5.20, 14.24).

9. One has to tolerate happiness and distress by understanding them as temporary like changing seasons (*2.14 mātrā-sparśās tu kaunteya…*)
10. Until death one must tolerate the urges of senses, desires and anger. (*5.23 śaknotīhaiva yaḥ soḍhuṁ…*)
11. Like an ocean that is still despite many rivers entering it, one should be undisturbed by the incessant flow of desires. (*2.70 āpūryamāṇam acala-pratiṣṭhaṁ…*)

Satisfaction

12. For a satisfied person, the threefold miseries don't exist. (*2.65 prasāde sarva-duḥkhānāṁ…*)
13. There is no entanglement for one who is satisfied with gain that comes of its own accord. (*4.22 yadṛcchā-lābha-santuṣṭo…*)
14. When one gives up all desire for sense gratification, which arise from mental concoction, finds satisfaction in the self alone. (*2.55 prajahāti yadā kāmān…*)
15. For a self-satisfied person there is no prescribed duty. (*3.17 tasmād asaktaḥ …*)
16. A self-satisfied person ultimately attains the Supreme. (*5.24 yo 'ntaḥ-sukho…*)
17. Satisfaction is the quality that endears one to Lord Kṛṣṇa (*12.14 santuṣṭaḥ satataṁ yogī, 12.19 santuṣṭo yena kenacit*)
18. A peaceful and satisfied devotee attains pure devotional service unto the Lord (*18.54 'mad bhaktiṁ labhate parām'*)

Obstacles

19. Uncontrolled mind and senses present various obstacles in cultivating equanimity, tolerance and satisfaction (See thematic compilation 5)

10. The Five Topics

The subject matter of *Bhagavad-gītā* entails the comprehension of five basic truths, namely – *īśvara* (the supreme controller Kṛṣṇa), *jīva* (the living entities), *prakṛti* (nature), *kāla* (time or the duration of existence of the universe or the manifestation of material nature) and *karma* (action and reaction). *Īśvara* is the energetic person and *jīva* and *prakṛti* are His energies. These three are mutually related. Some of the prominent verses related to these topics from the *Gīta* are given below.

1. Iśvara – See the Thematic Compilation No. 1 in p.208.

2. Prakṛti

- *Prakṛti* is of two types: inferior material nature and superior spiritual nature (7.4-5)
- Inferior material nature constitutes of 5 gross and 3 subtle elements. (7.4)
- *Jīva* is spiritual, but becomes conditioned due to contact with material nature. (14.5, 13.22)
- Material Nature acts under the direction of Lord Kṛṣṇa (9.10)
- Material Nature constitutes three qualities (*guṇas*) namely, goodness, passion and ignorance that carry out all material activities and bind the *jīvas* to this world. (3.27, 14.5)
- One who is engaged in unalloyed *bhakti* unto Lord Kṛṣṇa transcends the three modes of material nature. (14.26)

3. Jīva

- The *jīva* is a part of Lord Kṛṣṇa (15.7)
- The *jīva* is the superior spiritual energy of Lord Kṛṣṇa (7.5)
- The *jīva* is an eternal individual, never subjected to birth or death (2.16-21)
- The *jīva* is the witness and knower of the field of material body (13.2)
- The *jīva* is entrapped in this world due to material desires and material work born of their nature (7.27, 16.12, 14.6, 18.60)

4. Kāla

- Inexhaustible time is the representation of the Lord (11.32)
- The material world is periodically created and destroyed by Kṛṣṇa's will (9.7-8)
- Arjuna describes the *kāla-rupa* of Kṛṣṇa (11.19-25)
- Auspicious and inauspicious times of leaving body (8.23-26)
- Brahma's one day or *kalpa* is 1000 *yuga* cycles (8.17)
- The Supreme Lord and His pure devotees are not influenced by time

5. Karma

- The intricacies of *karma* are difficult to understand even by the wise (4.16-18)
- One who is greedy for the fruits of one's actions becomes entangled (5.12)
- One should responsibly perform prescribed duties with detachment (2.47)
- One who works with knowledge, renunciation, self-realization for the Supreme is a true *yogī* and is not bound by *karma* (4.41, 5.10, 6.1, 2.39)
- Only by working for Vishnu, one is free from *karma* (3.9, 9.28)
- With mind fixed on Kṛṣṇa, one will be liberated from bondage of *karma* (9.28, 12.7, 2.51)

Relationship between Īśvara, Jīva, & Prakṛti

- *Īśvara* is the source of *jīva* and *prakṛti*, which are His superior and inferior energies respectively (7.4-7).
- The *jīva* desires, the *īśvara* sanctions and the *prakṛti* facilitates. Thus they are the three doers. (5.13-16)
- *Īśvara* and *prakriti* – Material nature works under the superintendence of the Lord, but the Lord is neutral and aloof. (9.9-10)
- *Īśvara* and *Jīva* – The *jīvas* are parts of *īśvara*. The *jīva* is eternally atomic and dependent on *īśvara* while *īśvara* is eternally blissful, all cognizant, omniscient and fully independent (5.7, 15)
- Reciprocation between *Īśvara* and *Jīva*
    - *Īśvara* reciprocates according to the way the *jīva* approaches (4.11)
    - *Īśvara*'s special favor to the devotees (9.29-32)
    - *Īśvara* gives spiritual intelligence and guidance from within (10.8-11)

APPENDIX

1. Kṛṣṇa's Names in the Gīta

In the *Bhagavad-gīta,* Lord Kṛṣṇa is described as *Bhagavān*, the Supreme Personality of Godhead. Kṛṣṇa is also addressed with various other names in the *Gīta*, mostly by Arjuna while inquiring from Kṛṣṇa or glorifying Him. These names indicate various attributes and activities of Lord Kṛṣṇa. The great commentators of the *Gīta* have given specific explanations for many of these names, in relation to their context. The following is a list of Kṛṣṇa's names along with their meanings. Although some names appear repeatedly, in different contexts, only one instance and the common meaning are given here.

	Verse	Name	Meaning
1	1.3	*Keśava*	The killer of the Keśī demon
2	1.21	*Acyuta*	The infallible Lord who never fails in His affection for His devotees
3	1.32	*Govinda*	Lord Govinda
4	1.34	*Madhusūdana*	Killer of the demon Madhu
5	1.35	*Janārdana*	Maintainer of all living entities, killer of the atheists, chastiser of the enemies
6	1.36	*Mādhava*	Husband of the goddess of fortune
7	1.40	*Vārṣṇeya*	Descendant of Vṛṣṇi
8	2.4	*Arisūdana*	Killer of the enemies
9	4.6	*Īśvara*	The Supreme Controller
10	4.6	*Bhūtānām īśvara*	Lord of all living entities
11	5.29	*Mahā-īśvara*	The Supreme Lord
12	5.29	*Su-hṛdam*	The benefactor

13	6.38	*Mahā-bāhu*	Mighty-armed Lord
14	8.1	*Puruṣottama*	Greatest of all persons
15	8.2	*Adhiyajña*	The Lord of sacrifice; the Super-soul
16	9.5	*Bhūta-bhṛt*	The maintainer of all living entities
17	9.18	*Prabhu*	The Lord
18	10.12	*Ādi-devam*	The original Lord
19	10.12	*Ajaṁ*	The unborn Lord
20	10.12	*Divyam*	Transcendental
21	10.12	*Paraṁ brahma*	Supreme Truth
22	10.12	*Paraṁ dhāma*	Supreme Sustenance
23	10.12	*Pavitraṁ paramaṁ*	Supreme Pure
24	10.12	*Puruṣaṁ śāśvataṁ*	Eternal personality
25	10.12	*Vibhum*	The greatest
26	10.15	*Bhūta-bhāvana*	Origin of everything
27	10.15	*Bhūteśa*	Lord of everything
28	10.15	*Deva-deva*	The Lord of all devatās
29	10.15	*Jagat-pati*	Lord of the entire universe
30	10.17	*Yogin*	Supreme mystic
31	11.2	*Kamala-patrākṣa*	Lotus-eyed Lord
32	11.3	*Paramśvara*	Supreme Lord
33	11.4	*Yogeśvara*	The Lord of all mystic power
34	11.9	*Hari*	The Supreme Personality of Godhead, Kṛṣṇa
35	11.9	*Mahā-yoga-īśvaraḥ*	The most powerful mystic
36	11.13	*Ananta-vīrya*	The master of all potencies
37	11.15	*Deva*	The Lord
38	11.16	*Viśva-rūpa*	Form of the Universe
39	11.16	*Viśveśvara*	Lord of the universe
40	11.17	*Aprameya*	Who is immeasurable
41	11.24	*Viṣṇu*	All-pervading Lord Viṣṇu

42	11.25	*Deveśa*	The God of all gods
43	11.25	*Jagan-nivāsa*	The refuge of the universe
44	11.31	*Deva-vara*	The great one amongst the devatās
45	11.31	*Ugrarūpa*	Whose form is fierce
46	11.32	*Kāla*	The great destroyer of the worlds
47	11.36	*Hṛṣīkeśa*	Master of the senses
48	11.37	*Ādi-kartre*	The supreme creator
49	11.37	*Akṣaram*	Imperishable
50	11.37	*Ananta*	The unlimited Lord, there is nothing that is not covered by His influence
51	11.37	*Mahātman*	Great soul
52	11.38	*Ādi-devaḥ*	The original Supreme God
53	11.38	*Ananta-rūpa*	One who has unlimited form(s)
54	11.38	*Paraṁ nidhānam*	Supreme refuge
55	11.38	*Puruṣaḥ purāṇas*	Oldest personality
56	11.39	*Prapitāmahaḥ*	The great-grandfather, the father of Brahmā.
57	11.40	*Amitavikrama*	Having unlimited strength.
58	11.41	*Sakha*	Dear friend.
59	11.41	*Yādava*	Member of Yadu dynasty
60	11.43	*Apratima prabhāva*	Possessor of immeasurable power
61	11.43	*Guruḥ*	The Supreme spiritual master
62	11.43	*Pitāsi*	The Supreme father
63	11.44	*Īśa*	The Supreme Lord.
64	11.46	*Sahasra-bāho*	Thousand-handed one
65	11.46	*Viśva-mūrte*	Universal form
66	11.50	*Vāsudevaḥ*	Son of Vasudeva
67	12.7	*Samuddhartā*	Swift deliverer from ocean of birth and death
68	18.1	*Keśinisūdana*	The killer of the Keśī demon

2. Arjuna's Names in the Gīta

Just as the speaker of the *Gīta,* Kṛṣṇa is addressed with many names in the *Gīta,* Arjuna, the hearer of the *Gīta* is also described with many names. These names bring out Arjuna's qualities as a *kṣatriya,* a devotee and friend of Kṛṣṇa. The following is a list of Arjuna's names along with their meanings. Only one instance of the repeated names is presented here.

	Verse	Name	Meaning
1	1.14	*Pāṇḍava*	The son of Pāṇḍu
2	1.15	*Dhanam-jayaḥ*	The winner of wealth
3	1.20	*Kapi-dhvajaḥ*	He whose flag was marked with Hanumān
4	1.24	*Guḍākeśaḥ*	One who conquered sleep and ignorance
5	1.25	*Pārtha*	Son of Pṛthā
6	2.14	*Bhārata*	Descendant of the Bharata dynasty
7	2.14	*Kaunteya*	Son of Kuntī
8	2.15	*Puruṣarṣabha*	Best among men
9	2.26	*Mahā-bāhu*	Mighty-armed one
10	2.41	*Kuru-nandana*	Beloved child of the Kurus
11	2.9	*Parantapa*	Chastiser of the enemies
12	3.30	*Anagha*	Sinless one
13	3.41	*Bharatarṣabha*	Chief amongst the descendants of Bharata
14	4.31	*Kuru-sattama*	Best amongst the Kurus
15	6.40	*Tāta*	My (Kṛṣṇa's) friend
16	8.4	*Deha-bhṛtāṁ vara*	Best of the embodied beings
17	10.19	*Kuru-śreṣtha*	Best of the Kurus

18	11.33	*Savya-sācin*	Expert shooter of arrows to kill his enemies
19	11.48	*Kuru-pravīra*	Best among the Kuru warriors
20	17.12	*Bharata-śreṣṭha*	Chief of the Bhāratas
21	18.4	*Bharata-sattama*	Best of the Bhāratas
22	18.4	*Puruṣa-vyāghra*	Tiger among human beings
23	18.78	*Dhanuḥ-dharaḥ*	The carrier of the bow and arrow

3. Analogies

Any concept presented with an analogy becomes easily understandable. The great scriptures and their commentators often use analogies to explain philosophical concepts in a lucid manner, to help the audience assimilate the subject matter better.

The following is a list of pertinent analogies from the verses of the *Bhagavad-gīta* and the purports of Śrīla Prabhupāda. The analogies are categorized under various themes of the *Gītā* and the like terms of each analogy are colour-coded.

Īśvara – The Supreme Lord

1. The sun has three different aspects, namely **sunshine**, **sun's surface** and **sun planet** itself. Similarly the Absolute Truth has three features namely the **glaring effulgence of impersonal Brahman**, **Paramātmā** and **Personal form** respectively. (2.2 P)
2. The sky reflects both the **moon** and the **stars** in water but still they are not on same level. Similarly, the **Supreme Lord, Kṛṣṇa** and **individual spirit soul** are not on the same level. If both of them are deluded by the illusory energy, then there is no need of one being the instructor and the other the instructed. (2.13 P)
3. Just as two birds sit on the same **tree**, while one bird is **eating the fruits** and the other bird is simply **watching his friend**, similarly, in the **material body**, soul is **enjoying the fruits of his activities** and the Supersoul is simply **witnessing those activities** (2.22 P)
4. Just like the **sun** **rises** and **sets**, similarly the **Lord** **appears** and **disappears** in this world. (4.6 P)
5. The **proprietor** never desires the **low-grade happiness** that the **workers** might desire. Similarly, the **Supreme Lord**, being full in Himself, has no attraction for so-called **heavenly happiness** which the **devatās** might desire. (4.14 P)
6. The **rains** are not responsible for different **types of vegetation**, although without such rains there is no possibility of vegetation, Similarly the **Lord** is aloof from the **material actions and reactions**, although He is the ultimate cause. (4.14 P)
7. Just as the **pearls** are **strung** on a **thread**, **everything** **rests** upon **Kṛṣṇa**. (7.7)

8. The clouds cannot cover the sun, moon and stars, but they are not manifest to our limited vision. Similarly māyā cannot cover the Supreme Lord, but He is not manifest to the less intelligent men. (7.26 P)
9. The different governmental departments are nothing but the energies of the king resting on his power, although he is not personally present in every department. Similarly, different manifestations in the material and the spiritual worlds are resting on the energy of the Supreme Lord. (9.4 P)
10. A cloud that pours rain all over, regardless of whether it falls on rock, land or water. Similarly, the Lord provides all necessities of life to everyone, since He claims every living entity in all forms as His child. (9.29 P)
11. A citizen may know everything about his patch of land, but the king knows not only his palace, but all the properties of his citizens. Similarly, one may be the proprietor of his own body, but the Supreme Lord is the proprietor of all bodies. (13.3 P)
12. The sun appears to many persons in many places in all directions but at the meridian, it is situated in its place. Similarly, one Viṣṇu is present everywhere by His omnipotence appear as if divided but same time situated undivided in his personal abode. (13.7 P)

Prakṛti – The Material Nature

13. Just as a forest fire that blazes without being set by anyone, the perplexities of life automatically appear in this world without our wanting. (2.7 P)
14. Just as there is appearance and disappearance of winter and summer, similarly there is nonpermanent appearance and disappearance of happiness and distress in due course, one must learn to tolerate them without being disturbed. (2.14)
15. A big skyscraper becomes manifested from the earth and when dismantled, again becomes unmanifested as earth. Similarly, while creation the material elements are manifested from the subtle unmanifest state, and after dissolution again becomes unmanisfested. (2.28 P)
16. A father gives seeds to the womb of the mother for the child. Similarly, the Supreme Lord by His mere glance injects all the living entities into the womb of material nature, and they come out in their different species, according to their previous desires and activities. (9.10 P)
17. A scorpion seems to be born out of rice, which is not the cause of the scorpion. But mother scorpion lays its eggs in piles of rice. Similarly, living entities seem to come out as products of material nature, which is not the cause of their birth. The Supreme Lord is the seed-giving father. (14.3 P)

18. A person seated in a high-speed motorcar goes faster than the one seated in a slower car, though the drivers may be the same. Similarly, by the order of the Supreme Soul, material nature puts particular type of living entity in a particular type of body so that he may work according to his past desires. (18.61 P)

Karma – Action and Reaction

19. A sincere sweeper in the street is far better than the charlatan meditator who meditates only for the sake of making a living. Similarly a sincere person doing his prescribed duties without attachment is far better than a false pretender who adopts show-bottle spiritualism to cheat the innocent public. (3.7 P)
20. Just as the lotus leaf is untouched by water, similarly one who performs his duty without attachment, surrendering the results unto the Supreme Lord, is unaffected by sinful action. (5.10)
21. Just as a man bound by a rope cannot free himself, but must be helped by a **person who is unbound**, similarly the conditioned soul bound by three modes cannot free himself from bondage, but can be released only **by Lord Kṛṣṇa, or a guru.** (7.14 P)
22. A seed first sprouts and becomes a small plant, and later becomes a big tree and then bears flowers and fruits, enjoyed by the person who has sown the seed. Similarly, a man performs a sinful act which is in the form of a seed at first, and there are others which are already fructified and are giving us fruit, which we are experiencing as distress and pain. (9.2 P)
23. Just as fire is covered by smoke, every endeavour is covered by some fault. (18.48)
24. Smoke disturbs the eyes, but still one must use fire. Similarly, one should not give up his natural occupation because there are some disturbing elements. (18.48 P)

Jīva – The Living Entity

25. Just as the influence of a medicine spreads throughout the body, similarly influence of a minute spiritual spark spreads all over the material body as consciousness, and that is the proof of the presence of the soul. (2.17 P)
26. Just as the sunlight maintains the entire universe, so the light of the soul maintains this material body, otherwise the body begins to decompose. (2.18 P)
27. When there is light in the sky, we understand the presence of the sun. Since there is consciousness in the body, we understand the presence of the soul. (2.20 P)
28. Just as a person puts on new garments, giving up old ones, the soul similarly accepts new material bodies, giving up the old and useless ones. (2.22)

29. Just as the sparks of a fire, although one in quality with the fire, are prone to be extinguished when out of the fire, the individual souls who are prone to be covered by the illusory energy when they become separated from the Supreme Lord. (2.23 P)
30. Just like in a dream one may think of flying in the sky or becoming a king, but when wakes up sees oneself neither in the sky nor seated on the chariot, similarly material body has no factual existence in relation to the eternal soul. (2.28 P)
31. Just as a rich man or a diseased man has his symptoms by which he is known, similarly a devotee of Kṛṣṇa has specific symptoms in various dealings. (2.54 P)
32. Just as the leaves and branches are not separate from the tree, similarly a Kṛṣṇa conscious person who is very dear to every living being cannot think of them as separate from Kṛṣṇa. (5.7 P)
33. The individual self is the passenger in the car of the material body, intelligence is the driver, **mind** is the **driving instrument**, and the senses are the horses. (6.34 P)
34. Just as the mighty wind blowing everywhere, rests always in the sky, similarly all created beings rest in Kṛṣṇa. (9.6)
35. When a diamond set in a golden ring looks nice, and both the gold and the diamond is glorified at the same time. Similarly, when a living entity becomes inclined to the service of the Supreme Lord, both he and the Lord eternally glitter. (9.29 P)
36. The sky, due to its subtle nature, does not mix with anything, although it is all-pervading. Similarly, the soul situated in Brahman vision does not mix with the body, though situated in that body. (13.33)
37. Just as the sun alone illuminates entire universe, similarly the living entity illuminates the entire body by consciousness. (13.34)
38. Just as a tract of land is sometimes barren and sometimes green, the different species of life are manifested according to the particular material modes. (15.2 P)
39. Just as the air carries aromas, the living entity in the material world carries his different conceptions of life from one body to another. (15.8)

BHAKTI – DEVOTIONAL SERVICE UNTO LORD KṚṢṆA

40. By watering the root of a tree one automatically distributes water to the leaves and branches, similarly by acting in Kṛṣṇa consciousness one can render the highest service to everyone—namely self, family, society, country, humanity, etc. (2.41 P)
41. Just as a blazing fire burns everything within a room, similarly the senses can be controlled only by bhakti to Kṛṣṇa, who is situated in the heart of the yogī, and burns up all kinds of impurities. (2.61 P)

42. Just like an antiseptic vaccine protects a person from the attack in an epidemic disease, similarly, food offered to Lord Viṣṇu and then taken by us makes us sufficiently resistant to material affection. (3.14 P)
43. Just like the serpents become no more effective with broken fangs, one's mind in Kṛṣṇa consciousness becomes stronger than the strong senses. (3.42 P)
44. A patient who is suffering bowel disorder due to overindulgence in milk products is cured by another milk product, namely yogurt. Similarly the conditioned soul absorbed in material activities can be cured by Kṛṣṇa conscious activities. (4.24 P)
45. A tortoise in the water brings up its offspring simply by meditation on eggs laid down on land. Similarly, the devotee far away from the Lord can elevate himself to His abode simply by thinking of Him constantly by engagement in *bhakti*. (5.26 P)
46. A hungry man feels satisfaction and strength for every morsel of food he eats, similarly, a devotee feels transcendental satisfaction by discharge of bhakti as the mind becomes detached from material objectives. (6.35 P)
47. Expert treatment and appropriate diet cures the disease of the suffering patient, similarly hearing about Kṛṣṇa and eating His prasāda treats the mad mind. (6.35 P)
48. A swan in the water takes pleasure in digging into the lotus flowers. Similarly a devotee prays to die immediately when he is quite healthy so that his mind seeks entrance at the stem of Lord's lotus feet. (8.2 P)
49. One who can go to the top of a building by an elevator, need not go by the staircase, step by step. Similarly when one directly approaches Kṛṣṇa, one need not approach different energies of Kṛṣṇa indirectly. (9.18 P)
50. One follows the laws made by the government, and not by the officers. Similarly, worshiping the Supreme Lord will automatically satisfy different demigods who are His representatives. (9.23 P)
51. The spots that resemble the mark of a rabbit on the moon do not become an impediment to the diffusion of moonlight. Similarly, the accidental fall down of a devotee does not make him abominable from the path of saintly character. (9.30 P)
52. The vast ocean, although being filled with more water in the monsoon, neither gets agitated nor crosses beyond the limit of its brink. Similarly a person fixed in Kṛṣṇa consciousness, although demanded by the body for sense gratification, doesn't get disturbed by such desires. (2.70 P)
53. Just as the seed of a tree fructifies with regular watering, devotional service which is like a seed sown in the heart of a living entity, fructifies by hearing and chanting and gradually grows until it penetrates the covering of the material universe and enters into spiritual sky. (10.9 P)

54. Just as a fish cannot live without water, a person fully absorbed in love of God cannot live even for a moment without being in contact with the Lord. (10.9 P)
55. The letters in mailboxes authorized by post office naturally go to their destination without difficulty. Similarly, God has an authorized representation in arcā-vigraha, who accepts our service through that form. (12.5 P)
56. The staircase begins from the ground floor and reaches up to the top floor. Similarly spiritual path begins from lower stage of knowledge up to the point of realization of Kṛṣṇa. (13.8-12 P)
57. The servant of the king enjoys on an almost equal level with the king. Similarly when a devotee approaches the Supreme Lord, there is an exchange of six opulences of the Lord. (14.27 P)
58. A green bird enters a green tree not to become one with the tree but to enjoy the fruits of the tree. Similarly, a person can enter into the Supreme Lord's abode in one's individuality to be in His association and render service unto Him. (18.55 P)

Jñāna – Spiritual Knowledge

59. Just as a bee licking the bottle of honey from outside cannot taste it unless one opens it, a nondevotee cannot understand *Bhagavad-gīta* unless he becomes a devotee. (2.12 P)
60. There is no source of understanding the identity of the father except by the authority of the mother. Similarly, there is no source of understanding the soul except by studying the Vedas. (2.25 P)
61. Just like all purposes served by a small well can at once be served by a great reservoir of water, all the purposes of the Vedas can be served to one who knows the purpose behind them. (2.46)
62. Someone who lifts a struggling swimmer from the ocean is the greatest saviour. Similarly perfect knowledge received from the Supreme Lord is the path of liberation from this material existence. (4.36 P)
63. Just as a blazing fire turns firewood to ashes, the fire of knowledge burns all reactions to material activities to ashes. (4.37)
64. One process is to find the root of the tree, and the other is to water the root. Similarly by analytical study of the material world one finds the soul of existence and by devotional service to the Lord one renders service to the soul of the material world, Viṣṇu (5.4 P)
65. Just as the sun lights up everything in the daytime, knowledge reveals everything by destroying the nescience. (5.16)

66. The swine that eat the night soil do not accept sweetmeats made of sugar and ghee. Similarly, the foolish worker who hears of the sense-enjoyable tidings of the flickering mundane world, will have very little time to hear about the eternal living force that moves the material world. (7.15 P)
67. Just as a young boy and girl take pleasure in association, realized souls in Kṛṣṇa consciousness take continual pleasure in hearing transcendental literatures. (10.9 P)
68. Just as a shining lamp destroys darkness, the Lord dwelling in the hearts of everyone destroys the ignorance by giving knowledge as His special mercy. (10.11)
69. Just as lamplight is not required in sun, the original verses of Bhagavad-gīta, which are as clear as the sun doesn't require insights from foolish commentators. (11.51 P)

Mind and Sense Control

70. A tortoise draws its limbs within the shell. Similarly one who is firmly fixed in perfect consciousness withdraws his senses from sense objects. (2.58)
71. By restricting a diseased person from certain types of eatables, his taste for such eatables is not lost. Similarly less intelligent persons without Kṛṣṇa consciousness following rules and regulations to restrict sense enjoyment do not lose taste for dead material things. (2.59 P)
72. Just as a strong wind sweeps away a boat, similarly even one of the roaming senses on which the mind focuses can carry away a man's intelligence. (2.67)
73. There is always a chance of an accident, even on the royal roads. Similarly one may go astray, even when one does sense gratification under regulation. (3.34 P)
74. Just as milk in contact with sour tamarind is transformed into yogurt, the sense of love of God becomes transformed into lust with material mode of passion. (3.37 P)
75. Just as fire is covered by smoke, as a mirror is covered by dust, or as the embryo is covered by the womb, the living entity is covered by different degrees of lust. (3.38)
76. Just as fire is never extinguished by a constant supply of fuel, lust cannot be satisfied by any amount of sense enjoyment. (3.39 P)
77. Just as a lamp in windless place does not waver, the transcendentalist whose mind is controlled remains steady in his meditation on the transcendent Self. (6.19)
78. An acute infection may surpass the efficacy of medicine. Similarly although intelligence is supposed to direct the mind, the obstinate mind often overcomes even the intelligence. (6.34 P)
79. Trying to practice yoga while engaging the mind in material enjoyment is like trying to ignite a fire while pouring water on it. (6.36 P)

Author's Profile

Gauranga Darshan Das, a disciple of His Holiness Radhanath Swami, is a distinguished educator, prolific speaker, and bestselling author of over 43 books. He holds a Master's degree in Systems Science and Automation from the prestigious Indian Institute of Science (IISc), Bangalore, India. His outstanding contributions have earned him accolades such as the "Visionary Leader: Spirituality" award from Brand Vision Inc. and the "Spiritual Scientist" award from the Andhra University.

Before embracing monkhood in 2009, Gauranga Darshan Das had a brief yet impactful corporate career spanning two years. During this time, he conducted research at renowned organizations like TCS Innovation Labs, authored over 10 technical papers, and filed a provisional patent for his research.

Currently, he serves as the Dean of Bhaktivedanta Vidyapitha at ISKCON Govardhan Ecovillage (GEV), where he leads both residential and online spiritual education programs. With his ability to present timeless wisdom in a lucid and contemporary style, he connects with diverse audiences, including children, teens, professionals, and educators. His speaking and teaching engagements span India, Australia, the United States, the United Kingdom, New Zealand, Singapore, and other countries. He has addressed audiences in spiritual organizations, schools, colleges, and corporate sectors, and on prominent platforms like TEDx, ISRO, DRDO, and Hindustan Times. To date, he has delivered over 8,000 hours of lectures and conducted more than 50 online courses, available at www.vidyapitha.in.

As an accomplished author, Gauranga Darshan Das has written over 43 books. His works include study guides (such as the Subodhini series), storybooks, self-enrichment titles (From Chaos to Calm, Dhruva, Disapproved but not Disowned, and more), and children's literature (Mindful Me!, Bhagavatam Tales, and Gita Wisdom Tales series). He also runs a monthly e-zine, Bhagavata Pradipika, and contributes thought-provoking articles to Back to Godhead magazines in India and internationally.

Gauranga Darshan Das's dedication to sharing spiritual wisdom has made him a highly respected figure in spiritual, educational, and corporate circles. Learn more about his inspiring work at www.gaurangadarshan.com.